TOUCHED WITH FIRE

TOUCHED WITH FIRE

Morris B. Abram
and the Battle *against*
Racial *and* Religious
Discrimination

DAVID E. LOWE

Potomac Books
An imprint of the University of Nebraska Press

All rights reserved. Potomac Books is an imprint of the
University of Nebraska Press.
Manufactured in the United States of America.

Library of Congress Cataloging-in-Publication Data
Names: Lowe, David E., author.
Title: Touched with fire: Morris B. Abram and the battle
against racial and religious discrimination / David E. Lowe.
Description: Lincoln: Potomac Books is an imprint of the
University of Nebraska Press [2019]. |
Includes bibliographical references and index.
Identifiers: LCCN 2019015598
ISBN 9781640120969 (hardback)
ISBN 9781640122734 (epub)
ISBN 9781640122741 (mobi)
ISBN 9781640122758 (pdf)
Subjects: LCSH: Abram, Morris B. | Lawyers—United
States—Biography. | Civil rights—United States—History. |
BISAC: Biography & Autobiography / Lawyers & Judges. |
Social Science / Discrimination & Race Relations.
Classification: LCC KF373.A27 L69 2019 |
DDC 340.092 [B]—dc23
LC record available at https://lccn.loc.gov/2019015598

Set in Arno Pro by Mikala R. Kolander.

To Mom and Dad, with admiration and affection

Through our great good fortune, in our youth our hearts were touched with fire. It was given to us to learn at the outset that life is a profound and passionate thing.

—OLIVER WENDELL HOLMES JR.

CONTENTS

PREFACE

To get to Yarmouth Port, Massachusetts, you take the exit to Route 6A and drive the winding road toward Dennis. After passing the Cape Cod Center for the Arts and the Bass River Rod and Gun Club, along with multiple cape cod–style houses, garden nurseries, and art galleries, you are reminded that you are in the heart of New England by streets named Oxford and Canterbury, Longfellow and Walden Way.

When you reach the Elegant Inn at Cape Cod you make an awkward left turn onto Summer Street, and just down the road you take the third entrance into the Woodside Cemetery. It's not long before the names on the stones begin to sound less like the WASPish ones attached to those buried in the front of the cemetery and more like those who arrived on the Cape many generations later: Vogel, Ridman, Kaufman, and Epstein.

When you come to the simple dark stone covering his grave just off the narrow road, you realize that the person buried here was no ordinary summertime resident, but rather someone who lived through—and helped shape—a historic period of American history. The stone reads:

MORRIS BERTHOLD ABRAM

June 19, 1918–March 16, 2000
He established "one man, one vote"
as a principle of American law

ACKNOWLEDGMENTS

First time authors are more dependent than others on the kindness of strangers, not to mention friends and acquaintances.

My first debt is to Hillel Neuer, the talented executive director of UN Watch, who proposed that I put together a slideshow about its founding chairman for the organization's website. While working on this assignment at Emory University in the early part of 2017, I realized that my subject's rich life deserved fuller treatment.

Had it not been for the encouragement I received at the outset from a valued friend, the author David Evanier, the project would probably not have been undertaken. Along the way I have received support from many others. Special thanks go to Joshua Abram, who gave generously of his time throughout the project to fill in critical details and help me gain a more complete understanding of the personal side of his father. Many others took a strong interest in the project and offered assistance in various ways. They include Morris Abram's daughter Ruth Abram and his widow Bruna Molina, as well as the following: Cecily Abram, Elliott Abrams, Steven Bayme, Jonathan Cohen, Michael Colson, Larry Diamond, Stuart Eizenstat, Deborah Forman, Carl Gershman, Hannah Gaywood, Robert Hicks, Penson Kaminsky, Joseph Lefkoff, Mark Levin, Lynn Levine, Richard Lowe, Eric Singer, Allen Tanenbaum, Stuart Weisberg, and Stephen Whitfield. I am also grateful to Alan Lowe, who read entire chapters and made helpful suggestions.

I am most fortunate that my longtime colleague Marc Plattner was willing to give the manuscript a careful reading and make useful recommendations. At the University of Nebraska Press, Ann Baker provided steady direction to the project and Abigail Stryker and Christina LaRose offered valuable editorial assistance.

My agent, Ronald Goldfarb, gave me a solid education in how to write a book proposal and made some helpful suggestions related to the book's organization. I would also like to express appreciation to those who gave this project credibility by providing endorsements of my proposal: Abe Foxman, David Harris, Vernon Jordan, Bill Kristol, Alfred Moses, and Norman Podhoretz.

Let me take this opportunity to recognize the contributions of those unsung heroes whose expertise in locating relevant material not only lessened the burdens of research but also frequently made working in libraries such a pleasure: Kathy Shoemaker and her excellent staff at the Rose Archives at Emory University; Tim Myers and Sarah Braun at the Democracy Resource Center of the National Endowment for Democracy; Chloe Morse-Harding at the Goldfarb Library at Brandeis University; Charlotte Bonelli and Desiree Guillermo at the American Jewish Committee Archives; and the staffs of the Georgia Historical Society and the Dorot Jewish Division of the New York Public Library.

The following gave generously of their time to sit for personal interviews, providing indispensable insights about the Morris Abram they knew: Cecily Abram, Joshua Abram, Ruth Abram, Miles Alexander, Shulamit Bahat, Steven Bayme, Eric Block, Janice Rothschild Blumberg, Marshall Breger, Linda Chavez, Jacob Cohen, Jonathan Cohen, Michael Colson, Alan Dershowitz, Robert Destro, Gordon Fellman, Hamilton Fish, Deborah Forman, Abraham Foxman, Felice Gaer, Hannah Gaywood, Max Gitter, Jerry Goodman, Max Green, David Harris, Robert Hicks, Malcolm Hoenlein, Jeh Johnson, Vernon Jordan, Penson Kaminsky, Morton Keller, Billy Keyserling, Joseph Lefkoff, Mark Levin, Elliott Levitas, John Lewis, Seth Lipsky, Ted Maloof, Bruna Molina, Alfred Moses, Lamar Perlis, Anne Patterson, Norman Podhoretz, Bruce Ramer, Robert Rifkind, Sidney Rosdeitcher, Richard Schifter, George Shultz, David Schwarz, Eric Singer, Stephen Spitz, David Squire, Kenneth Sweder,

Mark Talisman, Herbert Teitelbaum, Jonathan Tepperman, Eric Yoffie, and Andrew Young.

My wife, Paula Lowe, whose good judgment I rely upon daily,
made frequently sensible suggestions while patiently putting up with
what has been my near obsession for the past two years.

I only hope that no one listed here will feel responsible for any
of my errors.

TIMELINE OF MORRIS B. ABRAM'S LIFE

1918   Born June 19 in Fitzgerald, Georgia, to Sam and Irene
        Cohen Abram
1934   Enters the University of Georgia (UGA)
1938   Graduates from UGA *summa cum laude*, Phi Beta Kappa;
        awarded Rhodes Scholarship to Oxford to begin in the
        fall term the following year
1939   Rhodes Scholarship program suspended on the eve of
        World War II; enters University of Chicago Law School
1940   Earns law degree from University of Chicago; accepts
        position at the Atlanta law firm Howell and Post
1941   Enters the U.S. Air Force as a second lieutenant at Fort
        McPherson, Georgia
1944   Marries Jane Isabella Maguire
1945   Birth of daughter Ruth
1945   Completes military service with the rank of major;
        awarded the Legion of Merit
1946   Moves to Oxford, England, with Jane and Ruth; enrolls
        in Pembroke College
1946   Spends the summer in Nuremberg, Germany, working
        on the U.S. prosecution team of the International
        Military Tribunal for Nazi war crimes
1948   Earns Oxford degree
1948   Returns to Atlanta and joins the law firm of Heyman,
        Howell, and Heyman
1948   Birth of daughter Ann

1950	Files first lawsuit challenging Georgia's county unit system of voting
1950	Birth of son Morris Jr.
1953	Becomes partner in the law firm of Heyman, Abram, and Young
1954	Runs unsuccessful campaign for the U.S. House of Representatives from Georgia's Fifth Congressional District
1955	Birth of son Jonathan Adam
1958	Appointed by Mayor Hartsfield to chair the Atlanta Citizens Crime Commission
1961	Serves as the first general counsel of the U.S. Peace Corps
1962	Appointed by Pres. John Kennedy to the position of U.S. Member, UN Sub-Commission on Prevention of Discrimination and Protection of Minorities
1962	Argues *Sanders v. Gray* case before U.S. Circuit Court panel, which declares Georgia's county unit system unconstitutional
1962	Joins the New York law firm of Paul, Weiss, Rifkind, Wharton and Garrison as a partner
1962	Birth of son Joshua
1963	Argues *Gray v. Sanders* case before U.S. Supreme Court on January 17; on March 18 the court upholds the Circuit Court ruling and establishes by a vote of 8–1 the constitutional standard of "one person, one vote"
1963	Selected as the youngest president in the history of the American Jewish Committee (serves until 1968)
1965	Appointed by Pres. Lyndon Johnson to co-chair the planning committee for the White House Conference on Civil Rights
1965	Appointed UN Representative to the UN Commission on Human Rights and Senior Advisor to UN Ambassador Arthur Goldberg
1965–81	Serves as chairman of the Field Foundation
1968	Inaugurated as the second president of Brandeis University

1969	Leads the university's response to the eleven-day student takeover of Ford Hall
1970	Resigns the presidency of Brandeis; rejoins Paul, Weiss
1971–80	Serves as chairman of the United Negro College Fund
1973	Begins treatment for acute myelocytic leukemia (AML) at Mt. Sinai Hospital in New York City
1974	Divorced from Jane Abram
1975–76	Heads the Moreland Commission's investigation of New York State's nursing home industry
1976	Marries Carlyn Feldman Fisher
1979	Receives final treatment for AML; declared cancer free
1979–83	Serves as chairman of the President's Commission for the Study of Ethical Problems in Medicine and Biomedical and Behavioral Research, following appointment by Pres. Jimmy Carter
1983–86	Serves as vice-chairman of U.S. Commission on Civil Rights, following appointment by Pres. Ronald Reagan
1983–88	Serves as chairman of the National Conference on Soviet Jewry
1987	Leads the mass Soviet Jewry rally on the Washington DC mall on Freedom Sunday, December 6
1987	Divorced from Carlyn Abram
1986–89	Serves as chairman of the Conference of Presidents of Major American Jewish Organizations
1989–93	Serves as ambassador to the European Office of the UN, following appointment by Pres. George H. W. Bush
1990	Marries Bruna Molina in his summer cottage on Cape Cod
1993	Begins tenure as the Founding Chairman of UN Watch
1999	Receives AJC's National Distinguished Leadership Award
2000	Dies on March 16 in Geneva; funeral and burial on March 19 in Yarmouth Port, Massachusetts

Introduction

Are you kidding? You don't know about Morris Abram?

O n April 29, 1962, the federal courtroom in Atlanta's old post office building was packed to the rafters. Leading members of the League of Women Voters and the United Church Women, along with state and local politicians and students from the local law schools, sat, dressed in suits and wearing hats in the darkly paneled third floor room. Reporters lined both sides of the courtroom ready to rush back to their newsrooms.[1]

The drama began to build as U.S. Circuit Court Judge Griffin Bell started reading in his southwestern Georgia drawl the decision in the case of *Sanders v. Gray*. Morris Abram had spent thirteen years waiting for this moment. He was worried, since he believed that Bell (the future attorney general of the United States), a recently appointed federal appellate judge and one of the youngest in the country, was "political to his fingertips" and "tied in with all the Russell's and everybody else who was a political force, including Herman Talmadge."[2]

Everyone in the courtroom knew that if the plaintiffs were victorious, the ruling would reverberate throughout the state of Georgia. The fate of the "county unit system," designed to entrench the practice of racial segregation by filling the state's executive, legislative, and judicial branches with politicians and judges prepared to fight any effort to challenge it, now rested with the opinions of three federal judges. The courtroom drama marked the penultimate fight of Morris Abram's lengthy battle against that system.

Since 1917, Georgia law required the state's political parties to use an electoral system in statewide primaries based upon unit votes assigned to each of Georgia's counties. (The number of counties in Georgia was capped by the 1945 and subsequent state constitutions at 159, a total second only to Texas.) The number of unit votes was so disproportionately granted to favor the smaller rural counties that the metropolitan areas could be safely ignored by candidates for statewide office. And since the state's Republican Party was virtually nonexistent, the winner was effectively the candidate who collected the most unit votes in the Democratic primary.

Eugene Talmadge famously declared that he never wanted to carry a county with a streetcar. And in fact, in the 1946 Democratic primary, Talmadge was nominated for governor despite losing the popular vote. (To the surprise of no one, he was officially elected in the fall for a fourth term.) After succeeding his father as governor following Eugene Talmadge's death two years later, his son Herman said that he and the unit system were the only bulwarks against federally mandated "race mixing."

Halfway through Judge Bell's slow reading of his seventeen-page opinion, it became clear to Abram and his colleagues that they were on the verge of achieving the result they had long sought. Atlanta's mayor William Hartsfield, whom Abram had represented in an earlier county unit lawsuit, turned to his lawyer friend and winked. When Judge Bell finished reading the unanimous decision, the mayor jumped in the air. Abram's daughter Ann walked to the front and gave her father a hug. Victory celebrations followed.[3]

But Morris Abram still had one more battle to fight. Although Judge Bell's opinion had overruled the unit system on grounds that it was discriminatory *as then constituted*, it left open the possibility that a different arrangement of unit votes might pass muster with that court. And Abram's ultimate objective was to eliminate any vestige of a system that violated the principle of "one man, one vote."

The court's decisions in *Sanders v. Gray* and a companion case involving the malapportioned Georgia state legislature were watched closely by a peanut farmer from the rural southwestern part of the state. Jimmy Carter, who considered the outcome of the county unit case "one of the most momentous judicial decisions of the century in Georgia," soon announced his candidacy for one of the newly created state senate seats located near his home in Sumter County.[4] His political career was launched after being declared the winner by a court in a disputed contest. He now represented a district located less than ninety miles from the small town where Morris Abram spent his childhood.

In the early months of 2017 I was asked by the executive director of the Geneva, Switzerland–based organization UN Watch to put together a slideshow of its founding chairman for the group's website. The assignment took me to Emory University, where Morris Abram's papers are archived. I knew of Abram from my own experience. In fact, I had met him once as an entering freshman at Brandeis University in the fall of 1968, where he was beginning his brief tenure as its second president. But my knowledge of Abram's career ran much deeper. Like my subject, I am a Georgia native. I grew up during the turbulent years of the struggle for civil rights, a struggle in which Abram played a key role. And later in life, I worked in the Civil Rights Division of the Anti-Defamation League during the same period in which he ascended to the national leadership of the American Jewish community.

But why a biography of Morris Abram? It's a question I have been asked many times, though never by those who knew him, or who were otherwise familiar with his lifetime of accomplishments. A former law partner from his days in Atlanta, Maurice "Ted" Maloof, said to me in an interview just months before his own death: "He was a great man, as you know. But I can't believe how many people never heard of Morris Abram. I ask people all the time, 'Do you remember Morris Abram?' And they say, 'No, I never heard of him.' When I remind them about his victory over the county unit system, then they remember."[5]

Jeh Johnson, whom Abram mentored during the 1980s at the New York law firm of Paul, Weiss, Rifkind, Wharton and Garrison, long before he served as General Counsel of the Pentagon and Secretary of Homeland Security under President Obama, remembers hearing from a young associate in his firm from rural Georgia that he would be arguing a death penalty case in Alabama the following week. "And I said, 'So you must know all about Morris Abram.' And he said, 'Who's Morris Abram?' I said, 'Are you kidding? You don't know about Morris Abram?'"[6]

In fact, Abram stands today as a mostly forgotten figure outside the American Jewish community where he played a leadership role during the second half of his life. Few beyond his native Georgia remember his successful effort to unmask the Ku Klux Klan, his lengthy battle to end the state's county unit system of voting that entrenched racial segregation, or his role as an intermediary in assisting Martin Luther King Jr. in his release from prison less than a month before the 1960 presidential election.

But his civil rights work in Atlanta during the 1950s and early 1960s marked only the beginning of Abram's public service, for which he was tapped by five U.S. presidents, from John F. Kennedy to George H. W. Bush. Beginning with his presidency of the American Jewish Committee in the 1960s, he became a leading voice in the worldwide effort to free the Jews behind the Iron Curtain. And his pioneering work in the field of international human rights spanned the years from his service on Justice Robert Jackson's prosecution team at Nuremburg shortly after World War II to his efforts in the final decade of the twentieth century to hold the United Nations to the high standards of human rights protections its founders had envisioned.

Abram's accomplishments are even more remarkable considering his humble beginnings. Growing up in Fitzgerald, a rural town in southcentral Georgia, his immigrant father struggled to support his family with earnings from a dry goods business that failed to provide a secure income for his wife and their four children. Abram's childhood haunted him throughout his life, and he frequently thought himself unworthy of the many accolades that accompanied his achievements. "He was smart, and he was charming," said Robert Hicks, a law partner in Abram's firm in Atlanta. "But he couldn't understand why people thought so highly of him."[7]

Still, growing up as a minority in a small town installed in Morris Abram a fierce ambition to succeed. His background as an "outsider," a Jewish southerner growing up in a racially segregated environment, played a major role in sensitizing him to the injustices he witnessed early in his life. He became an effective advocate in his home state for those who were being denied the protections he believed to be guaranteed by the U.S. Constitution and by a society committed to the rule of law. He carried that outspokenness to the national and international arenas on behalf of Soviet Jewry and the state of Israel.

According to his daughter Ruth, founder of the Lower East Side Tenement Museum in New York City, Abram's status as an outsider "was actually very much communicated to his family as a good position to be in. Not a thing to be afraid of, or try to change, since being an outsider had some advantages." When I spoke to her, Ruth was preparing to give a presentation on the relationship between the artist and the immigrant. "I will be speaking to the outsider theme," she said. "I'm sure I got that from him."[8]

During the mid-1960s, several years after his move to New York, Abram reflected upon the advantages his marginality had afforded him: "If one is a Jew and lives in a small Southern town, one is bound to realize early that a minority group has a different position than a majority. . . . By being one of such a small group, I was bound to get a certain insight that I would not have had as a member of the majority group."[9]

In a lengthy set of interviews he sat for with the writer Eli Evans after receiving his doctor's diagnosis of acute myelocytic leukemia, a disease most of his associates did not expect him to survive, Abram ruminated on where he should be buried: "I don't feel at home in Fitzgerald. I don't feel at home in New York. Who wants to be buried in one of those cemeteries on Long Island? I don't feel at home in Atlanta. At least I feel more at home than I did, but from the years 1948 to 1962 as a Jew confronting the system, I was not part of it and Atlanta was not really my home."[10]

Abram's ascendency to the leadership of the American Jewish community could hardly have been predicted in his early years. He told Evans only half-jokingly that he was raised as a Protestant. In fact, his hometown did have a tiny close-knit contingent of Jewish families, but under his mother's influence the Abram family had little association with them. Abram's intellectual curiosity as a teenager led him to an early fascination with Jewish history and culture that grew over the years into a strong personal identification as a Jew. Though never religious, he became a passionate public defender of the state of Israel.

Abram's life as an outsider followed him throughout his career: a student at the University of Georgia and later an Atlanta lawyer who vigorously opposed the predominant political and social views of the day; a partner in a highly regarded Northern law firm who never lost his genteel Southern manner and style; the president of an elite university to which he brought traditional liberal views during a time when those views were under assault from the New Left; and a pioneer of the civil rights movement, which turned against him as the result of his vigorous opposition to racial and ethnic quotas.

As the latter example indicates, Abram's career was not without its disappointments. When the Rhodes Scholarship he received during his senior year at the University of Georgia was cancelled just before the outbreak of World War II, Abram was able to accept an invitation to complete his legal education at the University of Chicago, thanks to the financial intervention of his college roommate's father. But following his graduation, anti-Jewish discrimination prevented him from being hired at any of Atlanta's prestigious law firms.

When Abram was in his late fifties, he wrote to his son Morris Jr., "Once I had rather vaulting ambitions to make contributions to social and/or political progress or even to history. The latter dream I discarded early—or was it only a day dream?" He had, after all, been president of his class at law school and president of his debating society at the University of Georgia. As he told Eli Evans, "I was always involved in political matters. I loved political matters."[11]

In 1954 Abram challenged Atlanta's incumbent congressman, a former judge and member of the Ku Klux Klan, but he lost in a race he later described as "the nastiest, meanest campaign in the world."[12] Reflecting on that campaign twenty years later, Abram said that his first speech in the small county he needed to win the election "went over like a lead balloon" since he was making the mistake of trying to reason with his audience. "I couldn't be a demagogue," he said, "and I am no good at speaking that requires wit and humor. I cannot even remember jokes very well."[13] As he told Evans, "I would never be a Madison Square Garden speaker. I am not good at shouting out one-sentence applause producing lines like a labor leader . . . and I do not like to speak in polemical terms. I like to reason in a speech."[14]

In the late 1960s, after moving to New York and establishing his reputation in both the legal and Jewish communities, Abram was considered a leading Democratic candidate for the U.S. Senate, but he dropped out of the race when he realized his call for a negotiated settlement to the Vietnam War prevented him from receiving the support of the Johnson White House. And after stepping down from the presidency of Brandeis University, his candidacy for New York's other Senate seat fizzled out before the Democratic primary.

But it was Brandeis that marked Abram's biggest career disappointment. A position for which he believed himself perfectly suited lasted less than two years, a memory that troubled him for the rest of his life. Many of the problems he encountered stemmed from a naiveté about what a university president could achieve during the campus upheavals of the late 1960s. "He got into Brandeis," said Rabbi Eric Yoffie, then its student council president, "and he realized very quickly that this was not the job for him. The whole university scene was not for him, particularly in the '60s."[15]

Abram also suffered personal setbacks. Although his first marriage to a talented journalist from a prominent Florida family brought much happiness and five children to whom he was deeply devoted, it fell apart shortly before he was diagnosed with the leukemia that nearly took his life. During the same period he experienced deep frustration trying to connect with his oldest son, Morris Jr., who had left the country and temporarily broken off communication.

Abram fought a lifetime of insecurity. As Robert Hicks told me, "I think Morris was a man in search of himself all his life. He had what I call a 'green pasture' syndrome. Everything was greener on the other side of the fence. He was always aggrandizing himself, pushing and climbing, climbing, climbing." He continued, "Morris was one of the most brilliant men I ever knew. Men or women; he just was smart. But he never was at peace. He wanted to get somewhere all the time."[16]

And he had his shortcomings. He went to great lengths, mainly through the use of extravagant flattery, to ingratiate himself with those whom he believed could advance his career. On separate occasions he got into trouble with important constituencies for making unauthorized statements to the press, first as president of Brandeis and years later as chairman of the Conference of Presidents of Major American Jewish Organizations. And his second marriage to a long-lost sweetheart from his early days in Atlanta did not survive her discovery of his infidelity.

Abram did marry for a third time at the outset of his final decade. The marriage to a European career woman over two decades younger was spent in his adopted home of Geneva with summers on Cape Cod. His wife Bruna described it to me as a happy one, and by then he had long since rebuilt his relationship with Morris Jr.

Alan Dershowitz, who found himself at odds with Abram on several occasions, told me that Abram was a proud member of the establishment, in contrast to his own career as an outsider. For someone like Abram, who grew up in one of twelve Jewish families in a rural Protestant southern town of six thousand residents, this may seem like a contradiction.

But Dershowitz's encounters with Abram did in fact come after Abram had ascended to one of the top New York law firms and the leadership of the organized Jewish community. In his mid-forties, Abram accepted a partnership at the law firm of Paul, Weiss, Rifkind, Wharton and Garrison, shortly before becoming the youngest president in the history of the American Jewish Committee, that most established of Jewish organizations. And a little over two decades later, special arrangements were made by the Conference of Presidents of Major American Jewish Organizations to enable him to become its chairman. He was now, indeed, a full-fledged member of the country's Jewish establishment.

By then Abram had parted ways politically with old friends and allies who could not fathom the fact that this crusader for civil rights had, in their estimation, abandoned his liberal views and "moved to the right." But in Abram's assessment it was they, and not he, who had compromised their position. Testifying before the Democratic National Committee's Platform Committee in 1984, he and fellow U.S. Civil Rights Commission colleague John Bunzel pointed out that "in the name of a new equality, the policy of color-blindness, which had long been the touchstone and mandate of our Constitution and is a requirement of the 1964 Civil Rights Act, has been severely modified."[17]

Abram was saddened to see the civil rights movement discard the concept of equal protection of law in favor of legally sanctioned racial preference—the very antithesis of what the authors of the key civil rights legislation had advocated. Toward the end of his life Abram wrote, "The transformation of the moral struggle for equality and integration into one for preference and separation has not been to the advantage of blacks and certainly not to the country."[18]

Morris Abram's story is, as his son Joshua describes it, an "American story," and for that reason alone it is worth telling. But what is most striking is its relevance to our times. In an opinion piece Abram wrote in 1978 that was quoted before the Senate Judiciary Committee by Senator Henry Jackson in his statement on behalf of Abram's nomination to the U.S. Commission on Civil Rights, he warned of the dangers of using race and ethnicity as political tools in a pluralistic society. "The State must not tag and assign rights on the basis of race, sex, or religion," he wrote. "If we do, we shall surely end up at each other's throats."[19]

One can only wonder what the early pioneers of the civil rights movement would think of the politics of identity that have moved to the center of our partisan battles today. Morris Abram, who knew with certainty the injustice of discrimination based on one's identity at birth, understood the price that is paid by a nation that abandons its commitment to the rule of law.

ONE

Childhood

In the South especially, Jews languished as the provincials, the Jews
of the periphery, not destined to triumph but just to survive.

—ELI N. EVANS, *The Provincials*

Morris Abram's hometown of Fitzgerald, Georgia had a deep
impact on him throughout his life. During his treatment for
leukemia in the 1970s, Abram told his psychiatrist that he never
really broke away from the town. From his mother, he said, he had
acquired the qualities of strength; from his father, he had gotten
his more "human" qualities. And while he believed his hometown
"gave shape to much of what I am," his childhood was not without
frequent feelings of alienation.

Abram cited numerous factors as essential to shaping his later life:
being born a Jew in the South "who had to face the majority world
which was hostile"; the cultural divide between his parents, one an
Eastern European immigrant, the other who claimed German Jewish roots that enabled her to condescend to those of different origin;
his small size throughout his childhood; growing up in a conventional environment of white Protestant fundamentalism in which
he absorbed views on morality, ethics, and sexual behavior; and the
enormous emphasis in his family on intellectual skills as contrasted
with the slight emphasis on athletic achievement.[1]

Abram spent his childhood in a town of six thousand residents that was unique in American history. He took pride in his hometown that, he believed, incorporated "a profound aspect of the American experience."[2] Located in the rural, piney woods of south central Georgia, Fitzgerald had its origins in the unlikeliest of places: the vision of an Indianapolis, Indiana newspaper owner and editor. Phylander (P. H.) Fitzgerald, a Union drummer boy in the Civil War, had watched in despair as the war's midwestern pensioners faced drought conditions in the 1880s that forced them to leave their homes. Fitzgerald sent out an appeal to prominent southerners for assistance, and it was Georgia's governor, William J. Northen, who answered the call by sending two trainloads of supplies to Nebraska, the state most hard hit by the drought.[3]

It wasn't long before Captain Fitzgerald and Northen were working together to establish a colony that would be a haven for Union veterans and others most affected by the drought and other difficult climatic conditions. In July 1895 Fitzgerald made the first payment on a large plot of fertile land purchased from two brothers who owned a sawmill in the tiny community of Swan. Word of the purchase spread quickly, as northerners and westerners began their journeys by wagon and train to the new colony. By the end of the year, more than twenty-five hundred settlers arrived and set up camps that would have to await the building of the town named for Captain Fitzgerald.

Some of the Union veterans seeking to spend their final years in the heart of Dixie had ridden with Sherman in his infamous march through the state. Others had been held under the harshest of conditions in the Confederate prison in nearby Andersonville. One had even witnessed the capture of Jefferson Davis a mere ten miles away. The original settlers were soon joined by locals from surrounding towns, many of whom had come originally as tourists to witness history being made.

While planning the layout of the town in a Midwestern-style grid, the leadership of the colony company realized that it would be foolish to alienate the locals, for whom bitter memories of the war remained. Thus, street names reflected the atmosphere of reconciliation that surrounded the building of the town. On the east side of

Main Street the avenues were named for Grant, Sherman, and other Union generals. Avenues running north and south on the west side bore the names of Lee, Jackson, and other Confederate generals. The drives in the central part of town were given the familiar names Monitor and Merrimac, as well as other naval ships from both sides of the conflict. The remaining streets were named for trees native to the state. The town's first big public works project was a four-story, 150-room hotel, the biggest wooden structure in the state at the turn of the twentieth century. Morris Abram's parents were among the first to hold their wedding reception at the Lee-Grant Hotel.

In addition to the joint naming of streets and buildings, the town did its best to integrate the two cultures. A wall poster located today in the town's Blue-Gray Museum reads: "The Yankee veterans brought to Fitzgerald their architecture, their churches, their town plan, their midwestern industries, their commercial habits, their family customs, their patriotism to the Grand Army of the Republic—and a host of reminders left behind. The local Confederates contributed their land, their knowledge of agriculture, their labor, their sense of justice for the Confederacy, their churches, their cuisine, their language, and a host of southern traditions."

At the opening of the town's large exposition hall in 1896, it was decided to keep the peace by dividing the parade into separate groups of Union and Confederate veterans. But as the band began playing, the soldiers decided to march side by side, carrying the American flag. The next year they formed Battalion I of the Blue and Gray, an unprecedented development.[4]

By 1900 Fitzgerald had its first Jewish resident, Isadore Goldenberg (née Solomon), who arrived with his new bride Bessie and opened a dry goods store. By the end of the decade, Goldenberg had two other Jewish immigrants as partners, including his nephew Sam Abram, who lived with the Goldenbergs as a boarder.[5] Morris Abram remembers "Uncle Ike" Goldenberg as "a gentleman, attractive and sweet," the most dapper man in town.[6] Abram's father Sam, a man short in stature, had grown up in the small village of Buchesti, Romania, where his large family were the only Jews. "Nobody bothered them," Sam's younger brother Shmule later reported. "Of course, when the goyim got drunk, they would usually beat up a Jew, but nobody paid any attention to that."[7]

Sam, or Schneur, as he was then known, was one of nine children born to Moshe Avram, a wood dealer, and his wife, Anna Zalman Avram, in 1883. Sam, who would later lose two of his brothers in World War I and a third to the horrific 1941 pogrom in the Romanian city of Iasi that took over thirteen thousand Jewish lives, was only nine when his father died. Apprenticed to a harness maker in nearby Vaslui, Sam eventually became head of the shop, but when he faced the prospect of being conscripted into the army, he began to weigh the decision to emigrate to America.

The source of much anxiety for his mother and siblings, the decision was not an easy one, as emigration was prohibited by the authorities. And, as his brother later estimated, only one in five who set out for America at that time was successful in reaching its shores. Engaged to be married, his fiancée's father forbade her to go with him. In the end, it was the infamous pogrom in nearby Kishniev in 1903 that led Sam Abram, at the age of twenty, to decide he would leave his native Romania for America.

In 1880, Morris Abram's maternal great-grandfather, Elias Eppstein, one of the first Reform rabbis in the United States, arrived in Kansas City, Missouri, to take over the pulpit of Congregation B'nai Jehudah. (One of its future congregants was Harry Truman's close friend and one-time business partner Eddie Jacobson.) Born in Saarwelling, Alsace-Lorraine and educated in France and Germany, Rabbi Eppstein had emigrated to the United States in 1851, accepting a Jewish educational position in Syracuse, New York. Before arriving in Kansas City, he served congregations in New York City; Jackson, Michigan; Milwaukee; and Detroit, where he initiated Friday evening services at Congregation Temple Beth El in 1867 and was the first rabbi to offer sermons in English.[8]

Rabbi Eppstein kept a journal during his three-year tenure at B'nai Jehudah. In his very first week on the job, he had the religious school partitioned into classrooms to provide age-appropriate education, enlarged the congregational choir, accepted a position as circuit preacher for surrounding communities, and received a commit-

ment from forty-two female congregants to organize a fair to raise
money to pay off the synagogue's mortgage. It was a great start for a
Rabbi working on an annual salary of $1,500.[9] The fair, held in Octo-
ber 1880, was particularly notable, with the streets surrounding the
Grimes Building on Delaware Avenue thronged with crowds on five
consecutive days and nights, and the mayor presiding at the opening and closing ceremonies. If the fair was a financial success, it was
also a reflection of the integration of the Jewish community into the
general populace of Kansas City. As the synagogue's account notes,
"their language was by now almost entirely English, their dress indistinguishable from that of everyone else, and their children imbued
with American ways." As a measure of just how far religious traditions had been publicly set aside, the fair's luncheon menu featured
shellfish, strictly forbidden by Jewish law.[10]

Rabbi Eppstein's tenure coincided with the beginning of the great
migration of Jews to the United States from Russia following the
assassination of Czar Alexander II. At first Rabbi Eppstein reported
that the community would gladly provide for those refugees reaching his community. He later tempered this generous outreach, however, by urging the Hebrew Emigrant Aid Committee in New York
to desist from sending any more to avoid placing a burden on the
next generation.[11] In his diary, Rabbi Eppstein noted how many of
the newcomers refused to become involved in the community and
declined to engage in charitable acts, while at the same time condemning fellow Jews who failed to observe the strictures of Jewish
law. Still, he asked, "Should we condemn the whole on account of
these hypocrites?"[12]

The rabbi's contract was not renewed upon the end of his term
in 1883. A sermon he had delivered the previous year on the subject
of "Retribution" had incurred the displeasure of a prominent con-
gregant, and the temple's patriarch was already looking to the first
class of graduates of the recently established Hebrew Union College
in Cincinnati, a center of Reform Judaism, as a recruiting ground
for Eppstein's successor.

Three of the rabbi's seven children remained in Kansas City when
he left for his next pulpit in Philadelphia. Among them was his daugh-

ter Mathilda, who became the first secretary of the Kansas City chapter of the National Council of Jewish Women. Her son Harold Kander, father of future Broadway composer John Kander, later served on the synagogue's board of trustees.

Among the children accompanying, Rabbi Eppstein and his wife, Fannie, to his next pulpit in Philadelphia was his fourteen-year-old daughter, Therese, known throughout most of her life as Daisy. There she met and later married a watchmaker named Morris Cohen, who decided to enter the medical profession after financing his sister Sarah's education at the pioneering Women's Medical College of Pennsylvania. Sarah graduated in 1879, later becoming a distinguished obstetrician. After completing his medical education at Jefferson Medical School in Philadelphia, Morris Cohen began to practice in a series of small towns, beginning in Quincy, Illinois, where his daughter Irene was born. From there he worked his way south until he ended up in Fitzgerald when Irene was seventeen or eighteen years old.

"He followed a moving star," Morris Abram said, and would have found Fitzgerald an interesting town in which to settle. Standing at five feet, eight inches, Cohen was remembered by his grandson as a "galvanic figure" of supreme self-confidence, a country doctor "who combined in his person all the traits of master technician and tribal shaman."[13] Abram recalled that his grandfather, although warm and lovable to his grandchildren, was an iconoclast who was on the outs with the other doctors in town, whom he regarded as "dummkophs." His distrust of the personnel at the local hospital led him to perform his surgeries in his office. His refusal to own a car resulted in him walking to see his patients or requiring the more affluent to drive to see him. When Morris was seven, his grandfather moved from Fitzgerald to Cleveland, leaving behind many fond memories of this somewhat mythic figure and his gentle and loving grandmother, whom Abram later described as "the delight of my life."[14]

It was Dr. Cohen who brought Morris Abram into the world on June 19, 1918, the second son of Sam and Irene Cohen Abram. Lamar Perlis, a successful property developer in southern Georgia, now in his mid-nineties, remembered Dr. Cohen's daughter Irene as "a very dominant, powerful woman. All the things people do today, garden club, you name it, she was involved. And they had a clothing store like everybody else. She was the one who decided whatever needed to be decided."[15]

When asked about Irene, Janice Rothschild Blumberg, whose friendship with Morris Abram went back many decades to his days in Atlanta, said, "It's been a long time, but I remember what she looked like and what she sounded like, and when she said 'Jump!' you jumped. I had the feeling that she really kept the family together."[16] Abram's daughter Ruth, the oldest of his five children, has fond memories of visiting her grandparents in her father's hometown, which he liked to show off to them while his parents were still alive. "My grandfather," she recalled, "was a tiny little person with a big pot belly. When he asked me to sit on his lap when I was a little girl, I was always wondering where to sit. My grandmother was much taller than he was and seemed to be the dominant force in that family. And they had a dry goods store, and my father used to love to tell the story of how he had watched his father put a dollar in a suit and say to a farmer that if you buy this suit you'll have the dollar. And he thought that was such a good trick. But as my father said, the place never really made any money and they were always on the edge."[17] Considering the deep personality differences between Morris Abram's parents, with his father's "scorned humanity" and his mother's "bitter power," it is not surprising that they frequently clashed. To the young Abram, who learned early on that his mother's marriage to Sam Abram had been against the advice of her parents, they were "utterly mismatched."[18] As he told Eli Evans many years later, "Mother had always depreciated Daddy and his family and Daddy deeply resented it and it would come out in explosive ways in which he would say that you just don't know how good people in my family were."[19]

The clothing store Lamar Perlis and Ruth Abram remember was not the first one Sam Abram owned after working for his uncle. That one was located on Grant Street, the principal business district of town. The store went bankrupt during the panic of the early 1920s when Morris was five years old. A second store named "Red Star," opened on Pine Street in a poorer part of town, also failed, and the elder Abram decided to open a shop on the same street that sold and repaired shoes. When the shoe business proved to be less than successful, he added clothing.

"He was not a good businessman," Abram recalled of his father.

He didn't keep accounts very well, he never planned, he just operated by the seat of his pants, and the only thing he knew was what he paid for something and if he got a little bit more for it that was fine, he would give credit to people who wouldn't pay him. He did not really read and write. Mother had to do all of this. He was really a good salesman and had a nice personality, except he was so bedeviled, I think, by his financial problems, and by the host of his angers and anxieties, and relationship with Mother [that he] wasn't putting his best foot forward.[20]

The young Abram, who worked in the store after school and on weekends, didn't like to be seen there, turning his head or walking inside when he saw a car with girls inside. While he felt good about his academic achievements, he felt very "cut down" by his family's position in the town, by what his father had to do to earn a living, and by his lack of success. He was struck by the fact that the other Jewish merchants in town, "those from Eastern Europe who married wives from Eastern Europe, were doing very well indeed. But I was sort of separated from those people by virtue of my mother's attitude about them."[21]

Abram's niece Cecily, the daughter of his brother Lewis, remembers the store as dimly lit, with clothes on one side and shoes on the other. If you had to use the facilities, you would need to go outside. "There were these lime steps leading to a ladder that took you into a tent, with a chain to let the water in and out of the toilet." Sam Abram enjoyed a close relationship with his customers. "My uncle was told not to make fun of them," Cecily Abram said. "And some of them were able to help his father financially when the business got into trouble."[22]

When Morris Abram, his wife Jane, and their second daughter Ann traveled to Vaslui, Romania in the mid-1960s to visit what remained of his father's family, its members were surprised to learn that their American relative spoke no Yiddish. When asked why his father never taught him the ethnic language of his fellow Jews of Eastern

Europe, Abram was too embarrassed to reply that he never heard him speak it at home.[23]

To his mother, the granddaughter of an Alsatian Rabbi with a degree from the University of Bonn, Judaism was emphatically a religion and, in all other respects, Jews were no different from their neighbors. Just as emphatically, said Abram, his mother's tradition taught her that Jews are not a distinct people: "The idea of a linkage between people around the world as if we are more than a religion, that we carry certain germ cells, that we carry certain traditions, that we carry certain baggage, that we are tied to certain destinies—not so!"[24]

There was, in fact, a tiny but tight-knit group of a dozen Jewish families in Fitzgerald during Morris Abram's childhood. According to Ruth Singer, who was Abram's one Jewish classmate throughout their school years, Fitzgerald's Jewish community became the hub for Jews who lived in the surrounding towns and who came together to celebrate Jewish holidays and other occasions. Singer's father and uncle, the latter of whom became active in local politics, brought with them from their native Lithuania the traditions and liturgies of their Jewish ancestry and were able to lead services in Hebrew.[25] The Jews of Fitzgerald met at the local Masonic Lodge, located on the second floor of a building in the business district, until they built a synagogue in the early 1940s that stands today and continues to hold services once a month and during High Holidays. But Irene Abram and her husband Sam, who followed her lead, never became a part of that community.

"I don't know where I assimilated the idea," Morris Abram told Eli Evans, "that somehow or other they [Eastern Europeans] were different or less valuable, whatever word of depreciation you want to use, but that idea clearly got through to me."[26]

But the relationship with the other Jews in Fitzgerald was also complicated by the fierce competition among the town's businesses. According to Abram, they were by necessity contesting for every customer. "It was a fairly competitive, vicious environment," he recalled, "and I suppose that's the reason for some of my family's feeling about those other Jewish members of the community because they were so much more successful than my mother and father."[27] In the late

1920s, the Hebrew Commercial Alliance was created to help those merchants who could not borrow money during the Depression. It was a credit cooperative that provided loans to its stockholders. The cooperative's liberal lending policy helped reduce the number of bankruptcies, and from the time he joined the alliance, Sam Abram never incurred another insolvency.[28]

Eric Singer remembers his mother Ruth telling him that the Abram family sought acceptance not from the other Jewish families but rather from Fitzgerald's Protestant society. But according to his mother, "the non-Jewish society resented it, and they were never really accepted." By contrast, "her family and the other Eastern European Jews were who they were, with their funny accents, and they got along fine with everybody."[29]

According to Abram, it was not really acceptance that his family sought, since their aspirations went beyond the world around them. As he told Eli Evans, "I suppose I always had, and maybe the whole family had, a vision that was a little broader, a little wider and a little higher than the people of that town. We always felt ourselves a little misplaced, always stronger, never really at home there, always looking to go somewhere else, and I think our aspirations were higher."[30] Despite his father's lack of formal education, Abram recalled that "he didn't give a damn about how far I could throw a football," certainly an important priority for many fathers in that part of the country. "All he cared about were those grades, and that's what I emphasized."[31]

Abram recalls those rare occasions when his family, which included his older brother Lewis and younger sisters Ruthann and Jeanette, made the ninety-mile trip to the western Georgia city of Albany to attend services at a Reform Temple. But he never had his own Bar Mitzvah service to formally enter the ranks of Jewish adulthood.

This did not mean, however, that the young Morris Abram was entirely removed from his Jewish roots. A bookish youngster, he fell under the influence of a neighbor named Isadore Gelders, a Jew of Dutch origin with politically progressive views who had started his own newspaper, the *Leader, Enterprise, and Press,* to rival the older and more prosperous *Fitzgerald Herald.* The paper supported the town's railroad workers in a bitter strike in 1921. Thirty-four years later, when Morris Abram ran for Congress in Atlanta, the paper ran an editorial endorsement that read, "The career of Morris Abram has proved once again for those who know him best that a good boy makes a good man."[32]

Although married to a Methodist woman who had seen to it that their five sons were baptized in the church, Gelders was a regular attendee of Friday night Sabbath services at the Masonic Hall and, after the synagogue was built, he donated a Torah to it. Today he is buried on the edge of Fitzgerald's Jewish cemetery. Like Irene Abram, a former schoolteacher who knew Gelder's wife from their membership in a women's club, of which Irene was president, Isadore Gelders was a regular at Fitzgerald's Carnegie Free Library.[33] Abram greatly admired the editor's feistiness in challenging the local political and business establishment. Gelders is credited today with making Fitzgerald the first city in Georgia to secure free books for its schoolchildren. When Abram was in high school, Gelders convinced him to start a rival school paper that he distributed with the *Leader*. The two frequently discussed politics, and Abram called out his mentor for his support for state politicians Eugene Talmadge and Tom Watson.[34] Gelders regarded both as populists, but Abram already was sophisticated enough to abhor their bigoted demagoguery.

It was from Gelders that the young Abram first heard that Western civilization was indebted to the Jews for promoting its highest values. Abram's curiosity about his heritage led him to turn first to the index entry on Jews during his frequent reading of books on history, politics, and philosophy. By the age of thirteen, he was being called upon to offer speeches at local Bar Mitzvah services in lieu of a rabbi, which the small Jewish community could not then afford.[35]

Abram's public speaking abilities were soon established not only in Fitzgerald but also in surrounding communities. Lamar Perlis, who was seven years younger, recalled watching Abram perform on stage during his teenage years. "We had a debating club in Cordele," he recalled, "and they [Fitzgerald] had a debating club. He was on the stage debating in high school and was recognized then as someone with exceptional talent. Whatever developed, that showed early in his life. What a debater this young man was! And his scholarship, if you knew anything about him, you knew how brilliant he was. And he had the command of the language even then."[36]

Abram later attributed his interest in performing publicly to "a feeling of inadequacy, insecurity, and inferiority" that resulted from several factors, including growing up as a minority in a small town and being fed by his parents with the notion that "you are really better than your circumstances and different."[37] Abram's father encouraged his teenage son's public speaking. When he was fourteen he made the two hundred mile trip to Savannah to address a convention of railroad workers on the topic "Our Shackled Railroads." The speech was based upon a paper he had written for school that his father had shown to local members of the railroad association. "I was a ninety-pound orator," Abram wrote, "who succeeded in inciting the burly workers, joined for the occasion with management, to loud huzzahs and a standing ovation."[38]

Abram's interest in politics, stimulated in part by his father's friendships with local politicians, started very early. On the eve of Jimmy Carter's nomination for president in July 1976, Abram reflected on his early fascination with the subject:

> Until the 1950s, most of the southern population was rural. In those days, the courthouse provided most of the community's drama and entertainment. Chief attractions were the trials inside and nonstop discussion and argument over political affairs in the halls, on the steps, and spilling into a wide radius of the street. The heroes of my youth (and I belong to the same generation as Jimmy Carter) were not movie stars, sports figures, or the smart set, but politicians. An aware boy grew up with politics in his blood. Local issues unleashed passion which burned like a brand; more remote topics dazzled youthful curiosity. Spurred by the obviously high regard of parents and community for the profession of politics, techniques of debate and persuasive demeanor were studied and assimilated.[39]

In 1932, when Abram was fourteen, he wrote a letter to the *Macon Telegraph*, the newspaper the family read at home, responding to a letter attacking Governor Richard Russell. Russell was seeking his first term in the U.S. Senate, one that would propel him to a four-decade career as one of its leading figures. He had gained the young Abram's support with populist rhetoric that painted his main opponent as a friend of the power companies and the political establishment.

The letter to the *Telegraph* attracted the governor's attention, and Abram and his father were invited to a vast hunting preserve in South Georgia for a deer hunt on the property of a Russell associate. Neither had ever shot an animal. Meeting the governor was a great thrill for Abram, and he stayed friendly with Senator Russell, who became the leader of the anti-civil rights bloc in Congress, until he began fighting the county unit system.[40]

Of all the stories Abram liked to tell throughout his life from his childhood, his favorite was his father's account of an encounter that took place when he was four years old and an Indiana KKK leader came to town. The Klansman offered the number one membership card to Fitzgerald's sheriff, Elijah Dorminey, a close friend of Sam Abram's, and the sheriff asked the Klansman what he stood for. When he replied "Americanism," and the sheriff asked him for clarification, he replied, "We're against n——, Catholics, and Jews." When the sheriff told him that was not what the term meant to him and the Klansman threatened to run him out of office, Dorminey made it clear that any improper behavior on his part would have serious consequences. The man left town after the sheriff discovered that he was wanted for crimes committed in another state. Abram took great pride in the fact that Dorminey loved his father, who helped run his campaigns behind the scenes.

Andrew Young, who admired Abram's early commitment to civil rights but who later opposed his nomination by President Reagan to serve on the U.S. Commission on Civil Rights, attributed Abram's enlightened views on race to the fact that he grew up in "an unusually liberal town." He compared Fitzgerald to the Louisiana county in which he himself grew up that produced Huey Long, and the city in Mississippi that produced Hodding Carter and his family (Greenwood).[41] In 1962 Abram told a reporter for the *Atlanta Journal-Constitution* that part of the reason he gravitated to liberalism was the peculiar characteristic of Fitzgerald's founding.[42]

While it is true that Fitzgerald was different from many deep South communities in terms of racial hatred—no lynching, for example, was ever committed in the county in which it is located, despite numerous ones in surrounding counties—the town was hardly free from racial bias. Abram told Eli Evans that he never knew an integrationist in Fitzgerald when he was growing up. "I never heard the term," he said. "There may have been some closet integrationists, but I didn't know any, and I didn't detect any difference between the northerners and the southerners on that point." Moreover, his own parents "accepted the then-conventional wisdom that blacks were stupid, unwashed, and unlettered, and that those who rose above it were the exception."[43]

Abram's own views growing up were not much different. He traced the beginning of his awareness of his own prejudice to a weekend when he was home from college tending to his father's store on Pine Street. While observing a group of white and black sharecroppers and field hands—ragged, dirty, and illiterate—he tested the idea of desegregation by asking himself how many of those blacks he would invite to his home. The answer was none, but he realized that it was the same for the whites.

Why, then, he asked himself, did he require that all blacks be acceptable before any could be, a standard he did not apply to whites? And wasn't the same double standard applied to Jews, whereby all are held accountable for the behavior of some? (Interestingly, this was the same question his great-grandfather, Rabbi Eppstein, had asked about Russian Jews, whose behavior he had found distasteful.) From that time on, Abram wrote, "segregation became an abomination to me and irreconcilable with the American tradition."[44]

As for antisemitism, no Jew growing up in the state of Georgia during the 1920s could have been unfamiliar with the case of Leo Frank, a New York–born factory manager in Atlanta wrongfully accused of murdering a young employee. His lynching in 1915 after the governor commuted his death sentence "hovered like a black cloud over the region, churning up insecurities and fear, at the same time the South was on the skids economically."[45]

Abram later told an audience that he refrained from dating non-Jewish girls in high school given "the reverberations" of that case. In the same speech, he recalled frequent readings in his public school classes of the passage in the Book of John that observes, "Jesus walked in Galilee. He would not walk in Jewry because the Jews sought to kill him."[46] As a youngster he had associated antisemitism with a lack of education, believing that "it was only the white trash, the ignorant, the illiterate, the unwashed, and the unlettered" who were its adherents. But it wasn't long before he discovered that his eighth grade Algebra teacher, an educated man, disliked Jews. He later described this insight as one of the shattering experiences of his life.[47]

Abram's profound sense of alienation in his hometown led to the creation of an alter ego, a character he named Stanley Withers, who stayed with him throughout his high school years. Although Stanley was advanced academically, what distinguished him from Abram himself was his prodigious physicality and athletic ability. "Here was a figure," Abram wrote, "who could harness space and conquer time."[48]

It was physical strength, though not that alone, that Abram greatly admired in his older brother Lewis. While Morris was a runt throughout his years in Fitzgerald, weighing just over one hundred pounds, he took satisfaction in the knowledge that his six-foot-tall brother could beat up everybody in the neighborhood. And he was in awe of the backbreaking labor Lewis was able to manage during summers working the machinery at the local railroad yards.[49]

His brother played an important role in Abram's life in a more significant way. Lewis Abram cut in half a two-year medical internship to return to Fitzgerald to open a medical practice. His purpose in doing so was to earn enough money to finance his younger brother's college education. (One of his patients during that period was the young Lamar Perlis, who traveled thirty miles from his home in Cordele to be treated by Dr. Abram for asthma.) After his service in World War II, Dr. Abram left Fitzgerald for good, taking over his uncle's allergy practice in Cleveland. Morris Abram told Eli Evans that his brother had set out for the University of Georgia at age fifteen to be a lawyer but changed to medicine when he realized that "lawyers have to lie."[50] Ironically, it was the medical profession and, for a brief time, the rabbinate, that Abram had in mind when he left his home in Fitzgerald for Athens, home of the University of Georgia, in the fall of 1934.

TWO

Education

What a marvelous thing it is, both for the country and me that I, the son of an illiterate merchant, am now going to see the president of the United States.

Morris Abram was sixteen years old when he entered the University of Georgia in 1934. At five feet, six inches tall, he had delivered his high school valedictory address at Fitzgerald High School standing on a stool to enable him to see over the podium. It did not take long, however, to reach his adult height, just short of six feet.

The state of Georgia was the first to charter a state-sponsored university. The university's first building, opened in 1801, was called Franklin College of Arts and Sciences in honor of Benjamin Franklin.[1] Abram had to travel two hundred miles from Fitzgerald to reach the university's main campus in Athens, located in the northeastern part of the state.

Coming from a rural town well outside Georgia's political and cultural center, Abram was at first overwhelmed by his new surroundings. Still, he found exhilarating the opportunities they afforded him to pursue the intellectual interests he had begun to cultivate as a teenager in Fitzgerald. Abram decided early in his freshman year that he had little interest in joining a Jewish fraternity. He was, he later wrote, far too proud to assimilate with Gentiles, far too "antisemitic" to associate with exclusionary Jews, and far too socially inept to fit in with assimilated German Jews. When invited to join, he responded that he was personally opposed to groups that were segregated by race or religion.[2]

Still, the interest in Judaism he had cultivated largely on his own growing up in Fitzgerald led him to flirt early on with the idea of becoming, like his great-grandfather, a Reform rabbi. Attending Friday night services on campus, he befriended the local rabbi, who agreed to meet with him twice a week. But there were two problems. The first was his difficulty with the Hebrew language, whose alphabet he had not learned during his childhood. The second was his discovery through his exposure to the rabbi in Athens that his role was to be "the ass kisser to the rich in the congregation and to visit them on all occasions."[3]

One of the ways the university opened a new world for Abram was by exposing him to students from the larger cities of Georgia and from outside the state. Some were Jews from New York to whom Abram took an immediate dislike. Loud and "ostentatiously Jewish," he nevertheless found himself drawn to them with their ability to comprehend and talk freely about politics and high culture. Their world, he wrote, "was big, foreign, and full of new ideas."[4]

One who had a large impact on Abram's thinking was a graduate student named Joe Gitter, who had come to Athens on a teaching fellowship while pursuing a master's degree. A mathematician, philosopher, and "a first-class mind," Gitter had attended New York's City College, a haven for smart New Yorkers who could not afford its private universities. His wife Naomi was the sister of Mannheim Shapiro, head of the Community Services Division of the American Jewish Committee. The Gitters lacked the arrogance of others on campus from a similar background, and Abram found that their discussions of fundamental questions helped bring about a maturation in his political outlook.[5]

Abram's most lasting friendships at the university grew out of an introduction that was made by a university administrator who also headed the campus YMCA. Bobby Troutman, a devout Catholic, whose father was the general counsel of Coca-Cola, came from an old-line, wealthy Atlanta family. Gus Cleveland, a future head of the Georgia State Bar, was a Baptist from South Georgia. Troutman, Cleveland, and Abram soon began traveling the state under the auspices of the Religious Voluntary Association, a program of the YMCA, preaching the virtues of interreligious tolerance.

One of the trio's themes was the similarity of the three religions' traditions. Reflecting on the experience in later years, Abram noted that their discourse was made possible by papering over the enormous gulfs between their religious beliefs. The appreciative crowds reflected the fact that "we were telling people what they wanted to hear."[6]

Abram came to realize that he was speaking in those days the Judaism of his mother. "The idea of the identity and peculiarity and singularity of the Jewish tradition," he told Eli Evans, "just didn't occur to me. I was very anti-Zionist, those nuts who were going to interfere with this sweet and easy flow of amity between Jewish Americans and other Americans by creating a state which was bound to create dual loyalties, and which was bound to create all kinds of questions in the minds of people who otherwise were very sensible and had agreed to a peaceful coexistence with Jews in this country."[7]

Abram's family background—his grandfather, great aunt, uncle, and brother were all physicians—drew him early on to the study of medicine, which he pursued during his freshman year. But an inability to excel at drawing what he saw under a microscope, particularly in comparison with the other pre-med students, combined with a fear that a career in medicine would be insufficiently stimulating, led him to abandon the idea of becoming a doctor.[8] What had fascinated Abram from his childhood was the drama of the local courthouse. Now he was attracted even more to the law's more intellectual underpinnings. At the university he began his lifelong appreciation of the "majestic prose" of the U.S. Constitution, especially the words of the Fourteenth Amendment that guaranteed "equal protection of the law."[9]

Abram's teenage success as a public speaker in his hometown led him shortly after his arrival at the university to seek out the two literary societies—in reality, debating associations—on campus. His first choice, Demosthenon, named for the Greek orator Demosthenes, was one of the first literary societies in the United States, founded in 1804, the same year the university graduated its first class. A leading member was Abram's classmate Herman Talmadge.

Talmadge's father Eugene, who had succeeded Richard Russell as the state's governor two years earlier, was on the verge of establishing the machine that enabled him to dominate Georgia's politics for the next two decades. Abram was already familiar enough with his rants against FDR and organized labor to steer clear of any group with which his son was closely associated. Instead, he joined a rival organization known as Phi Kappa, founded in 1831, that carried on a friendly rivalry with Demosthenon.

The debating coach in the university's English Department got wind of Abram's walkout at the older institution because of the younger Talmadge's involvement in it and arranged a debate between the principals of a burgeoning political rivalry. Georgia governors then served two-year terms and Herman Talmadge's father was up for reelection that fall. The topic was whether Eugene Talmadge should be reelected governor.

Talmadge whipped up the working men with whom he had packed the large audience in the campus chapel in the same way his father did with his supporters on the campaign trail. Abram countered by accusing his opponent of a lack of originality. "I don't believe he would be very proud of his son tonight," Abram asserted. The tactic worked with the judges, who ruled that Abram won the debate over Talmadge.[10] The two would remain bitter political enemies throughout Abram's battles against the county unit system while Talmadge was fighting to preserve it after succeeding his father as governor in 1948. (Years later they would become friends and even business partners after working together on a fundraising project for the university.)

It was during Abram's junior year that he became president of Phi Kappa. Shortly thereafter, he came up with the idea of inviting President Roosevelt to become a member in order "to put one over on the Demosthenon." FDR had established his "Little White House" in the state's Warm Springs, which he frequented to receive treatment for polio.

Abram was astonished and delighted when the president accepted his offer to become an honorary member of Phi Kappa. Because his disability created logistical obstacles to receiving his membership in Athens, Roosevelt invited Abram and his fellow members to join him in Warm Springs for the induction. "I thought," said Abram, "what a marvelous thing it is, both for the country and me that I, the son of an illiterate merchant, am now going to see the President of the United States. It just filled me with pride."[11]

Abram invited his father to travel from Fitzgerald for the induction. Although he agreed to make the trip, Sam Abram chose to wait outside the gates of the Little White House during the ceremony. Following Abram's presentation and the president's acceptance, father and son left "with a great feeling of elation and accomplishment."[12]

But in the glare of what he called "celebrity and the high places," situations in which he frequently found himself later in his life, Abram often identified with his father, standing awkwardly outside the gates of the Little White House. Many years after the ceremony, when Abram drove his wife and youngest son to the site where he had personally inducted President Roosevelt into his college literary society, he stopped before the entrance where they all got out of the car in tribute to Sam Abram.[13]

During Abram's junior year at the university, the year he began his formal legal education, he competed for a Rhodes Scholarship, a goal he had set for himself as far back as his high school days. Although he advanced beyond the state competition, he fell short in the regionals. With assistance from his roommate Bobby Troutman, who told Abram he needed to stop speaking "like a hick," he succeeded in his senior year. Graduating *summa cum laude* in 1938, having achieved no grade during his four years below 90, he was accepted into Oxford's Pembroke College for the following fall.[14]

But Abram never set sail for Great Britain, as planned, during the fall of 1939. When Hitler's troops invaded Poland on September 1, the trust that operates the Rhodes Scholarship moved quickly to suspend the program. As Abram's hopes of studying at Oxford faded, the University of Chicago's law school announced an offer of tuition scholarships for all would-be Rhodes Scholars similarly affected by the breakout of World War II. But even with free tuition, Abram lacked the resources to cover his living expenses. Robert Troutman Sr. stepped forward to make it possible for his son's friend to complete his legal education at the highly regarded law school.

Abram found his year of study there particularly challenging, entering as a transfer student "with poor preparation" to a university whose law school had earned a reputation for academic rigor. For better or worse, he wrote to his friend Bobby Troutman, the school emphasized the philosophical underpinnings of the law, leaving the more technical aspects to be learned on one's own.[15]

Although Abram had been accepted at Harvard with a scholarship, the university offered only one year of credit for the two years he spent at the University of Georgia Law School. Chicago offered credit for both years, enabling him to enter as a third-year student. Despite his status as a Rhodes Scholar, he was frightened "not of failure but that I would not excel here."[16] Still, as he wrote to Troutman, a student at Harvard Law School and the roommate of Joseph Kennedy Jr., the older brother of JFK, he was enjoying the work more than he did at Georgia. And while he found the students not as friendly as those he had met in Athens, he developed relationships with many. They breathe the air of intellectuality, he noted, and while that could grow stale, "that is a dislike all Southerners must not carry too far."[17]

Abram quickly befriended several members of the faculty, including Fritz Kessler, a leading authority in Europe on Anglo-Saxon law who had fled Nazi Germany in 1934 with his Jewish wife. Kessler, an adherent of the school of legal realism, became best known for his work on contract law. Abram described him to Troutman as his ablest professor, with a magnetic personality and "the most delightful man I have ever known."[18]

By November he was telling his friend that he no longer needed financial support, having taken a position that paid forty dollars a month. "I can never thank you and your father enough for your help," he wrote. "Always I shall try to be the sort of person that your father would want to see whom he had helped become."[19] The job was assistant director of the Hillel Foundation, which serviced the Jewish students on campus and gave Abram the opportunity to put into practice ideas and principles he had begun developing as an undergraduate. In this role his mentor was Rabbi Maurice Pekarsky, who headed the Hillel Foundation program at Northwestern and who had taken on the task of setting up a chapter at Chicago.

Abram had met Pekarsky shortly after his arrival at the university, and the rabbi asked him shortly thereafter to lead one of the graduate seminars the foundation was sponsoring. As the relationship grew, Pekarsky became a Jewish role model, and for the first time Abram was made to feel "that Jewishness could be quite different from Protestant practice without being incomprehensible to me personally and out of phase with the American social setting." A disciple of Mordecai Kaplan, founder of Judaism's Reconstructionist Movement, Rabbi Pekarsky helped Abram restore his Jewish identity, which had been diminished during his ecumenical travels for the YMCA with his Christian friends at the University of Georgia.[20]

Abram's correspondence with his friend Bobby Troutman records a deep concern about his future as well as an uncertainty about the direction he should take in starting out his legal career. One possibility was to seek a position in Washington, but he was discouraged from doing so by the senior Troutman, who believed it would burden him with a specialization that would close off future possibilities.[21]

Abram began exploring his options in Atlanta. Janice Rothschild Blumberg remembers meeting him at the home of Leonard Haas, a prominent Atlanta attorney who was the ACLU's first lawyer in Georgia. Abram's accomplishments as an undergraduate, she said, "made him well-known particularly to interested Jewish attorneys in Atlanta. I knew a couple of them who were close to my parents who frequently invited him to their homes. Their wives had intentions of getting to know him because they would have a brunch party on Sunday and would invite all the single girls in Atlanta, I mean we were all single, the girls in our crowd who they thought were reasonably intelligent, to meet him."[22]

But Abram was already attached. During his junior year in Athens he began a romance with a young woman named Virginia Somerville from the small town of Rockmart in the northwestern part of the state. Abram described her as "tall and willowy, attractive, very sweet, reasonably intelligent and quite believing in Jesus, though thoroughly accepting of me." Although he dated other women during his year in Chicago, he told Bobby Troutman that "every other girl is dim beside her."[23]

Abram told Eli Evans that he and Virginia didn't have sex because this was not done "unless you intended to marry the person." And marriage was never really in the cards for them. For one thing, Abram said, "her horizons were limited," and "I knew very well that I had more potential in me than she had in her." And he did not think he could spend his life with someone "who genuinely believed in Jesus." But she was loving and "I had many a pleasant day with her." Although they ceased to go out with one another in 1943, they stayed in touch for many years afterward.[24]

In view of Abram's degree from a prestigious law school, his legal career got off to a surprisingly rocky start. During his undergraduate days at the University of Georgia, Abram had spent many weekends at the Troutman home at 132 Peachtree Circle in the affluent Ansley Park section of Atlanta, where the family had a live-in butler and maid. Abram was grateful to his friend, who "opened up Atlanta" for him.

But if he expected to receive an offer from the firm of Spaulding, Troutman and Meadows upon his return to Atlanta following graduation, he was soon to be disappointed. "Here was a man," he said, referring to his best friend's father, "who thought I was very bright, invested money in me, would never let me repay him, and never thought of inviting me into his law firm, where his son was then practicing, nor did the son think of it."[25]

Miles Alexander, who became a senior partner in the Atlanta law firm Kilpatrick, Townsend and Stockton, knew Abram early in his career by reputation and later through his involvement in the local chapter of the American Jewish Committee. Alexander said that in those days, "Atlanta firms did not take women, did not take blacks, and many did not take Jews. I know that early in Morris's career that left a real mark on him because his closest friends in college were Bobby Troutman, Gus Cleveland, and Harry Baxter, and they went with the prestigious firms."[26]

Many years after Abram's failure to find a place in the Spaulding Troutman law firm, the younger Troutman's sister told Abram that he was acceptable "until I got mixed up with the colored question or the county unit, and then, brother, she said, they were steering clear of me but really because they didn't want to be tarred."[27]

Although he had friendly conversations with the principals of seven law firms, including Haas, he received only one offer.[28] Allen Post, who had served on the committee that had selected Abram for the Rhodes Scholarship, took him into his practice after he received his JD from the University of Chicago in the summer of 1940. Allowing himself only ten days to prepare for the Georgia Bar exam, Abram was stunned to learn that he had failed it and would need to retake it later that year. He later claimed the reason he didn't pass the exam was because he had atrocious handwriting, and the panel of examiners was old and didn't want to bother reading his responses. The evidence he offered was that the only difference between his first and second attempt was that in the latter successful effort he took more care with his handwriting.[29]

Nonetheless, while waiting for the results of the retake of the exam, Abram was offered a position in the firm Howell and Post at the standard wage of seventy dollars per month. The senior partner in the firm, Hugh Howell, a former chairman of the state Democratic Party's Executive Committee, had been a close adviser of Eugene Talmadge early in his career. When Talmadge ran for governor two years earlier, Abram had campaigned against him.[30] By the time Abram joined the firm, Howell and the senior Talmadge had become enemies.[31] To make matters even more complicated, a senior associate at the firm of Howell and Post, himself a Klansman, was the son of the Grand Dragon of the Knights of the KKK.[32]

Abram did have one more opportunity when the head of the Fulton National Bank offered him a position there. But a career with the bank, he believed, would restrict his political views and the work would be "damn dull." But there was another reason. Abram saw no Jews in high places in any of Atlanta's banks, and he wasn't about to enter an institution in which there would be some lid on where I could go."[33] Many years later, recalling the experience during his presidency of the American Jewish Committee, he took the opportunity at a gathering of one thousand and five hundred of the country's top bankers to chide their industry for not advancing Jews to management positions.[34]

At first Abram was encouraged by the opportunity to practice law in Atlanta. Allen Post, he informed Bobby Troutman, "I find to be a brilliant man, but even more than that. He is fair and friendly as well. Mr. Howell has his limitations, but there is no man I have known who is more genuinely kind or willing to help whenever he can."[35]

But for the most part, he found the work disappointing. Post, who had gained a first in law from Oxford's Bailliol College, had little time for mentoring and Howell lacked the ability to do so.[36] What was most significant about this interlude between the completion of his law degree and Abram's decision to join the U.S. military was his introduction to Carlyn Feldman, the daughter of a prominent member of the Atlanta Jewish community who had founded the Puritan Chemical Company. Abram was drawn to her extraordinary beauty. Although the two began seeing one another, marriage was out of the question, since she was still in her late teens. As he wrote to Bobby Troutman, "she is still so young there is no need for much pressure."[37]

But with war approaching, Abram was beginning to feel financial pressure. He was determined to follow the example set by his older brother in enabling him to afford college by doing the same for his younger sister Jeanette. He was already a second lieutenant in the Air Force reserves from his ROTC days, and by enlisting he could choose his desired location: Fort McPherson, a base near Atlanta.

Abram spent the war years entirely in the United States. During the early months after his enlistment, he was telling Troutman that he had intentions of marrying Virginia Somerville.[38] But two years later his life took an entirely different turn. A friend of his at the University of Chicago had told him during his year there about his girlfriend, a woman from a prominent Florida family. Abram was more than intrigued by her photo and the letters she sent to his friend.[39]

Toward the end of 1943, Abram's friend from his days in Chicago gave him an introduction to his now former girlfriend Jane Maguire in Orlando as she prepared to participate as a sponsor for the Orange Bowl in Miami on New Year's Day. A twenty-three-year-old graduate of the Florida State College for Women, Jane Maguire was a reporter and feature writer for the *Orlando Morning Sentinel*. To Abram, she represented the perfect mate for someone seeking to move from the world of his childhood to one to which he aspired. Jane's father, Raymer Maguire, was a past president of the Florida Bar Association, a leading candidate for national ABA president, and chairman of the state board of regents. Jane's mother, Ruth McCulloch Maguire, was a cousin of the founder of the McCrory chain of five and dime stores. In addition to her role as a journalist, Jane was a member of the Orlando Welfare Association and the Spinsters Cotillion.[40]

To Abram, "this was all I was looking for in terms of family," a gate opener who satisfied all his ambitions. Coming from a well-connected family, Jane Maguire was beautiful, elegant, and well-dressed. In short, she had "all the graces to open all the doors and to make me feel more comfortable socially with all the gaucheries" that came from growing up in Fitzgerald.[41] They were married in a formal ceremony by the pastor of Orlando's First Methodist Church at the home of a friend of Jane's parents, who were separated. Neither Raymer Maguire, who gave his daughter in marriage, nor his wife was told that Morris and Jane had been married first by the Reform rabbi in Albany, Georgia, two weeks before.[42]

The year 1944 marked brief stints for the newlyweds as part of Abram's military service in Illinois, Alabama, Washington DC, and Texas. The following year, as the war was winding down and his wife was pregnant with their first child, they moved to Santa Ana, California, where Abram, now a major, was sent to direct the public relations effort at the country's largest Air Force base. There he met Gus Tyler, who as a young socialist had argued passionately against rearmament in the 1930s to prepare for a Second World War. With Tyler as his tutor, he gained an understanding of the bewildering factional distinctions that characterized the American political left. As the war was winding down, Abram and Tyler organized a conference to address the needs of returning soldiers, and its success helped garner for Major Abram the Legion of Merit.[43]

Abram had not abandoned his dream of studying at Oxford. Shortly after the war he began making inquiries about how to enroll for the term beginning in January 1946. By then the trust that runs the program had relaxed the rule about the scholars bringing their wives, but children were not allowed to accompany them. On the advice of the trust's American secretary, Swarthmore president Frank Aydelotte, Abram traveled to England with both Jane and their young daughter Ruth and managed to enroll without incident.[44]

The two years spent in England were for Morris Abram an idyllic time. The sweeping beauty of his surroundings, the university's rich cultural traditions, and the intellectual stimulation he received from some of the world's most brilliant minds were more than he could have hoped for. But the living conditions they faced were less than ideal. Morris, Jane, and Ruth lived in a mews flat infested with mice. It had a potbelly stove and an insufficient amount of coal to deal with what Abram described as the coldest place he had ever experienced. Jane would ride her bicycle to the coke ovens and as soon as the coke came out would bring twenty-five cents worth home to keep the baby warm.[45]

Jane, though not able to advance her own career, was more than up to the domestic challenges they faced. "We lived in a tiny attic apartment that could only be reached through a trapped door," said Ruth, "but that didn't stop my mother from entertaining university dons who had to enter through that trapped door to reach the modest flat. It never embarrassed her; she was a princess and he was a king."[46]

At Oxford, Abram pursued a BA in politics, philosophy, and economics on the advice of his tutor after abandoning his original plan to study for a PhD.[47] It was the relationship Abram developed with Arthur Lehman Goodhardt, the Regius Professor of Jurisprudence, that opened the door to a life-changing experience. Born into an American Jewish family, Goodhardt was the grandson of one of the founders of the Lehman Brothers investment banking house. During Abram's first year at Oxford, the professor visited U.S. Supreme Court Justice Robert Jackson in Nuremburg, Germany, where he was serving as the Chief Prosecutor of Nazi war criminals and returned with an enthusiastic evaluation of the conduct of the trials.

Jackson agreed to Goodhart's request to take Abram on during his summer recess at Oxford as a member of the chief prosecutor's staff. In Nuremburg the Abrams lived in luxury at the Grand Hotel where the staff was housed, a welcome contrast to their meager accommodations in Oxford. In the Grand Hotel, he recalled, "we were the rulers."[48]

Abram's assigned task was to comb the trial record of the top Nazi leaders to come up with evidence that could be used against those German industrialists who had fueled the Nazi war machine. He was convinced that all those in this defendant category were guilty, and that the ultimate tragedy was that "the sons of bitches never got their just desserts." Most guilty, he had no doubt, were Hjalmer Schact, the banker, well known and respected in the West, and Franz Von Pappen, a friend of the pope. Abram believed their source of protection was the fact that both had powerful friends in the United States, including Gen. Dwight Eisenhower and such high U.S. officials as Lucius Clay and John J. McCloy.[49]

Abram learned much about trial techniques during his summer in Nuremburg. He was highly impressed with the British prosecutor who questioned Julius Streicher, the publisher of the notorious Nazi publication *Der Stermer*. Rather than dwelling on Streicher's Jew-baiting, the counsel concentrated on his incitement that led directly to the destruction of Nuremberg's great synagogue in a speech that had lasted nearly two hours. By contrast, Abram was disappointed with the performance of Justice Jackson, whose early cross-examination of Hermann Goering dealt with Nazi philosophy, enabling the war criminal to run circles around his inquisitor.[50]

Abram's experience at the Nuremburg trials included, in addition to hearing oral testimony, seeing graphic photographs, films, and written documentation of the slaughter of the millions of Jews and others designed and carried out by the Nazis. It taught him unforgettable lessons that shaped many of his future views about international law, strengthened his belief in a homeland for the Jews, and brought him closer to the Jewish people. The Nuremberg experience, he said, did as much as anything to establish his identity.

During the trials, Abram wrote, he "began to ponder the links that bind all Jews to some common fate." No longer was that bond strictly religious, as defined by their enemies. The anti-Semite had now broadened the definition of Jews to include the genes of a single grandparent.[51]

Abram strongly defended the legality of the Nuremberg trials, which he believed were conducted with scrupulous adherence to due process. Far from a kangaroo court, many of those on trial he believed to be guilty were declared innocent. Regarding the charge that the trials were *ex-post facto*, he argued that the Hitler regime had clearly violated international treaties that Germany had signed. And perhaps most significant, it was important for the sake of history to know what the defendants did and why they were being punished. Guilt was established by written documents that provided indisputable proof.[52]

When Abram was a student at the University of Chicago, despite his interest in the subject of legal philosophy taught by future Attorney General Edward Levi, he could never quite grasp the idea of natural law. The concept, going back to the ancient Israelites, Christians, Greeks, and Romans, posits that there are laws that transcend the rules adopted by a particular society or state. It was not until that summer of 1946, while working on Justice Jackson's staff in Nuremberg, that Abram began to realize what the Nazis had violated was "a system of right and justice binding on all humanity."[53]

For Abram, the experience provided a powerful intellectual and emotional awakening. During the year Canadian corporate lawyer Eric Block worked at UN Watch, Abram spoke with him about working for Justice Jackson at Nuremberg and being moved by the experience, and by the evidence that was supplied. As Block recalled, "I think Morris knew about the Holocaust, but at Nuremberg he came face-to-face with the evidentiary record which just astonished him. Not just evidence about the slaughter of Jews but how the people on trial at Nuremberg were more than willing participants."[54]

During his years as an undergraduate, Abram had considered himself an anti-Zionist. The first time his position on that issue changed was the summer he was forced to confront firsthand what had befallen the Jewish people. As Jane Abram expressed it, "either you're a Jew with no heart or a Zionist." Abram said, "It flummoxed me, that she, a non-Jew, should see things so clearly."[55]

But beyond that insight, Nuremberg exposed Morris Abram to complicated legal questions and courtroom practices that would occupy his mind and influence his outlook on fundamental questions for the rest of his life. Upon the completion of his Oxford education, Abram began to incorporate many of those lessons when he returned to Atlanta to practice law.

THREE

Atlanta Lawyer

He had the reputation of being a kind of modern Atticus Finch, who
was willing to take on these tough race cases.

M orris Abram sought advice from Supreme Court Justice Hugo
Black when deciding whether to return to Georgia when his
Rhodes Scholarship to Oxford came to an end in 1948. He told
Justice Black that he intended to do battle with the county unit system, did not accept segregation, and tended to question traditional
premises on which current Southern economic, social, and political life were based. Black did not sugarcoat his response: "If you
return to Georgia and pursue your beliefs," he told the young lawyer, "expect to get your head beaten in."

Three decades later, when delivering the Hugo Black lecture at
the University of Alabama Law School, Abram recalled that he went
back to his native state and fought the county unit system, said and
did what he pleased in public life, and survived very well. "I was
never thrashed," he said, "but sometimes threatened."[1]

After a brief stint working in Washington DC as the assistant to the
director of the Committee for the Marshall Plan, Abram returned to
Atlanta to resume his practice of law. He began by contacting Hugh
Howell, the former pro-Talmadge candidate for governor and senior
partner of the small firm with which he had been associated during
his brief period in Atlanta following law school. Howell, who was no

longer involved in politics, introduced Abram to his partners Arthur Heyman, then in his eighties, and his son Herman.

Coincidentally, Abram knew the younger Heyman's son, one of his students at the Sunday school where he had taken a part-time job in 1940 to earn extra money to make ends meet. After receiving glowing recommendations of Herman Heyman from the senior Troutman and from Allan Post, the senior partner at the firm where he worked before the war, Abram decided to join the firm.[2]

He would never regret it. Robert Hicks, who began practicing law in Atlanta in the early fifties, regarded Herman Heyman as "one of the finest men I ever met in every sense of the word. He was extremely brilliant, Phi Beta Kappa. Just an elegant man, too, and his wife was an elegant lady. He was President of The Temple and the two of them were important people in Atlanta in the Jewish community."[3]

Abram took a job with the firm that paid him $300 a month. He and Jane rented a two bedroom apartment with a monthly rent of $95.[4] Herman Heyman became a mentor to Abram, leaving him free to develop in the law and encouraging his public role. Abram's involvement in issues of concern to the black community began very shortly after his return to Atlanta. "He had the reputation," recalled Andrew Young, then a young preacher pastoring in South Georgia, "of being a kind of modern Atticus Finch, who was willing to take on these tough race cases."[5]

Abram's thinking on matters of race had undergone a transformation since his days as a youngster growing up in a segregated community. And it required him to face the prospect of a very uphill battle against prevailing opinion. In his 1972 address to the graduates of Emory University, he recalled the time during his senior year at Georgia when a black graduate from a good college indicated that he wished to apply to the university's law school. The young man had circulated a tactful letter to the student body seeking, if not their support, at least their non-resistance. Abram never forgot the response of "one brilliant and otherwise open-minded law student" who spoke in opposition to the almost uniform rejection and disdain of the black student's plea: "Let him in but let him understand that he must sit in the back of the class and move to the side of the sidewalk as whites pass."[6]

In 1949 Abram drafted an *amicus* brief on behalf of his firm in a challenge to the state's New Voter Registration Act. The law imposed either literacy or knowledge of citizenship tests on voters, with the results left to the discretion of the local white registrars. It was a clear effort to disenfranchise the few blacks who had the courage to show up to vote. "In a world where tyranny is so widespread," Abram wrote, "American jurisprudence is firmly grounded on the proposition that the freedom for all and all of our freedoms are safe only in a system of law. As Cicero said: We are in the bondage of the law, in order that we may be free. . . . The unconstitutionality of this Act results from the Legislature's willful disregard of the organic law of the land."[7]

Abram persuaded then attorney Elbert Tuttle, later one of the leading pro-civil rights southern federal judges, to join the brief in the case of *Franklin v. Harper* before the Georgia Supreme Court. Tuttle was very pleased with the brief, writing the young lawyer, "I think you have done a marvelous job and I am very glad to be with you on the brief."[8] Abram also received a letter from Ellis Arnall, Georgia's progressive governor from 1942 to 1946, praising the brief: "Let me again tell you how very excellent I think it is."[9]

Grace Towns Hamilton, who was the executive director of the National Urban League's Atlanta chapter at the time, recalled how the black community had been dealt an unfair allocation of bond funds for the erection of separate but equal schools. When she asked Abram to intervene with the city's power structure, he brought their case before business leaders as well as the president of the school board and the superintendent of schools.[10] Hamilton admired Abram as a man of principle: "He supported me in my efforts to improve medical facilities for blacks in the public hospital," she wrote. "He supported my successful efforts to bring black physicians on its staff; he fought to make land space available for blacks to live on; we worked for middle class housing in which blacks could live; and of course, he was a leader in the fight to get rid of the county unit system which was the pillar of racist politics." Hamilton, who later became the first black woman elected to the Georgia legislature, said that Abram practiced his beliefs "when very few southern whites surfaced in our struggle."[11]

Hamilton's biographers note that of all the programs sponsored by the Atlanta Urban League (AUL) during her time as its executive director, housing was its biggest success.[12] In 1946, Atlanta's black population, which encompassed 33 percent of the population, accounted for only 16 percent of its living space, with 71 percent of its housing deemed to be substandard. Instead of pressing for integrated housing, which would have stimulated violence, the AUL's approach was to seek areas of land expansion that were not taken by the post–World War II flight of whites to the suburbs. Abram played a key intermediary role in these transactions. In the case of "Western Land," a corporation formed to establish a beachhead for black ownership in the area, of the twenty-three investors, Abram was the only white. When R. A. Thompson, the AUL's point person on housing, was asked if two additional tracts purchased to create moderate priced homes for blacks would have been sold had this ultimate purpose been known, he replied, "Might have, we don't know. It was just easier for Morris to buy it, since he was white."[13]

In 1951, Herman Heyman and Abram formed a new partnership. They took with them as an associate Robert Young, who would later become the county attorney of Fulton County. Abram's office on the fifteenth floor of the Healey Building featured sculptures of Rodin's "The Kiss" and the "Scales of Justice." Maurice "Ted" Maloof, the son of Lebanese immigrants and a young lawyer looking for a like-minded firm to associate with in the late 1950s, was attracted to Abram's law practice: "I had heard of him as a liberal and we were liberals. And I knew he had brought cases to bring down the county unit system to declare it unconstitutional. It was the kind of law I wanted to practice."[14]

Miles Alexander recalled Abram as "bright, liberal, an outstanding trial lawyer." When the Lennox Square shopping mall was being developed in the 1950s, the city of Atlanta was using eminent domain to put in roads that were wiping out a small black neighborhood in the upscale Buckhead section where maids, chauffeurs, and those who worked and had jobs in white homes lived. "Morris was challenging the amount of money the state was giving them for their homes," recalled Alexander. Abram used an innovative argument that these homes were irreplaceable, since there was no other area where black residents could buy homes where there was no juvenile delinquency, where the schools were good, and where their children could have contact with white children. As a result, he contended, the compensation for their homes should be the fair market value of homes in their area, not in terms of what they were worth then but what they would be worth to willing buyers and sellers in the black community who wanted to be there.[15]

This kind of approach, according to Maloof, led to Abram's exclusion from the city's social clubs where the lawyers in what he termed the "silk-stocking" firms congregated. "Morris was respected for his intelligence, but they did not like him handling all these cases that he handled." Those cases garnered Abram a great deal of publicity.[16] One such case marked the first successful malpractice suit brought in the southern United States against a highly respected doctor. Abram's client, Agnes Railey, was the victim of ill-advised brain surgery to cure epilepsy that left her unable to lead anything resembling a normal life.

During his two years at Oxford, Abram had had pangs of regret that he hadn't pursued the medical education he had abandoned during his undergraduate years. "I'm a frustrated doctor," he told Eli Evans. "I guess that's why I've been so extraordinarily successful in litigating malpractice cases."[17] Railey's suit against a prominent Atlanta neurosurgeon required three trials and two years of flying to numerous cities in the United States and Canada to gather evidence. In the end, Abram's exhaustive research paid off for his client.

The case enabled Abram to display a wide array of talents, including an impressive lay understanding of medicine, an aggressive courtroom manner, and an unyielding determination to challenge the forces arrayed against him, which included the Georgia medical establishment and expensive insurance attorneys. The suit on behalf of Mrs. Railey resulted in the largest judgment ever received in a DeKalb County court up to that time. According to Maloof, "The silk-stocking lawyers liked Herman and used to ask him, 'Herman, how did you partner with this guy?' They saw Morris as an ambitious go-getter. They didn't embrace him. Of course, Morris didn't need to have anyone embrace him. He knew who he was and was very satisfied with that."[18]

As Abram's success as a trial lawyer grew, so did his local reputation along with his ability to receive press notice. According to Maloof, Abram had a nose for publicity. But "he wanted people around him to get recognition, too. He tried to get recognition for all of us. In the county unit case it was all him, but he wanted them to list in the article the names of all the people who worked on it. Which was nice for us and not necessary. But he was that way. He wasn't trying to hog at all."[19]

Elliott Levitas, who would later become the U.S. congressman from Georgia's Fourth Congressional District representing Atlanta's growing suburbs from 1975–85, first met Morris Abram when he was invited by the Abrams to dinner after being named a Rhodes Scholar at Emory University in 1956. Levitas recalled how his admiration for Abram grew over the years: "I was very impressed with him. He became for me something of an aspirational role model because he had the reputation of being a good lawyer, he was active in a community that needed representation and visibility, and I knew of his background and that was also inspirational." Levitas later joined the team of young lawyers who provided research and other assistance to Abram and his law partners when they were working on the county unit system cases.[20]

Following the demise of the white primary and two unsuccessful challenges to the county unit system, the second led by Abram shortly after he returned to Atlanta, his old nemesis from his University of Georgia days Herman Talmadge, now sitting in the governor's seat, began the first of two campaigns to institutionalize the system by implanting it into the state's constitution and extending its reach beyond party primaries to include general elections. Abram played a major role in those campaigns, which were successful in turning back these efforts. In 1952 he chaired a committee organized by the state chapter of the League of Women Voters called Citizens Against the County Unit Amendment.[21]

Joining Abram and his colleagues from the League and other civic groups was an attorney from a prominent and very conservative

Macon, Georgia family named Charles Baxter Jones Jr. As Abram said, Jones was born with a garrote in his hand to use against his father. "He could make the most radical idea sound conservative," he recalled, "and he would get an orgasm over doing so." This quality he contrasted with his own ability "to take a conservative idea and make it sound radical."[22]

In 1952 Jones took on the sitting congressman from Georgia's Fifth Congressional District, James Davis, a former state judge who had been a member of the Ku Klux Klan during the 1920s. As a state assemblyman, Davis had sponsored a bill passed into law requiring a card index of all Georgians indicating whether they had a trace of Negro blood. Abram, who raised funds for Jones, looked on as the congressman conducted a smear campaign against his candidate, centered on his part-time position teaching business law at a local black college. While Jones won the popular vote, he lost the county unit vote, returning Davis to Washington.

It was the second time that Davis had won his seat while receiving a minority of the vote, and Abram was convinced that he could make a credible run for the seat himself in 1954 by making this fact the centerpiece of his campaign. It wasn't the first time that he had thought about entering politics. While completing his Rhodes Scholarship at Oxford, Abram considered returning to his hometown of Fitzgerald to run in Georgia's Third Congressional District, which included the city of Columbus.[23] When he appeared before the Fulton County Commission in January 1950 with his friend Grace Towns Hamilton, the black head of the city's Urban League chapter, he allowed her to introduce herself rather than violate the racial norms of the day by using a polite title for her, an act which would have jeopardized his political viability.[24]

But to say that Abram was in for a rough ride during his campaign for Congress is an understatement. That the race issue would dominate the campaign became inevitable shortly after Abram announced his candidacy when in May, the U.S. Supreme Court handed down its unanimous decision in the groundbreaking case of *Brown v. Board of Education*. During the campaign, Abram, while avoiding the issue of desegregation, did say that the law of the land had to be obeyed.[25]

The Fifth Congressional District consisted of three counties: Fulton, the more urbanized part of Atlanta; DeKalb, the home of James Davis, which was then primarily rural; and the small county of Rockdale, whose population at the time was under 8,500. The problem for a candidate with Abram's political orientation was that in the Democratic primary, which invariably determined the eventual outcome, it was rural Rockdale's two unit votes that determined the winner of races in which one candidate carried Fulton and the other DeKalb. As an editorial in the *Atlanta Journal* during the 1952 campaign pointed out, in a close race, Rockdale's 1,500 voters could determine who would represent the Fifth CD.[26]

On the last day of July, Abram kicked off his Rockdale campaign by riding a two-horse buggy into Conyers, Georgia, the heart of Rockdale County, with his wife Jane and his three children, Ruth, Ann, and Morris Jr. Parking the buggy on the courthouse lawn, he stood on the back seat and took aim at the incumbent congressman. Abram blasted Davis for his failure to do anything positive for the Fifth Congressional District, for his unwillingness to defend the Democratic Party against what he called "GOP slander," and for his blocking of America's fight against Communism and its efforts to achieve world peace. In a county that benefitted greatly from the county unit system, Abram said he would abolish the undemocratic system.[27]

The audience applauded when Abram explained how his family's home in Fitzgerald had been saved by a federal agency during the Depression and how, with that action, "Morris Abram became a Democrat for the rest of his life." Asking why the congressman could not get in step with Georgia's senators Richard Russell and Walter George, he criticized Davis for voting against his party 67 percent of the time. Abram ended his oration with a passage about the Lord's kingdom "from the prayer book I use in my religious life."[28]

Two days later, readers of the *Atlanta Journal* found in their morning newspapers a four-page paid advertisement supplement highlighted by what Abram regarded as the key issues of his campaign, namely, economic development and an end to the undemocratic county unit system. "In his busy legal career," the supplement noted, "he is in the middle of the District's diverse economic activities, its role of leadership in finance, in wholesale and retail trade, in service enterprises, in transportation and communications. He will be on top of the problems and needs of all these activities, as only an intelligent, forward looking young man can be." The supplement included a statement by his campaign manager, Stephens Mitchell, brother of the famed Atlanta author of *Gone with the Wind,* on why Morris Abram would be a positive force for progressive growth in the district.[29]

Regarding the county unit system, Abram pointed out in the supplement that in non-statewide races, the practice was not required by law and not even sanctioned in the Fifth Congressional District by custom, having been substituted for free, popular voting in 1946. He also noted that the Congressional nominee appoints the District Democratic Committee that determines whether the unit system will be applied, and that in both 1950 and 1952, both Fulton and DeKalb counties had voted overwhelmingly to defeat the proposed amendments giving the system state constitutional protection.[30]

During the 1952 campaign to add the county unit system to the state's constitution, two of its leading opponents, Jones and Abram, had been attacked during the height of the Red Scare as Communist sympathizers.[31] Two years later, the former Klansman Davis highlighted Abram's membership in the American Civil Liberties Union, which the congressman claimed was giving clandestine aid to the Communist Party.[32] He attacked Abram as the candidate of the most radical elements of organized labor and of the Negroes.

Hovering over Abram's campaign was what he later described as an "undercurrent" of antisemitism, which he regretted not confronting.[33] Atlanta's Jewish community was still traumatized by the 1913 trial, conviction, and subsequent lynching of Leo Frank. Abram recalled how he was frequently reduced to collecting money for his campaign, anonymously, so it wouldn't be known that he was the recipient.[34]

Miles Alexander, then a summer law associate, recalled attending several debates between the two candidates, one with Barbara Hillman, the future wife of his good friend Elliott Levitas:

> I remember being very disappointed in Morris's inability to cope with James Davis, who would interrupt him and speak over him during their

debates. Morris was used to a certain civility in exchanges. He could not compete in that realm of someone who would lack any courtesy and who would not let him talk without interrupting him. Babs and I both had the same reaction that he was losing the debates despite being a much better speaker. Morris was not able to finish his sentence before Davis interrupted him with some irrelevant and usually pejorative comment. It was not his lack of speaking ability. It was his lack of ability to cope with someone of that ilk.[35]

Years later Abram attributed the nastiness of the campaign to the fact that the *Brown* decision had been handed down the very month he announced his candidacy. And there was no question that the state's segregationists were watching in a state of alarm. Georgia's most well-known segregationist, Governor (Herman) Talmadge, noted that there had been an unbroken chain of what he referred to as "bloc voting" since the white Democratic primary was declared unconstitutional by the U.S. Supreme Court. "In the 1954 Congressional race in Atlanta," he wrote, "Congressman James C. Davis, who was reelected, received only 540 votes in these bloc-vote controlled precincts to 5,558 for his opponent," not mentioning Abram by name.[36]

In the end, Abram carried Fulton County but lost the unit votes of both DeKalb and Rockdale. Throughout his life he would contend that it was the county unit system that had led to his defeat, but he also lost the popular vote by a five thousand vote margin. Ralph McGill would later write that Abram was defeated in 1954 by "demagoguery, prejudice, and the county system."[37] As Mayor Hartsfield pointed out in his affidavit to the Supreme Court in the case of *Gray v. Sanders*, under the unit system it was not customary for people in the urban counties to register or vote in anything like the proportionate numbers they were to the population because of the fact that their votes didn't count.[38]

Looking back on that election over two decades later, Abram told Eli Evans that he was far from the ideal candidate: "I'm not a political animal. I think I am, but I'm not. I don't like to see my name in headlines in the *New York Times*. I don't like to self-advertise myself on a billboard I've paid for, I don't like to hear spot announcements about myself for Congress. I don't like to get up early in the morning and shake hands. I don't like chicken dinners, the tyranny of political clubs."[39]

Although elected office eluded him, Abram did receive a key public position in the summer of 1958 when he was called upon by Mayor Hartsfield to head up a crime committee for the city of Atlanta composed of leading citizens. The mayor had been stung by a *Time* magazine story that said Atlanta had the second highest crime rate in the country. He charged the committee, headed by the young lawyer with whom he was working closely to abolish the state's county unit system, to propose recommendations to the city, the counties of Fulton and DeKalb, and the state legislature.[40]

Joseph Lefkoff was a recent Emory Law School graduate when he was recommended to Abram by Charles Weltner, a Georgia liberal who became the first Fifth District Congressman elected after the demise of the county unit system and later served on Georgia's Supreme Court. Lefkoff recalled meeting Abram when the young lawyer spoke to his law school's honorary society. Invited to dinner at the Abrams with his wife following the Weltner recommendation, Lefkoff recalled voicing his differences with Abram about the legality of the Nuremberg trials. This, however, did not prevent Abram from offering the recent graduate a position at Heyman, Abram and Young. As Lefkoff recalled,

> the bar in Atlanta in 1960 was very interesting. Everyone knew everyone else. There were not a lot of Jewish practitioners in Atlanta, particularly in the larger firms. Herman Heyman, who was the senior partner, had an incredible reputation. He was as well respected as any lawyer in Atlanta. And to some degree Morris had benefitted from Herman's reputation. He [Abram] was considered a maverick of sorts in that he would undertake some cases that other lawyers might not be willing to jump into. And of course, Morris was a brilliant trial lawyer. If you ever tried a case with him or against him, you would have respect for him.[41]

Lefkoff recalled the medical malpractice case Abram brought that had been tried twice, resulting both times in hung juries. The third time he tried it, he involved his good friend Osgood Williams. "Osgood was a country lawyer," Lefkoff remembered. "He used Osgood to read medical depositions to the jury. And Osgood had trouble, stumbling over all the medical terms. He humanized the case. And it resulted in a substantial medical malpractice verdict that Morris took great credit for."[42]

Abram's relationship with Osgood Williams stretched back to the early 1950s after he coauthored a pamphlet for the local office of the Anti-Defamation League. The publication included five pieces of model legislation aimed at weakening the Ku Klux Klan, a fact that was used to paint him as the candidate of the blacks in his 1954 campaign for Congress. Abram recalled from his childhood the incident when the sheriff of Ben Hill County, a friend of his father, had stood up to an outside organizer for the Klan. The legislation he proposed would restrict cross-burning and, most significantly, unmask Klansmen during their hate-filled demonstrations.[43]

In 1950, Williams, then a recently elected state senator from a rural north Georgia county, showed up in Abram's office offering to introduce the Klan legislation in the Georgia legislature. It was a gutsy thing to do at the time, given the anger he knew it would generate back home. Williams was also only one of fifteen state senators to oppose the Talmadge amendment to expand the county unit system to include general elections.

Not surprisingly, Williams promptly lost his bid for reelection when the Talmadge political machine contributed heavily to his opponent and threatened elderly voters with the loss of their pensions. He moved to Atlanta, where he set up a law office in the same building where Abram's firm was located. The two struck up a friendship that would last the remainder of their lives.[44]

After he moved to New York, Abram maintained close contact with the man he referred to as "the Wizard," who became a Superior Court judge in Atlanta. According to Joseph Lefkoff, "Morris loathed certain aspects of Atlanta, but he loved his good friend Osgood Williams. Probably on an average of once a week we would have to get on the phone. He would call, and I would have to get Osgood on the phone and we would sit and just blabber for 30 or 40 minutes. I don't know who he was billing his time to."[45] When asked by a reporter to describe Williams, Abram said that his friend was "moral, but not moralistic. He doesn't wear his goodness on his sleeve." According to Lefkoff, "I cannot overstate the importance of Osgood Williams to Morris."[46]

In 1988, Judge Williams was honored by the Litigation Section of the Atlanta Bar Association as the first recipient of its new annual award. Asked by the dinner chair to offer comments, Abram sent the following message from New York: "Osgood Williams is a 20th Century Original. To find a counterpart, one would have to go back to a previous century and a lanky country lawyer of wit and wisdom who left his farming community for positions of greater scope and service. Jimmy Carter became the first Georgia president of the United States. Had Osgood Williams been born a decade later, that distinction could have fallen on him. If that had occurred, the country would have been well served."[47] When Williams died in 1994, Abram returned to Atlanta from his home in Geneva for the funeral and delivered the eulogy.

Ted Maloof recalled the congenial atmosphere of the Heyman, Abram, Young law firm: "It was just a great place to work. Everybody was dedicated. Everybody loved Morris. Morris was never mean; everybody who worked with him thought he was God. He had a good relationship with people in the firm. He would do a lot of laughing and a lot of practical jokes."[48]

One of those jokes Abram's partners played on him backfired badly when President Kennedy offered him the ambassadorship to the newly independent East African country of Tanganyika, then on the verge of achieving its independence from Great Britain. Knowing that Abram had sought a more prestigious position in the new administration, they conspired to send the president a letter complaining of the offer while Abram was in the country representing the United States in its independence ceremonies. Abram was furious when he read a blind copy of the letter on his desk upon his return before realizing it was bogus.[49]

During this period in Atlanta, Abram began his associations with the regional offices of two prominent Jewish "defense" organizations, the American Jewish Committee (AJC) and the Anti-Defamation

League (ADL). His involvement with the Jewish community was originally based on simple economics. Abram supplemented his legal salary by teaching Sunday School, serving as secretary to the local AJC chapter, and providing counsel to the ADL. He speculated to Eli Evans that "maybe this is how I got caught up in Jewish Affairs—I needed to earn extra money."[50]

According to Robert Hicks, who joined the Heyman, Abram and Young firm in the late 1950s, Abram's Jewish identity was far less than what it would later become:

> I was really touched by the way Morris became, in his later years, a real Jew. I mean he was proud of it, he was delighted with its ancient history, its culture, the divine causes of Judaism. But he was not a Jew in the sense that I'm describing when I was with him in Atlanta. I don't mean he was hostile in any way. But his law practice was heavily gentile, representing corporations that didn't have any connection to Jews at all. Herman [Heyman] was in the Jewish community in a much stronger way than Morris was. I know he [Abram] had friends at the Temple and he would go to ceremonies and things like that, but I don't think he was a regular attendee.[51]

Ted Maloof agreed. "Morris was not into Jewish causes to speak of when he first came to Atlanta from Fitzgerald. He wasn't in the Jewish community in the sense that he was fighting for Jewish causes." Maloof said it was Harry Elson, an Atlanta businessman and later business partner, whose legal matters Abram handled, who recommended that he become involved in Jewish causes.[52]

When asked what role Judaism played in their family life, Ruth Abram responded, "Hardly any. We didn't celebrate Passover at home. We went to the Elson family for that. I think there was some attempt to light Hanukah candles. We didn't go to Sunday school and we didn't go to the Temple."[53]

By the time of the 1960 presidential campaign, Abram's reputation as one of the most prominent liberals in Atlanta had been firmly established. During the highly competitive race within the Democratic Party for the 1960 presidential nomination, Abram was introduced to Senator John F. Kennedy by Bobby Troutman, a close friend of Kennedy's older brother at Harvard Law School who became active in his campaign. Troutman's plan to keep Kennedy friendly with both the large conservative camp in Georgia and the small but influential group of liberals connected to the state's blacks was to set up a dinner in Georgetown that included the Kennedys, the Talmadges, and the Abrams.[54]

As the 1960 election drew near, Martin Luther King Jr. and fifty-one student activists were arrested on October 19, 1960 by Atlanta police after being refused service at the Magnolia Room, a segregated restaurant at Rich's, the city's largest department store. King and the students were charged under Georgia's new anti-trespassing law. After charges were dropped against many of the trespassers, King and thirty-five students were held in custody after refusing to post bail.[55]

Harris Wofford, a Yale Law graduate and a devotee of Gandhian political activism, had befriended King after the 1955–56 Montgomery boycott, introducing him to the Mahatma's tactics of civil disobedience. He joined Sargent Shriver's team during the Kennedy campaign, concentrating his efforts on strengthening the senator's support in the black community. Acting on a personal basis, without wanting to drag the Kennedy campaign into public controversy, Wofford sought the assistance of someone who could prevail upon Mayor Hartsfield to get the city involved in King's release. He found the perfect candidate among his Atlanta contacts in Abram, who had represented Hartsfield on litigation to abolish the county unit system.[56] As Oliphant and Wilkie explain, "Abram was part of an influential coterie of whites in Atlanta who were helping to build the city's reputation as a refuge from backwoods violence and injustice."[57]

When he received the phone call, Abram was on his way to take his twelve-year-old daughter Ann out for a special day. Abram contacted the mayor, who was already engaged in discussions with the city's black leadership. He invited Abram to join them and to bring Ann along with him. When he arrived, he learned that King and the imprisoned students would not leave the jail until all charges against them were dropped. However, since they were being held in the county jail, the matter was beyond the mayor's jurisdiction.[58]

When Hartsfield heard from Abram that he had received the

call from Wofford, whom he knew was part of the Kennedy campaign, the mayor believed that his hand would be strengthened by invoking the candidate's name. Instead, it created panic in Kennedy's inner circle and fury among its Southern strategists, including Bobby Troutman. Troutman and others believed it would upend the political tightrope the campaign was walking between black and segregationist voters.[59]

After the local prosecutor agreed to drop the charges against King and the students, the reverend was immediately confronted with a more serious problem. Because of the trespassing charge, King had violated his probation on an old violation in neighboring DeKalb County of driving with an out of state license. The penalty, astonishing for a misdemeanor charge, was four months at hard labor in a state road gang, a potentially dangerous prospect that alarmed his wife Coretta, pregnant with the couple's third child. Mrs. King was terrified when her husband was taken out in the dead of night from the DeKalb jail and transferred to the maximum-security state prison in Reidsville.

Wofford prevailed upon his campaign boss Sargent Shriver to meet the candidate at the Chicago airport between campaign appearances and to convince him to make a supportive phone call to Mrs. King. At the time of the call, she was dressing for an appointment with Abram that had been arranged by her father-in-law, "Daddy" King, a client of Abram's, to see what his lawyer could do to get her husband released.[60]

When Robert Kennedy, the candidate's campaign manager, heard about the call and how Shriver and Wofford had engineered it, he was furious and dressed them down for insubordination and jeopardizing his brother's electoral chances less than two weeks before the election. But before Abram could become involved, King was unexpectedly released from Reidsville as the result of the involvement of none other than the younger Kennedy, who took the questionable step of calling the judge from a phone booth in New York outside a campaign event. Kennedy's phone call was the result of quiet intervention by Georgia's governor Vandiver at the behest of the presidential candidate himself. The governor contacted one of the judge's closest friends, who got the judge to agree to release Dr. King but only if contacted personally by either Kennedy.[61]

Martin Luther King Jr. had earlier in the campaign made clear to Wofford that he would not be endorsing either candidate for president. Although his father had previously taken the position of many Baptists, black and white, who opposed Kennedy on religious grounds, the actions taken by the campaign had changed his mind about voting for him. At the urging of Abram, Daddy King agreed to let his congregants know of these intentions, promising to deliver a "suitcase" full of votes for Senator Kennedy. At Ebeneezer Baptist Church on the Sunday before the election, he kept his promise.[62]

Following the election, Martin Luther King Jr. telephoned the White House and offered the president-elect several recommendations for positions in the new administration. For the important position of Solicitor General, the individual responsible for preparing and presenting the government's cases before the Supreme Court, he recommended Morris Abram. He repeated this to the new attorney general, but the Kennedys had already settled on Harvard Law professor Archibald Cox, who had been an advisor to the campaign. As Bobby Kennedy told Dr. King, despite thinking highly of Abram, they had already committed to Cox.[63]

Abram turned down the offer of the Ambassadorship to Tanganyika after his visit to the country. He opted instead to accept a temporary position as the first general counsel of the newly established Peace Corps, which he did by commuting to Washington from Atlanta during its first year of operation and traveling home on weekends.[64] The corps idea had been proposed by Senator Kennedy toward the end of his campaign in a rousing speech to a crowd of students at the University of Michigan. In it, he issued a challenge, asking how many of them would be willing to serve their country by living and working in the developing world.[65]

As general counsel and a close aide of its founding director, Sargent Shriver, Abram's main duty was to prepare legislation to supplant President Kennedy's executive order creating the organization. In an interview he gave three days after the order was signed on March 1, 1961, Abram described the corps as "the most original act of foreign policy" America has seen in years. He also expressed the view that Shriver was one of the best appointees named by the new president.[66]

One of Abram's jobs was to determine the legal status of a volunteer, since he or she would not be a civil servant or a soldier, but rather needed to have the advantages of an insurance program and the protection of the U.S. Health Service while overseas. Abram warned of the potential dangers involved: "It is going to be hard and tough and the romantic idealist who thinks it will be wonderful to be in an exotic country for two years will not be able to survive."[67]

In October 1962, shortly before he left Atlanta, Abram accepted an invitation to debate William F. Buckley Jr. before a packed audience in the Glenn Memorial Auditorium at Emory University. The event was sponsored by the conservative young adult group, Young Americans for Freedom. The debate centered on U.S. foreign policy and the proper role of the federal government in domestic affairs. The two clashed on U.S. policy on Cuba, the effectiveness of U.S. policy in the Cold War more broadly, and on their respective assessments of the late Senator Joe McCarthy. Abram contended that he was "not a McCarthyite," and that the two of them differed "on the issue of freedom." When he asserted that "McCarthy was an enemy of freedom," Abram drew big applause.

To Abram, the duty of the federal government is to help the people do things together that would not be done so well individually. If the states or private industry lag, the federal government should take up the slack. The example he offered was FDR's creation of the Tennessee Valley Authority, which made possible the electrification of the region of South Georgia in which he grew up. Conservatives, Abram asserted, view the world as "black and white, saved and damned, good and bad, which is a respectable viewpoint, widely held in the Middle Ages."[68]

For his part, Buckley accused Abram of having "done his best to present a caricature of the conservative point of view," and contended that conservatives are much less concerned about communists or traitors within the United States than "about the Abrams and the Kennedys of the world who did not recognize Fidel Castro for what he was even after he had kept his firing squads working day and night." Buckley said, "The people who cause catastrophes in government are not Communists but people like Mr. Abram." In response, Abram argued for complete academic freedom, including "the clash of ideas" at colleges and universities. As he remarked, "I glory in the excitement of the pursuit of truth." Buckley responded that "certain truths have in fact been found," and that "college presidents should only have faculty members whose set of values are identical with theirs."[69]

It had been fourteen years since Justice Black had warned Abram about the potential consequences of returning to the city he had lived in briefly after college and challenging the legal establishment. But it had been a success on many fronts: he had established a successful legal practice; he had emerged as one of the leading voices of a newer, more progressive South; and he and his wife Jane had established a rich family life and developed friendships that would last for many years. And his most ambitious project, to rid his native state of its archaic and regressive electoral system, was about to reach its climax.

FOUR

Victory

It's the biggest thing to hit Georgia since Sherman.

Shortly after Morris Abram began practicing law in Atlanta in the late 1940s, he was approached by Helen Douglas Mankin, the first woman ever elected to the U.S. Congress from Georgia. Mankin, an early feminist widely known as a progressive for her positions on race and labor issues during her tenure in the Georgia General Assembly, had won a surprise victory in a special election held in February 1946 to fill the seat of retired Fifth District Congressman Robert Ramspeck. She won with over one thousand votes from the last box counted, the overwhelmingly black Ward 3-B.[1]

Mankin's election sent shock waves throughout the Talmadge-led state Democratic Party establishment, already reeling from the prospect of losing forever the white primary, the Georgia practice of prohibiting blacks from voting in Democratic primaries, then under court challenge. Under the Neill Act, each congressional district had the option of using either the popular or county unit vote to determine the party's nominee for the U.S. House of Representatives. Mankin's predecessor Ramspeck, a member of the House's Democratic leadership, had used his control over the Fifth District's Democratic Executive Committee to eliminate the unit voting system for the three counties in the Atlanta area over a decade earlier. He knew that with his moderate voting record in Congress, he would otherwise be vulnerable to losing two of the three counties that constituted the district.

By the time of the 1946 primary held only months after her special election, the white primary had been declared unconstitutional and the district's Democratic Party establishment knew that the only way of defeating Representative Mankin was to reinstate the county unit system in the Fifth Congressional District.

Meanwhile, Eugene Talmadge, looking for a fourth term as governor, considered the coalition of poor whites, blacks, and organized labor that elected Mankin a threat to the state's political order. Making the black scare a major feature of his campaign, he went around the state railing against the newly elected congresswoman whom he dubbed "the Belle of Ashby Street," after the location of the black housing projects in Atlanta that had provided her margin of victory.[2]

In addition to reinstating the county unit system in the Fifth District, the DeKalb political bosses, who dominated the district's Democratic Executive Committee, recruited the white supremacist James Davis, then a state superior court judge, to run against Mankin in the upcoming Democratic primary. In the July primary, Mankin won the district's popular vote by carrying Fulton County by a wide margin. But the fix had been in at the time the unit vote was reinstated, and by winning his home county Dekalb and tiny Rockdale, Davis prevailed. The statewide results followed the same pattern. Although Talmadge lost the popular vote to lawyer and future Lockheed executive James Carmichael, he carried the unit vote by a comfortable margin.

Less than three weeks later, on August 3, 1946, two separate lawsuits were filed in federal court challenging the victories of Talmadge and Davis on grounds that the county unit system violated the Fourteenth Amendment to the U.S. Constitution guaranteeing equal protection of the law. As Mankin's biographer points out, the plaintiffs were "a coalition of progressive whites who were appalled by the racism that blew like a tornado over the state" in the wake of these victories.[3]

But the plaintiffs had two problems. Just two months earlier, Supreme Court justice Felix Frankfurter, writing for the court in a case seeking to overturn the malapportioned legislative districts of

Illinois, had proclaimed that it was not the responsibility of courts to enter a "political thicket" that was the province of the political branches of government.[4] The second was more immediate. As the three-judge panel convened to hear the case pointed out, not only had the primary election already been held, but ballots were already printed for the general election. The court ruled in the case of *Turman v. Duckworth* that the unit system challenge was moot as a result.

By the time Morris Abram was engaged to help Mankin continue her fight against the county unit system, she had lost two more elections to Davis: a write-in effort in the 1946 general election and the Democratic primary two years later. The latter was particularly painful, as Mankin won less than 40 percent of the popular vote, losing even her home county of Fulton. But far from being finished, "Mankin was as determined as ever to push ahead with her suit against the county unit system, to take it if necessary to the Supreme Court, no matter what the cost in cash, health, or friends."[5]

Abram had been drawn into the case by Mankin's nephew, Hamilton Douglas III, an Atlanta lawyer who knew Abram from their days as students at the University of Georgia. Despite her insistence that she be allowed to sue the state for damages in her own name, both Abram and Douglas believed it would undermine the case to have the appearance of a political motive behind it.[6] Instead, they enlisted an automobile parts dealer from Fulton County named Bernard South as plaintiff. South, a southern Baptist, had not been involved in politics or associated in any way with opposition to the county unit system. But as added insurance they brought in Harold Fleming, a staff member of the progressive Southern Regional Council, to be the co-plaintiff in case Mr. South was pressured to withdraw by pro-Talmadge forces. When asked many years later why he considered South's desertion a possibility, Abram replied, "because the pressure [was] terrific; and he was in business. He was selling automobile parts, and you don't sell automobile parts just to liberals."[7]

Mankin had a strong personality and did not get along well with Abram. Had he not been brought into the case by her nephew, the only member of her family with whom she had warm relations, he might not have remained on the case. While Abram thought of

Mankin as "strong medicine," she complained that he was using the case to further his political ambitions. While he prepared the legal arguments, Douglas kept his aunt away from him.[8]

The case of *South v. Peters* was filed in January 1950 in U.S. District Court in Atlanta and came up for argument the following month before a federal three-judge panel. The timing was critical, because given the dismissal of the 1946 cases, Abram knew that he would have to get the case to federal court before the Democratic primary. But the problem for the plaintiffs was that, technically, the county unit system did not have to be employed if the state's Democratic Committee decided to use a convention to nominate its candidates. And until the date of the primary was set, the court could dismiss the case as premature. As Abram put it, "we were always teetering between prematurity and mootness."[9]

Abram effectively disposed of that possibility on the first day of the federal trial by getting James Peters, the state's Democratic Party chairman and the defendant in the suit, to admit on the witness stand that the party would not be nominating its candidates "behind closed doors."[10] The three-judge federal panel hearing the case was presided over by Judge Samuel Sibley, the senior judge on the Fifth Circuit Court of Appeals, who had presided over the 1946 county unit case. Following Felix Frankfurter's reasoning in the Illinois reapportionment case, he dismissed the case as not a matter for the courts to decide. In a per curiam decision, the Supreme Court refused to accept the case.[11]

But there was an encouraging sign for Abram and other opponents of the county unit system in the form of a dissent issued by Justice William Douglas (and signed onto by Justice Hugo Black) in which he asserted, "The creation by law of favored groups of citizens and the grant to them of preferred political rights is the worst of all discriminations under a democratic system of government."[12]

Abram's brief noted the unit system's reinforcement of racial discrimination. In his dissent, Douglas remarked, "The county unit system has indeed been called the 'last loophole' around our decisions holding that there must be no discrimination because of race in primary as well as in general elections."[13] In a 1951 article published in the *Georgia Bar Journal*, Abram expressed his confidence that it was only a matter of time before the unconstitutionality of the county unit system would be recognized by federal courts. In a democratic system governed by a constitution, he argued, how could a practice so blatantly discriminatory be permitted? "At best," Abram wrote, "the place where the voter resides is a constitutionally irrelevant fact and cannot form the basis for discrimination. Would anyone doubt that a law permitting red-headed people no votes, black-headed people one vote, and blondes sixty-five votes, would on its face violate equal protection requirements?"[14]

After establishing the discriminatory nature of the system and its unconstitutionality with respect to both the Georgia and U.S. constitutions, he addressed the question of whether such discrimination might serve some reasonable or higher purpose, whether protecting county (as opposed to personal) interests, preventing the growth of city machines, or meeting the needs of good government. Counties, he argued, are not political entities, but simply geographical and administrative subdivisions in which people live. Constitutional guarantees run not to these entities but rather to the people who live in them. Regarding the rise of political machines, those operating in Georgia owe their support not to city but rather to rural interests. And besides, "a person's franchise cannot be deprived him because of the ruling government's fear of the manner in which he may use it."[15]

In refuting the purely hypothetical argument that the unit system might further good government, Abram turned to the Bible, comparing the county unit rule's all-inclusiveness to Herod's command ordering the death of all male children born on a certain day because one of them might someday cause his downfall. Even if people living in large counties are bad citizens, "can we not, as in Sodom, find ten righteous men amongst Fulton's 468,000?" The first demand of the classifier, argues Abram, "is that he obey the demand of justice to the individual. Group guilt is unknown to our jurisprudence."[16]

The same year his bar journal article appeared, Abram was back in court fighting the county unit system, this time with Baxter Jones Jr., the lawyer from Macon who would challenge James Davis for the congressional seat the following year. Although the target was the same, the strategy shifted from stopping the voting practice outright to seeking damages for his client, thus making the practice too expensive to continue. This, Abram believed, could best be achieved in state court.[17] According to the argument on behalf of plaintiff Cox, his vote was "diluted, devalued, and reversed," by the method of counting it, and therefore he was entitled to damages.[18]

But once again, the challenge to the county unit system was denied. The argument offered by Georgia's state supreme court on appeal was disingenuous and particularly frustrating for the challengers. According to the court, nothing in the Georgia state constitution "makes any reference to a party primary." Furthermore, "primaries are in no sense elections for an office, but merely methods by which party adherents agree upon candidates whom they intend to offer and support for ultimate choice by all qualified electors."[19] The appeal to the Supreme Court was dismissed "for want of a substantial Federal question." Once again, Douglas and Black registered their dissents, noting that the heavy black population in the large cities was substantially disenfranchised by the unit system.[20]

Among the state's prominent citizens, the only one as determined as Morris Abram to help bring about the demise of the unit system was Atlanta's longtime mayor, William Hartsfield. First elected in 1937, Hartsfield would become the longest-serving mayor in Atlanta's history (1937–41, 1942–61). During his tenure, the city's population grew tenfold to over one million. Under Hartsfield, who built a biracial coalition to secure repeated reelection, the city peacefully integrated its schools and solidified its reputation as "the city too busy to hate."[21]

Preparing for the 1958 election, Mayor Hartsfield asked Abram to bring another county unit case. Arguing that the unit system would dilute his vote, he sought an injunction to enjoin the state Democratic primary from being held later that year. The *South* case had been rejected in part on the fact that it sought equitable relief (i.e., preventing the next primary election from taking place under the usual terms). But the year before the Hartsfield suit, Congress had passed the 1957 Civil Rights Act which, among other measures, gave federal courts equitable powers in voting cases. Abram believed that this legal provision had the chance of meeting the Frankfurter objections to granting jurisdiction to those challenging the unit rule.[22]

First, Abram needed to find a judge who understood the legal subtleties involved. He believed he found the solution outside his Atlanta home district. One spring morning he traveled fifty miles to the courthouse and post office in Gainesville, where he knew Judge Boyd Sloan would be working on a Saturday. According to Abram, the judge was "madder than hell" and asked why he hadn't served the chief judge in his own hometown. Abram replied, "Judge Hooper doesn't work on Saturday."[23]

But if he thought the strategy would work, Abram was mistaken. Telling him that his case had already been decided, Judge Sloan refused even to convene a three-judge panel to hear it. Abram took the unusual step of "mandamusing" the judge in the U.S. Supreme Court to force him to convene the panel, something he admitted was "a tricky business." This prompted his wife Jane to ask, "Morris, can't you beat the county unit system without suing a federal judge?"[24]

In the 1958 case of *Hartsfield v. Sloan* (357 U.S. 916), the Supreme Court refused to order the empaneling of a three-judge federal court to hear the county unit case on its merits, upholding Judge Sloan's denials by claiming there was no substantial federal question raised. But since the previous two unit cases, President Eisenhower had made several appointments to the Supreme Court. Although the court voted against hearing the case of *Hartsfield v. Sloan*, this time two of the new appointees, Justice William Brennan and Chief Justice Earl Warren, jointed Justices Douglas and Black in dissent.[25] Abram was more than encouraged by this development. "We're naturally disappointed," he said. "We note that the decision was by a very narrowly divided court. I am positive that someday the judiciary will invalidate the Georgia county unit system."[26] Abram now knew that he needed to turn only one more justice against the Frankfurter doctrine that the unit system was simply a "political" matter to get a future case heard by the country's highest court. As he later remarked, "This fourteen-year struggle really, fundamentally eroded the Supreme Court's position gradually, gradually, like drops of water."[27]

It was not long before Abram found what he regarded as the perfect vehicle for reaching his goal of getting the Supreme Court to
act. He was approached by a voter from Savannah following the 1958
election in Georgia's First Congressional District where the unit system was used to nominate candidates for Congress. The man was
seeking damages, since the candidate he voted for had lost the election because of the unit system.

But Abram's maneuver was undermined by Judge Frank Scarlett
of the Southern Federal District of Georgia, who had served on the
panel that had turned away the original 1946 unit case. Abram knew
that Judge Scarlett would dismiss the case, as indeed he indicated to
Abram at its first hearing. But the judge simply refused to take any
action at all, effectively bottling up the case and frustrating completely Abram's strategy of getting a reversal in the Supreme Court.[28]

On March 26, 1962, Mayor Hartsfield learned from a reporter
friend that in a case from Tennessee, *Baker v. Carr*, the Supreme
Court had just overruled the 1946 reapportionment decision that
had prevented the county unit cases from receiving a hearing in the
federal courts. He immediately called Abram with the news, including the fact that the court's opinion in *Baker* had included references
to the county unit decisions, including *Hartsfield v. Sloan*.

Abram told Hartsfield that everything was ready to go with another
lawsuit, and that his name was on the complaint. The mayor hesi-
tated, realizing he would have to check first with "the cigar" to see
if he approved Hartsfield's name appearing on what could mark the
downfall of the state's voting system. The "cigar" was Robert Wood-
ruff, the man behind the international success of Coca-Cola and his
most important supporter. Hartsfield called back with the news that
Abram needed to find another name.[29]

The replacement of Hartsfield's name on the lawsuit by Atlanta
businessman James O'Hare Sanders did not dampen the mayor's
enthusiasm for the prospects of at last overturning the unit system.
In the calls he made to friends and reporters from Morris Abram's
office following the filing in the U.S. District Court for the Northern District of Georgia of the case of *Sanders v. Gray*, he said over

and over that "This will be cataclysmic in Georgia politics," adding, "it's the biggest thing to hit Georgia since Sherman."[30]

While Abram was similarly thrilled with this prospect, he did regret that circumstances prevented him from getting his cases to the Supreme Court before *Baker v. Carr*. In 1978 he told Lorraine Spritzer, "I regretted—when they finally held the issue of geographic representation justiciable, that it was in the *Baker v. Carr* case which came at the right moment after the court had already been eroded to the point of five-four in the *Hartsfield v. Sloan* case."[31] This was because there was a clear distinction to be made between the county unit case, where the issue was the equality of each vote, and the reapportionment cases, which revolved around the population of legislative districts, which could only approximate numerical equality.

The 1962 *Baker* decision created a sense of panic for the Georgia political establishment. Herman Talmadge, now a U.S. senator, issued a statement that read, "It is beyond the comprehension of anyone who ever has been exposed to a law book how a court at any level could compel a state legislature to take or not to take action on any question."[32] Governor Vandiver called the state's General Assembly into emergency session on April 16. Two days after Abram filed the *Sanders* suit, a case was brought challenging the apportionment of state legislative districts, not surprising given the fact that the number of House seats was tied closely to the number of unit votes in each county.[33] With the 1962 elections only months away, the assembly faced the prospect of a court forced reapportionment.

More than two dozen bills were introduced during the special session to alter the system in the hope of passing muster with the panel hearing the *Sanders* case. Under the bill that was signed into law, a majority of the population would still have only 33 percent of the unit votes.[34]

When the new statute was sent to the judges hearing the *Sanders* case, the defendants moved for immediate dismissal on the grounds that it rendered the plaintiff's complaint irrelevant. But Abram and his team had prepared amendments to their complaint for every bill that had been proposed. When the motion was presented, they promptly produced an amendment that mirrored the statute, including its inequities, and enabled them to proceed with the case.[35]

Following the successful *Sanders* decision before the three-judge panel led by Judge Bell, the state turned to the Supreme Court for a stay, but its appeal was rejected by Justice Black, thus throwing the upcoming September Democratic primary into turmoil. The demise of the unit system, along with the decision overturning the state's unequal apportionment of legislative seats, had led to the need to create an entirely new structure of legislative districts. Jimmy Carter soon announced his candidacy for one of the newly created state Senate seats.[36]

The decision also led to a turnaround in the electoral fortunes of moderate candidates for governor, such as Carl Sanders and later Carter and George Busbee. When Sanders, who had represented the city of Augusta in both the Georgia House and Senate, was elected in 1962, the first held following the *Gray* decision, he was the first governor elected in a non-rural county since the 1920s.[37] The *Sanders* decision also made it possible for the voters of the Fifth Congressional District to retire James Davis, who lost to Atlanta attorney Charles Weltner. Two years later Weltner became the only Georgia congressman, and one of only a handful throughout the South, to vote in favor of the 1964 Civil Rights Act.

Following the federal panel's decision in *Sanders v. Gray*, the chairman and secretary of the Georgia State Democratic Executive Committee, and the Secretary of State of Georgia, took their case to the Supreme Court, which for the first time in a Georgia county unit case, accepted jurisdiction. The oral argument was set for hearing on January 17, 1963, before any of the numerous related reapportionment cases that were waiting to be heard.

On December 21, Abram, who had recently left Atlanta to join the law firm of Paul, Weiss, Rifkind, Wharton and Garrison in New York, received a letter from Solicitor General Archibald Cox, asking if he would cede some of his time to the government to allow it more than a half hour to present its brief, which favored the lower court's ruling.[38] Abram was reluctant to comply with the request. But two weeks later, he received another letter from Cox, writing with the extraordinary news that Attorney General Robert F. Kennedy had decided to argue the government's brief himself. As a result, he would no longer need the extra time he had previously requested.

Since no announcement about the attorney general had been made to the press, Abram was to keep the information confidential, even from his co-counsel and client. Since by Supreme Court tradition Kennedy was not expected to receive questions from the Justices, "This means that you will probably have to bear the brunt of questions ranging broadly into the basic philosophy concerning the Fourteenth Amendment and the standards of adjudication that apply in the election and reapportionment areas."[39]

The practice of having the U.S. attorney general present a brief before the Supreme Court was not unprecedented. But what was unusual in this occasion is that Robert Kennedy had never argued a case of any kind. Indeed, he had never even entered a courtroom. Cox and Burke Marshall, the Justice Department's civil rights chief, had determined that the county unit case would be a relatively easy one for Kennedy to argue.[40]

But there was another reason as well. According to Bruce Ferris, who worked in the solicitor's office, after arguing the government's position in *Baker v. Carr* that the federal courts should become involved in cases involving voter inequality, and after being questioned harshly by Justice Frankfurter, Cox had whispered to him on the way out of the courtroom that Frankfurter's position was the correct one. His misgivings about the government's position explains why Justice Department officials were eager to have Kennedy argue the case and why Cox was prepared to defer.[41]

Ferris helped prepare the attorney general for the oral argument. Kennedy spent two weeks during the Christmas and New Year's holiday period studying the case. His material included a memorandum that had been prepared for him by Cox. The memorandum noted that the Supreme Court had not set out a standard it believed the equal protection clause of the Fourteenth Amendment imposed on states in their apportionment of voting power. While Georgia's county unit system was clearly discriminatory, Cox believed that none of the Justices beyond Douglas and Black would go so far as to rule that the Constitution mandated that all votes be given equal weight. Rather, as the government was arguing in its brief, it was at least theoretically possible that some form of county system, one not blatantly discriminatory, could pass muster.[42]

The afternoon before the oral argument, Abram traveled to Washington at Cox's request to meet with himself, Kennedy, and Civil Rights Division chief Burke Marshall. Cox wanted to coordinate the two arguments, which puzzled Abram, since he knew that the government's position was at odds with the one he would be taking. While the solicitor's brief essentially supported the lower court's decision, Abram would be insisting on the "one man, one vote" standard that the lower court had stopped short of declaring.

During the meeting, Abram pressed his point about the impossibility of devising a unit system that adhered to the equal protection doctrine of the Fourteenth Amendment. When Kennedy told Cox that he agreed with Abram, Cox made it clear that the government had already filed its brief, and that was the one Kennedy was going to argue. Baldy, the *Atlanta Constitution's* political cartoonist, drew a cartoon of Abram holding up a book to the attorney general and saying, "Read here, Bobby." In fact, Abram was not pleased that his thunder was being blunted, if not stolen, by Kennedy's personal intervention in the case. According to Abram's law partner Joseph Lefkoff, who assisted him on the case, "Morris was upset that Bobby Kennedy chose to make that case his only appearance before the Supreme Court. Morris, bless him, enjoyed the glory, and that sort of took the shine away from him."[43]

It was clear to Supreme Court observers on the morning of January 17, 1963, that this day in court would be different, if not historic. The courtroom audience included members of the Kennedy family, including the attorney general's mother, his wife Ethel, his brother Senator Ted Kennedy, and his sister-in-law Jacqueline, the First Lady. In addition to supporting the attorney general, they were present to see Ted sworn in as a member of the Supreme Court Bar.[44]

Arguing for the state of Georgia, two attorneys in the state attorney general's office, B. D. Murphy and E. Freeman Leverett, defended the county unit system as one that went back to the founding of the state of Georgia. According to Leverett, counties were governmental units in Georgia before it entered the union and had their voice in the councils of government on the state level through representation. From the very earliest, Georgia had accorded a high degree of autonomy to its counties.

In trying to justify deviations from pure equality of the vote, Leverett gave the example of the U.S. Constitution's establishment of such institutions as the Senate and the electoral college, but Justice Stewart, for one, was unimpressed. Unlike the United States, he pointed out, Georgia wasn't created by several counties getting together and voluntarily giving up some of their sovereignty to create the state. Leverett argued that the constitution does not prevent the states from choosing any electoral structure it thinks best suited to "the interest, temper and customs of its people." As Mr. Justice Frankfurter's dissenting opinion in *Baker v. Carr* points out, the idea of equality of voting power is not implicit in the history of American institutions.[45]

Abram, who had waited many years for this moment, opened his remarks by addressing the point of opposing counsel that there is no distinction to be made between legislative voting classifications and electoral ones. While you can protect a minority in voting for legislators either by proportional representation or by drawing boundaries between districts, classification in the case of voting must necessarily involve discrimination, since "if you give a man more than a vote, you're necessarily giving another man less of a vote."[46]

Pressed by Justice Stewart on whether age, literacy, and other requirements are therefore not legitimate, Abram agreed that they are, though once they are established, you can't make distinctions among voters simply by where they live. So, for example, even if the state made holding property a requirement, it couldn't then make the vote of one property holder greater than another.

The appellants had reminded the court that the unit system under review was not the one that had been in effect in previous years, but rather the one that the people of Georgia had passed the previous year through their elected representatives. To this argument, Abram pointed out that the lower house, which approved that law, represented 22 percent of the people and the state senate, a mere 5.5 percent. In both 1952 and in 1950, Abram pointed out, amendments to embed the county unit system in the state constitution passed by two-thirds of both houses of the legislature. Yet, when they were submitted to the people of the state for their approval, each was defeated soundly. Furthermore, the system was particularly detrimental to blacks. In counties benefitting from the system with large black populations, they were disenfranchised, whereas "where the Negroes were voting and of reasonable proportion of their population, their votes didn't count."

When asked by Justice Brennan whether the court had to rule the unit system unconstitutional per se, Abram responded that he was arguing for doing so because if the court writes an opinion, it would want to set guidelines on the actual way in which the constitution should be interpreted. He closed with the following words: "I do not think there is any way that you can uphold this system even if you don't say a system is *per se* unconstitutional, until you can say that two equals four or feel that 50¢ is the proper amount of change for a dollar or that you can give eight ounces per pound. I think a qualified voter is a qualified voter, is a qualified voter, and a vote, is a vote, is a vote."[47]

For his part, the attorney general stuck to the script prepared by Archibald Cox. He got a laugh from the audience when he struck a personal note into his remarks: "We used to have, and I repeat used to have, a saying in my city of Boston which was vote early and vote often. If you live in one of the small counties in the state of Georgia, all you have to do is vote early and you accomplish the same result."[48]

Unlike previous attorneys general who had argued before the Court, Kennedy welcomed questions from the bench.[49] Under questioning by Chief Justice Warren as to whether there was any place for a weighted system such as Georgia's county unit system, Kennedy's initial response was that he didn't think it necessary to reach that point. But then he added, "I do say that although I have given it a great deal of thought, I have difficulty coming up with any system that makes any sense which a unit voting in connection with a statewide election is."[50] According to Abram, who was sitting next to the solicitor general, when Kennedy gave this response, "Archie almost died."[51] Abram later sent a letter of protest to *Time* magazine, which had reported that Kennedy read the brief his department had prepared for him. Abram wrote that RFK delivered an oral argument without any notes and responded to questions from the court.[52]

Under questioning from the chief justice, the attorney general also distinguished Georgia's county unit system from the U.S. Electoral College, which was the result of a compromise between the small and larger states. (As Abram told William F. Buckley on his PBS program two decades later when discussing the state voting inequality in the U.S. Senate, the Fourteenth Amendment protects people, not states.)

The attorney general closed his remarks with an eloquent statement of what was at stake:

> The great miracle of the Constitution is that we've been able to deal with the problems of the twentieth century as well as the problems of the eighteenth century. These are the great problems that are facing the United States at the present time. And this kind of invidious practice that exists now and has existed before and the Georgia County Unit System strikes at the very heart of the United States. If we can give equal protection to those who feel that they've been deprived of their economic rights, certainly we can give equal protection to those who have been deprived of the most basic right of all, which is the right to vote. If we cannot protect them, then the whole fabric of the American system, our whole way of life, is irreparably damaged.[53]

The Supreme Court's decision in the case of *Gray v. Sanders*, announced on March 18, 1963, went well beyond upholding the lower court's ruling and beyond the U.S. government's supporting brief. It was entirely appropriate that the court's opinion was penned by Justice Douglas, who had dissented in the previous county unit cases the court had refused to hear. His words vindicated Morris Abram's longtime position regarding voter equality: "The conception of political equality from the Declaration of Independence, to Lincoln's Gettysburg Address, to the Fifteenth, Seventeenth, and Nineteenth Amendments can mean only one thing—one person, one vote."[54]

FIVE

Jewish Imperatives

The underdog had triumphed, and many of our Christian allies vanished.

R uth Abram remembers an incident from her teenage years that explains why she had no reservations about her father's decision to move the family from Atlanta to New York in 1962:

> When I was thirteen, I went to the Westminster School and that was, and I think still is, Presbyterian. And on my first day, when like everyone else going to a new school I was a bit scared, at least I had my friends, I had my poodle skirt, I had my bobby socks and my crinoline and my amulets to ward off all the dangers. At that point, all the girls I had grown up with circled me and said that from now on I couldn't come to any of their parties or go to anything they were doing because I was Jewish. They explained it wasn't them, they would love to have me, but it was their parents.[1]

For Morris Abram, the decision to leave Atlanta was not so simple. Still, his daughter's painful experience in school was not unrelated to the feelings of social isolation he also felt despite his many professional accomplishments. His closest friends from his University of Georgia days had abandoned him for the company they could keep at social clubs, which excluded Jews. These feelings of alienation were amplified by his sense that the southern environment in which he never felt entirely comfortable was both parochial and suffocating.

Besides, Abram's early legal career in Atlanta had led to a growing desire to perform on a larger stage, motivating him to seek challenges more in line with his talents and ambitions. His law partner
Ted Maloof expressed it this way: "Morris had some of the best talent of anybody. He was absolutely brilliant, he was articulate, and
he could really argue a case or anything else. He had all the attributes to be an outstanding international lawyer. I'm only speculating,
since he never said anything about this, but I thought with his talent
he could make a lot more money and go a lot further in New York
than he could in Atlanta."[2] To his partner Robert Hicks, the move to
New York was entirely consistent with Abram's growing ambitions.

The one job that would have kept Abram in Atlanta was a federal
judgeship, but that was precluded by his political convictions. He
later said he would have given his "eyeteeth" to have been appointed
to the bench. But "I knew goddamn well Herman [Talmadge] was
never going to let me be a judge. It would have been his political
life to recommend me or to let me, by 1962, which was when I left."
Abram said he often wondered if he had stayed in Georgia whether
President Johnson would have appointed him to the bench.[3]

Invitations in the late 1950s to join two organizations based in
New York engaged in public policy advocacy and research provided
openings for Abram to satisfy his growing professional desires. The
first was the Twentieth Century Fund (now known as the Century
Foundation), composed largely of former prominent New Dealers,
including Adolph Berle, Benjamin Cohen, and David Lilienthal. The
second was the Field Foundation, the board of its New York branch
headed by Adlai Stevenson. The foundation provided grants to organizations supporting poverty reduction, civil rights, and child welfare, among other efforts to promote social reform on a national scale.

A move to New York would also facilitate Abram's growing involvement in the New York–based American Jewish Committee (AJC),
for which staying in Atlanta would complicate his ability to assume
a national leadership role. In anticipation of his move, AJC's executive vice president, John Slawson, helped Abram secure an offer to
join the prestigious New York law firm Proskauer Rose, whose leading partner, Joseph Proskauer, had served as AJC's president from

1943 to 1949. But after some probing, Abram turned down the offer, judging the firm "too much interested in success and money."[4]

It was through the Field Foundation that Abram met Lloyd Garrison, the great-grandson of the famous abolitionist, a noted political reformer in his own right, and a highly successful Wall Street lawyer associated with the firm Paul, Weiss, Rifkind, Wharton and Garrison. The firm had a reputation not only for the political celebrities it hired, such as Adlai Stevenson and JFK speechwriter Ted Sorensen, but also for the pro bono work it accepted on behalf of often unpopular causes. Although Paul, Weiss had a policy of not taking on "laterals" as partners, preferring to promote its own associates, it did make exceptions such as Sorensen, Ramsey Clark, and Arthur Goldberg.

The firm's leading figure was former federal judge Simon Rifkind, at the time one of the country's leading litigators. Robert Rifkind recalls hearing Abram's name for the first time in the late 1950s, when his father told him "there was this bright, very able and energetic lawyer in Atlanta who had stood up rather courageously to the forces of evil in the segregation world. And there had been some discussions of his joining Paul, Weiss."[5]

A final reason for the move to New York was Abram's growing interest in international human rights and the opportunity to put it into practice in an international arena. In 1962, UN Ambassador Stevenson recommended to President Kennedy that he appoint Abram to serve as the U.S. expert on the UN Sub-Commission for the Prevention of Discrimination and the Protection of Minorities, an appointment he took up shortly after the move to New York.

When Abram was approached by Lloyd Garrison to join his law firm as a partner, he was still weighing the costs and benefits of leaving Atlanta. After all, there was the question of supporting a family that by now included a fourth child and was about to include a fifth. And it was ironic that he would be leaving his native state just as the old system he helped to destroy was bringing on a new generation of more progressive political leaders like himself.

Abram's commute to Washington during the weekdays while serving as general counsel to the Peace Corps in 1961 gave him a taste for what it was like to live outside Atlanta.[6] A respected associate and friend reminded Abram that he would never be fully accepted in Atlanta on his merits alone. And another asked him point blank whether he would prefer playing with the New York Yankees or the Atlanta Crackers, the local Triple-A baseball team.[7] In the end, the prospect of joining a firm like Paul, Weiss made the decision much less difficult.

In the fall of 1962, Abram moved his family to a three-story brick home near Long Island Sound in Larchmont, a prosperous New York suburb located in Westchester County. From there he bicycled daily on his secondhand Schwinn to the local commuter train, his journey ending at his twelfth floor office at Paul, Weiss overlooking Madison Avenue in midtown Manhattan.[8]

Among the items on Abram's resume that made him attractive to the firm was his rising position at the American Jewish Committee. The committee was founded in 1906 by a group of prominent American Jews, most of them the sons of German immigrants, in the wake of a series of pogroms in Russia and parts of Eastern Europe. The first of these pogroms three years earlier in the city of Kishniev had resulted in Sam Abram's decision to immigrate to America.

AJC's founders were concerned not only with the fate of fellow Jews abroad but also with the well-being of recent Jewish immigrants to the United States. During its early years, the committee fought to maintain the country's liberal immigration policy, organized relief for European Jewry, recognized the Balfour Declaration, helped the Jewish community in Palestine survive during World War I, and fought for the rights of Jewish minorities in peace treaties following the war.[9]

By the early 1960s, although the organization had become more diverse in its staff and lay leadership, an image study found that American Jewish leaders across the country still regarded AJC as an agency composed of wealthy German Jews with an assimilationist orientation and program. The organization began a public relations effort to educate the Jewish community about its work, to recruit from religious denominations other than the Reform Movement, and to energize younger members.[10]

One year after his move to New York, Abram became, at age forty-five, the youngest president in the history of the American Jewish Committee. Two attributes that had attracted the national leadership of the organization to the young lawyer were his commitment to civil rights and his advocacy skills. As David Harris noted, "In the sixties we were one of the central civil rights institutions. If you map the civil rights moments of the fifties and especially the sixties, AJC was very close to the center of it all. So, his own experience would have been very helpful in that regard as we dealt with our own positions, but the fact of the matter was that at heart, Morris was a superb advocate. His courtroom skills, his legal skills, made him the perfect advocate cum diplomat or diplomat cum advocate."

Harris continued,

> he had an extraordinary courtroom manner that was both deceptive and disarming. Morris had a deceptively folksy down to earth charm ing manner about him, but he brought with him a razor-sharp mind, an extraordinary ability to juggle complex ideas and convey them clearly and concisely and understandably. When he would stand up, whether in front of AJC's board of governors, or before the rally in Washington with two hundred and fifty thousand people, or the court of public opinion wherever it may have led him, he was a natural as an advocate.[11]

Since his move to New York, Abram had not been terribly happy with his new life, with its oppressive sense of anonymity that accompanied his daily commute to the big city. The metaphor he used to describe it was "the shuffle," the short-stepped march he and hundreds of others experienced walking off the commuter train at Grand Central Terminal.[12] Now, however, he was energized by the prospect of working on a host of important issues, including Israel, Jewish-Vatican relations, and the policy of the American Jewish community on desegregation. "I became President of the American Jewish Committee," he recalled, "and things picked up a great deal for me."[13]

Among the early success the organization had begun to enjoy at the time of his accession was in the removal of barriers to Jews in corporate, educational, and associational positions as well as in access to housing and leisure facilities. Studies by AJC staff and cam-

paigns by local chapters were given impetus by the public accommodations provisions of the 1964 Civil Rights Act. The Los Angeles
chapter was successful in opening the city's three most important
social clubs, and Abram's intervention with the American Bar Association resulted in its canceling all social events at the discriminatory Miami Beach Bath Club during its 1965 annual convention.[14]

Abram's leadership of the American Jewish Committee overlapped
with his work at the United Nations. When he was appointed by
President Kennedy to address human rights issues at the UN, Abram
saw an opportunity to bring to the position his experience working
on civil rights issues in the United States. But his work on the sub-
commission would soon expose him to the harsh realities of international politics at a time when the Soviet Union was stepping up
its campaign against Jews at home and America's ally Israel in the
international arena.

While working on an international antiracism law in the fall of
1962, Abram insisted that it include antisemitism, an issue on which
he sparred with his Soviet counterparts while calling attention to its
prevalence behind the Iron Curtain. Largely because of this controversy, two separate treaties were proposed by the subcommission,
the Convention on the Elimination of All Forms of Racial Discrimination and the Convention on the Elimination of All Forms of Religious Intolerance. But over the following two years in which these
documents were hammered out, the idea of including antisemitism
in either one was successfully contested by the Soviets.[15]

During the debates in the subcommission on these treaties, Abram
insisted that they must not infringe on the fundamental freedoms of
speech and press. In arguing the contrary position, the Soviet representatives had given assurances that "a new society had so per-
fected human nature that harmony between races and creeds now
prevailed." So much so was this the case that "no one wished to
express un-neighborly views, and therefore laws impressing these
imposed no actual restraint."[16]

Abram reacted with incredulity to a report by the Ukrainian Soviet
Socialist Republic and issued by the UN secretary-general in August
1963 that "there are no instances in the Ukrainian SSR of racial preju-

dice or of national or religious intolerance, either *de jure* or *de facto*." The report went on to state that although there are penalties in the criminal code for such behavior, such was unnecessary since "chauvinism, nationalism and racialism" are alien to the Ukrainian people, given that they are incompatible with Communist ideology. A similar report had been issued by the Soviet government that September.[17]

Those words proved hollow when that fall, Abram received from an Israeli source a viciously antisemitic book published by the Soviet controlled Ukrainian Academy of Sciences entitled *Jews Without Embellishment*. The book, by academy member Trofim Kichko, argued that a worldwide Jewish conspiracy, having played a role in Hitler's 1941 invasion of Russia, was operating to subvert the Soviet Union. The book's caricatures of Jews bore strong resemblance to Nazi propaganda. In February 1964 Abram called a press conference at the UN to denounce the book.[18]

Writing to his Soviet counterpart Boris Ivanov, Abram reminded him that during the debates on adopting the convention outlawing racial discrimination, Ivanov had led the charge to include ethnic and national discrimination. Indeed, Abram wrote, "you would have included all conduct, including propaganda which 'promoted' discrimination." Abram continued, "If ever I saw a book which both promotes and incites hatred and discrimination, this is one."[19]

Sending him a copy of the book, Abram asked for Ivanov's opinion as to whether the draft convention the subcommission had presented to the Human Rights Commission "is specific enough to reach the evil of the state organs publishing this book." After stalling for a month, Ivanov replied with a press release from the Washington Embassy of the Soviet Union on "Jews in the USSR" and another from the Soviet Mission to the UN characterizing the book as "one of several works on the problems of atheism published in Ukraine lately." His one concession was that the book "contains some slipshod formulations."[20]

Undeterred by his colleague's disingenuous response, Abram continued to seek answers to his original questions throughout the year, but to no avail. In December, the secretary-general's report on measures to implement the UN Declaration on the Elimination of All

Forms of Religious Discrimination included an assertion by none other than the Ukrainian SSR that all "principles and provisions" of the declaration had been implemented.[21]

In his statement to the subcommission on the Kichko incident, Abram drew several conclusions: first, no economic system is a guarantee against discrimination and intolerance; second, where it is known that actual instances of human rights deprivations are claimed, these should be met on their own terms candidly, and not by "repleading" the country's constitution; third, "some organ of the UN must be given the power and the authority to study intensively beyond the government reports, to challenge them if need be, to check fact against claim and hope against reality"; and fourth, the subcommission needs to spend more time on its annual review and increase "our facilities for making it effective." Concluding, he called for making our work "mean something to the oppressed and persecuted."[22]

In the spring of 1965 Abram was appointed by President Johnson to the position of U.S. Representative to the UN Human Rights Commission in Geneva.[23] It was the same position first held by Eleanor Roosevelt when she presided over the drafting of the Universal Declaration of Human Rights. In a memorandum to the president recommending Abram's appointment, Secretary of State Rusk wrote that he considered him "one of the most knowledgeable persons on Human Rights in this country. His leadership for the past two years as the U.S. expert member on the UN Sub-Commission on Prevention of Discrimination and Protection of Minorities has been outstanding."[24]

In the spring of 1967, Abram brought before the Human Rights Commission a proposal to appoint a UN High Commissioner for Human Rights. The idea, dating back to the 1950s, had originated with Jacob Blaustein, the Baltimore oil man and past president of the American Jewish Committee who had been an emissary of President Roosevelt to the founding meetings of the UN. It called for a neutral legal official to investigate human rights violations from an apolitical perspective.

During the debate, Soviet delegate Yacov Ostrovsky launched a personal attack on Abram, charging him, as a Jew, with serving "two masters." When Abram objected, his Soviet counterpart cut him off, noting with sarcasm that this was not a meeting of "the Zionist organization of which you are president." Abram countered by pointing out that the organization he headed fights injustice "regardless of race, color or creed," adding that he had seen the Soviet delegate when he personally visited the committee's human rights library.[25]

While making the case for the High Commissioner for Human Rights, Abram again referenced the Kichko book and accused the Soviets of the crudest antisemitism. He also revived the proposal to include antisemitism in the not yet adopted second of the two anti-discrimination conventions, the one dealing with the prevention of religious intolerance. While the High Commissioner proposal was tabled that fall, the attempt to include antisemitism in the second convention met the same fate as the earlier attempt to include it in the first.[26]

David Harris, who began a lengthy tenure as AJC's executive director nearly three decades later, said that Abram's exposure of the Kichko book and his confrontations with Soviet UN delegates received a great deal of attention both inside and outside the Jewish community. "Morris was very much exposed to this Soviet diet of anti-Semitism which in 1967, when the Soviets broke diplomatic relations with Israel as a result of the Six-Day War, very quickly morphed into anti-Zionism." The Soviet Union and its Third World allies would later exploit the UN conventions of the 1960s to secure the General Assembly's endorsement of the "Zionism is Racism" resolution in 1975.[27]

Perhaps no issue engaged Abram during his early tenure at the American Jewish Committee more than that of the position of the Catholic Church in its teachings on Jews and Judaism. In the summer of 1964 he led an AJC delegation to the Vatican to raise the subject directly with Pope Paul VI. For decades the organization had worked to root out passages in parochial school textbooks that were prejudicial to Jews. As part of those and related efforts, AJC staff and lay leadership had cultivated relations with Catholic leadership in the United States and around the world.[28]

Pope John XXIII convened the Second Vatican Council in the fall of 1962 to address the relationship between the church and the modern world. Angelo Cardinal Rocalli, a diplomat for the church during World War II, had released church documents resulting in the rescue of thousands of Jews. Under Pope John's tenure, unofficial relations between the Vatican and Israel became warmer.[29] AJC's efforts to get the church to liberalize its teachings on Jews were dealt a setback with his death in June 1963.

There had been hopes that the Vatican II Council would repudiate the Church's deicide charge against the Jews that had for centuries fueled antisemitism. Abram had done his best to explain to his own children the Christ-killing taunts aimed at them in school before they were in their teens. In May 1964, the American Jewish Committee was granted an audience with John's successor, Pope Paul VI, through the offices of the International University of Social Studies, Pro Deo, in Rome. The audience coincided with a gift by the widow of the former head of AJC's Los Angeles Chapter to Pro Deo to establish a research and action center to combat prejudice.[30]

The previous month, Abram and AJC Executive Director Slawson had paid a visit to the residence of New York's venerated Cardinal Spellman, in which they appealed to the cardinal to denounce the deicide charge at an upcoming AJC dinner. This the cardinal did emphatically before an audience that included Secretary of State Dean Rusk and other dignitaries. Prior to leading the committee's delegation to the Vatican, Abram flew to Washington and received Rusk's permission to share with the pope his endorsement of Cardinal Spellman's remarks concerning the deicide charge. Abram's goal for the visit was "to pin the Pope down."[31]

At his private meeting with AJC's delegation, Pope Paul began by reading a statement articulating the church's beliefs about the equality of all men and deploring the ordeals that the Jewish people have endured. But Abram and his colleagues were not going to be satisfied coming away from the meeting with little more than platitudes. Abram pressed Pope Paul on the deicide question. When the pontiff indicated that the matter was under formal consideration, Abram saw an opening, informing him that both the U.S. Secretary of State and the leader of New York's church were united in their conviction that the charge was "absurd." The pope replied that he agreed with their assessment.[32]

Much to the surprise and delight of the delegation, the pope also agreed to allow Abram to release the result of this dialogue upon their return to New York, a clear victory for those seeking continuity of the current papal regime with its predecessor in its approach to antisemitism. At his press conference in New York on June 1, 1964, Abram said that the pope had informed the delegation that Cardinal Spellman's address at AJC's dinner in April had been forwarded to him and that he had read it "with much satisfaction." Abram said that as a result of the audience with Pope Paul, AJC felt greatly encouraged about the prospects of the upcoming session of the council adopting the decrees regarding Catholic attitudes toward Jews and other non-Christian groups.[33]

Making use of the papal endorsement, Abram and other AJC officials traveled to Latin America where they lined up support for a declaration against the deicide charge from key church leaders at the next session of the council. Atlanta attorney Miles Alexander, who later assumed the chairmanship of AJC's Atlanta chapter, was attracted to the organization in part because of what it began to do behind the scenes: "I was really impressed with their going to various cardinals around the world and lobbying to end the blaming of the Jews for Jesus' death. Morris led that effort. I think the College of cardinals supported it, and I attributed a lot of that to the lobbying of the American Jewish Committee and Morris's behind the scenes work."[34]

Word got back to AJC's leadership later that summer that the Vatican could not pass the decree regarding Jews in its current form without facing serious diplomatic consequences in its relationship with the church in the Middle East.[35] Cardinal Sheehan of Baltimore, who had a close relationship with former AJC President Jacob Blaustein, and four other American prelates, prevailed upon the pope to keep the declaration back on the agenda of the council when it reconvened that fall.[36]

The final declaration voted on from October 14 to 15, 1965, did not specifically mention the word "deicide," but it did remove the teaching of contempt from the church's textbooks. This marked a radical departure from previous church teachings and a significant step forward in Catholic-Jewish relations. To Dr. Steven Bayme, AJC's director of Contemporary Jewish Life, he and his colleagues today regard the organization's work on Vatican II as "AJC at its finest," since both staff who worked on inter-religious matters under the leadership of Rabbi Marc Tanenbaum, and laymen led by Abram, worked closely together in helping to secure the declaration.[37]

Five days after it was decreed, Abram received a personal message from Richard Cardinal Cushing, Archbishop of Boston. "Dear Morris," it read, "I really think that the declaration by the Council on non-Christians was the very best we could get. At least we can now follow it up by having some of the hideous phrases especially relative to the Jews, eliminated from the Catholic liturgy. They appear to me to be relics of former ages."[38] At a dinner celebrating AJC's sixtieth anniversary the following May, past president Joseph Proskauer remarked that if the organization had done nothing else in its sixty-year history than the work it did on the fourth section of *Nostra Aetate, dayenu!* (It would have been enough.)[39]

The other major event during Abram's AJC tenure with consequences for the American and world Jewish communities was Israel's Six-Day War of June 1967. Although the committee had maintained a non-Zionist posture as late as World War II, it had welcomed the establishment of the State of Israel in 1948 as "an event of historical significance."[40] Still, as Bayme pointed out, "Without question, the place Israel assumed on the American Jewish agenda writ large, including AJC, was that pre-1967, Israel was always on the map but not central; after '67, so much of the agenda revolved around Israel. In that respect, June of 1967 was a decisive turning point."[41]

A month prior to the start of the war, AJC had reiterated its opposition to mass rallies, a relic of its longstanding preference for quiet diplomacy in pursuing its mission. On the fourth day of the war, seeing no need to consult with the committee's board, Morris Abram became the featured speaker at a rally held in Lafayette Park across the street from the White House. This was the largest demonstration held by the American Jewish community in the nation's capital prior to the one in 1987 on behalf of Soviet Jewry.[42]

To Abram what was most significant about the Lafayette Park rally was the reaction to it among many of Israel's longtime friends. In his speech he called upon allies in the liberal Christian churches to join the Jewish community in support of Israel. But by the time of the rally, the military tide had turned in Israel's favor, and many mainline Christian supporters in its more liberal ranks were beginning to side with those they now considered the "underdogs" of the region.

"The underdog had triumphed," wrote Abram, "and many of our Christian allies vanished. Yet, Israel's cause was not less valid on the fourth day of the war than on the first." Abram was forced to revise his long-held view "that the orthodox forms of religion were the chief obstacles to the development of warm ecumenism between Jews and Christians."[43] The experience foreshadowed many of Abram's future efforts to defend the state of Israel against attacks from those who no longer saw it as David fighting Goliath but rather as the region's dominant power.

Within the Jewish community, the Six-Day War marked a pronounced shift in its perception of Israel. It also brought about a shift in Abram's own perception of himself and his appropriate role as a Jewish leader.[44] When he began his association with AJC, Abram had avoided using the phrase "the Jewish people." By the time he handed over the presidency of the committee to his successor Arthur Goldberg in 1968, Abram saw no conflict between the idea of being both a proud American and a dedicated Jew.[45]

In addition to the opportunity to serve in a leadership role at the American Jewish Committee, New York opened additional doors for Abram as well, including his active involvement with the Field Foundation. The foundation was established in 1940 by Marshall Field III, the grandson of the founder of Chicago's famous department store. In the wake of the Great Depression, Field became a strong supporter of the New Deal and filled the board of the foundation with some of the country's leading social scientists, scholars, business leaders, and judges. Field believed passionately in racial integration and involved the foundation in matters related to race and juvenile behavior.[46]

In 1960, the foundation was split into two separate entities, one based in Illinois headed by Field's son and the other in New York, led by his widow Ruth. While the Illinois entity was more focused on local activity, the Field Foundation of New York maintained its national perspective, including on matters of race. It was that focus that led Ruth Field, shortly after the division of the foundation, to arrange a dinner in New York for board members to meet with Abram and Atlanta Mayor Hartsfield to discuss the race issue. The group included Adlai Stevenson, Lloyd Garrison, and Ralph Bunche, the first African American to win the Nobel Peace Prize.

At the dinner, Abram noted the centrality of Georgia among all the southern states to determining the direction of desegregation. But until the abolition of the county unit system, very little could move forward on that front. He injected an important dose of reality into the discussion of race by pointing out that it was the class issue that was burdening the South every bit as much as racial prejudice. Closing the class gap, he argued, would be critical to solving the race issue. Shortly thereafter, Ruth Field asked Abram to join the foundation's board, and he succeeded Adlai Stevenson as its president after Stevenson died in 1965.[47]

In May 1966 the American Jewish Committee celebrated its sixtieth anniversary at its annual meeting, which included a televised conversation involving Senator Robert Kennedy, New Jersey senator Clifford Case, and Morris Abram. The conversation addressed the topic "Extremism in America Today." In assessing the difference between a right-wing extremist and a genuine conservative, Abram noted that the latter accepts the need for gradual social change, "but he is concerned with preserving that which is wholesome and worthy of retention in our society." By contrast, a right-wing extremist views all social change as inherently evil. While the true liberal is less sentimental than the conservative about the past, he would accelerate the process of social change.

Thus, while liberals and conservatives take a different approach to change, they share a "faith in the American people and hold sacred the democratic process." By contrast, extremists of all stripes "would take the basic decisions away from the people and substitute their own judgments of right and wrong. And—most important of all—the extremists, left and right, are convinced that the end justifies the means."

As to which form of extremism posed the greater danger, Abram left no doubt where he stood. While demonstrating with a Viet Cong flag and burning draft cards are to be deplored "because they clog the channels of debate rather than they contribute to rational discourse," the greater danger comes from those on the far right "who are apt to equate any kind of dissent with disloyalty," regarding all who oppose them as guilty of treason. Such an attitude, he continued, "makes it impossible for democracy to solve its problems, which can only be done by debate, discussion, consensus, or at least a vote, and the acceptance of the will of the majority."[48]

Abram's years in New York, while broadening his interest in public policy both domestic and international, also brought him closer to his Jewish roots. His involvement with the local chapter of the American Jewish Committee in Atlanta had begun largely as a way of supplementing his modest income at a time when his family was growing. But years of lobbying on behalf of Jewish causes at AJC and fighting antisemitism at the United Nations not only made him one of the leading spokesmen for the American Jewish community but also led to a turning point in his worldview that would last for the rest of his life.

Bayme has a clear recollection of a debate between Abram and Albert Vorspan that took place in May 1983 at AJC's annual meeting. The debate centered around the question of Jewish universalism versus Jewish particularism. Vorspan, who headed the Commission on Social Action of Reform Judaism, expressed his concern about "a growing JDL-type mentality" within the Jewish community, making reference to the militant defense group led by Meir Kahane. In doing so, he was decrying the shift toward particularism in the Jewish community that had been sparked by the Six-Day War. As Bayme pointed out, "What Vorspan was trying to say, I think inelegantly, was that in the balance between universalism and particularism, we have tilted too much toward particularism." In other words, Jews were abandoning the principle of Jewish universalism.

For his part, Abram did not object to a Jewish stake in a universal imperative. Precisely because Jews have done so well in America, he said, we have a moral imperative to those less fortunate. But "there is no question he was becoming more particularistic as the years went on. What he was saying was let us not forget about Jewish imperative in the name of the universalist banner."[49]

In 1983 Abram was asked to join an international panel established by the head of the Jabotinsky Foundation to honor individuals with the Shield of Jerusalem Jabotinsky Prize for their defense of the rights of the Jewish people. The award was named for the intellectual father of the "revisionist" movement within Zionism that challenged the more established leadership for its lack of militancy in pressing the British for a Jewish homeland during the 1930s. The first awardees were the late Senator Henry Jackson, the Soviet refusenik Yosef Begun, and the French human rights advocate Simone Veil. A special award was given to former Prime Minister Menachem Begin, a protégé of Jabotinsky.[50]

The day after the award ceremony, Abram addressed the Southern Jewish Historical Society on the topic of taking another look at one's own past. He started by noting that his involvement in the selection of the recipients of the Jabotinsky prize had impelled him to go back and learn more about the man. "Oh, I can remember what I thought about him when I was a young man in college and I first heard his name. I thought, of course, the very worst things about him, the very worst. He represented every tradition in Jewish life that I regarded as false." But the more Abram learned about this son of Odessa, including his extraordinary mastery of the Hebrew language, leading to highly regarded translations of Dante and Edgar Allen Poe, the more he could understand why Jabotinsky had been honored with a state funeral in Israel thirty years after his death.[51]

In the last decade of his life Morris Abram was invited to be the guest speaker at an AJC dinner honoring the historian Naomi Cohen with the Akiva Award for Jewish scholarship. The award is named for Rabbi Akiva, the legendary sage who was the most important spiritual leader of the Jewish people following the destruction of the Second Temple. Bayme recalled that one of the reasons to choose Abram was that "while he himself was not a scholar, he was someone who valued Jewish scholarship. That interest intensified over the years. I doubt he could have given a speech like that or chosen to give a speech like that fifteen years earlier."

According to Bayme, Abram clearly was very upset by the level of antisemitism and of the unfair treatment of Israel internationally. And in his speech that evening, he said that a strong Jewish identity is the key to Jewish survival. "So I think in that sense his perceptions of anti-Semitism or anti-Israelism as the case may be in many ways set a very strong nurturing sense that the Jewish world and the world of Jewish values is the world in which he felt most anchored."

Morris Abram, who began his career looking outward to champion political and social reform, "became increasingly conscious of the degree of hostility Jews faced, increasingly proud of what Jews had done as a people, and increasingly convinced that the Jews cannot relax their guard, but the key to Jewish survival lies with strong Jewish identity, Jewish education, Jewish culture."[52]

SIX

Continuing the Struggle

I want every damn delegate quivering with excitement and
anticipation about the future of civil rights and their future
opportunities in this country.

In June 1963, President Kennedy summoned a group of leading members of the American Bar Association to the White House, among
them Morris Abram. The president, Vice President Johnson, and
Attorney General Robert Kennedy challenged the attorneys present
to join, however belatedly, the fight for equal justice in the South.

Abram, now a full-fledged New York attorney, stepped forward
to take up the first case of the newly established Lawyers Committee for Civil Rights Under Law. The scene was Americus, Georgia, the county seat of Sumter County, less than ninety miles from
where he spent his childhood. Abram's return to southwest Georgia marked an important symbolic turning point in his transition
from civil rights attorney in Atlanta to partner in one of New York's
most prestigious firms.

During the spring of 1963 a team of students from the Student
Nonviolent Coordinating Committee (SNCC) conducted a voter
registration drive in Americus and used pickets and sit-ins in an
attempt to integrate the local movie theater. The authorities reacted
by sending nearly one hundred local teenagers to jail.[1] Several weeks
later, following a mass meeting at a church, two hundred young
people marched through the streets of Americus. The police, after

ordering the group to disburse, fired warning shots and closed in on those protesters bracing themselves for arrest. As the police began to wield their clubs, protesters reacted by throwing bricks through windows. A state trooper broke a black demonstrator's leg, and another black man was fatally shot in the back as he walked through a white neighborhood.[2]

SNCC fieldworkers Ralph Allen, Don Harris, and John Perdew, who had launched the voter registration and community organizing drives as part of the Southwest Georgia Project, were arrested, joined one week later by Minnesota-born agricultural worker Zev Aeloney of the Congress of Racial Equality (CORE). The four were charged with insurrection, which carried the death penalty under Georgia's 1871 Anti-Treason Act. The county solicitor used this particular charge to keep the demonstrators jailed indefinitely, which was mandated in capital cases. Their arrest captured national headlines, and the "Americus Four" became a cause célèbre for civil rights advocates nationwide. Still, the U.S. attorney general decided against federal intervention, as his office found no merit in charges of police brutality and refused to challenge the charge of sedition.[3]

Abram's junior associate in the case, Sydney Rosdeitcher, had joined the Paul, Weiss firm shortly before Abram after working, coincidentally, for Abram's brother-in-law Harold Reis at the Justice Department. The strategy pursued by Abram's team was to get the case against the civil rights workers moved into federal jurisdiction. Rosdeitcher recommended that they make use of a precedent from the 1939 case involving Jersey City's notorious mayor Frank Hague and his use of a local ordinance to suppress a recruitment meeting planned by the Congress of Industrial Organizations. The lower federal court in that case, upheld by the Supreme Court, had held that federal jurisdiction could be applied if it could be demonstrated that constitutional issues were not likely to be enforceable within that community, particularly when there was a history of disregard for the U.S. Constitution in the state courts.[4]

"And so," said Rosdeitcher, "we effectively put the city of Americus on trial." Abram and his young associate questioned everything from the juvenile court system where a judge put blacks into outside concentration camps, to the hospital system in which blacks could not receive emergency care without being sent sixty miles away to a hospital that would accept them. "And a black person," he said, "could never enforce a contract in a county court or in a local court if they were enforcing it against a white person."[5]

Rosdeitcher was struck by a curious dichotomy in the treatment of Abram's legal team:

> One thing I remember about the case was that everyone was gracious to us during the day, but at night when we were walking in the streets they would scream out things like, "Go back to New York!" which had a connotation of not just that we were from there but also about our religion. But the odd thing was that they bought Morris. He was terrific as a legal advocate in the way he tried the cases. But he also had this wonderful Southern approach that during one break one of these guys came up to him and said, "Why can't you be on our side? We could really use you." They couldn't understand why he wasn't joining their side in the fight against desegregation and admired him. But I don't think they desired the result. We won.[6]

A three-judge panel led by Elbert Tuttle, one of the South's most courageous jurists of the civil rights era whom Abram had recruited fourteen years earlier to join him in his *amicus* brief in support of overturning Georgia's unconstitutional voter registration law, was convened to hear the case. The prosecutor who had brought the insurrection charge admitted that its purpose was to keep the civil rights workers locked up in order "to convince them that this type of activity is not the right way" to achieve their goals.[7]

On October 31, 1963, the panel voted 2–1 to release the civil rights workers, who had been imprisoned for three months, along with a black teenage girl who had been locked up in a prison in a nearby county by the local juvenile judge. Abram had insisted that her case be included in the trial. The panel also declared the state's insurrection statute unconstitutional.[8]

Abram's new status as an outsider was underscored by the fact that not a single member of the Georgia Bar accepted his invitation to join him in fighting an unconstitutional statute that threatened civil rights workers with the death penalty. Nor could he count on the support of the local state senator, a future president of the United States, who refrained from taking any public position. Referring to state senator Jimmy Carter's absence from the civil rights movement, Abram asked an interviewer fifteen years later, "What kind of a man would stand aside—what kind of a man must he be? Obviously, a man who has got sense enough to know where his bread is buttered. But what kind of a man is he?"[9] Abram recalled, "It felt good to return to Georgia on a civil rights case, backed now by the pillars of the national legal establishment and no longer dependent on a livelihood in Georgia."[10]

Abram returned to his native state that same year, summoned personally by President Kennedy for another mission that involved the civil rights of black Americans. This time it was in Atlanta, the city in which he had practiced law for fourteen years, and the target was its reformist mayor, Ivan Allen Jr. Despite his city's progress in desegregating public facilities during the early 1960s, Allen had been unsuccessful in convincing restaurant and hotel owners that it was time to open their doors to black customers. As these meetings continued with little result, in early 1963 President Kennedy proposed civil rights legislation that included a strong public accommodations provision. This action was met with hostility throughout the South and was opposed even by moderate Atlantans who considered it unfair to private enterprise.[11]

While Allen was trying to determine his own position on the provision, Morris Abram paid him a visit in his city hall office. Abram told the mayor that President Kennedy had asked him to solicit Allen not only for his support for the bill but also his agreement to testify in favor of it before the Senate Commerce Committee. Despite Allen's belief that doing so would destroy his chance for a second term, he eventually agreed to testify following a personal call from the president.[12]

Although a firestorm of controversy back home followed his testimony, Allen was able to survive reelection by a comfortable margin two years later. When he campaigned in the black community, he took with him a leather-bound copy of his Senate testimony from which he would read. "To say that my reading from that testimony was regarded with great reverence at Negro rallies," he wrote, "would be an understatement." Reminiscing on his final day in office in January 1970 about his eight years as mayor, Allen looked at the rocking chairs arrayed around his desk, calling to mind "the day Morris Abram sat in one and told me President Kennedy wanted me to testify in Washington."[13]

Abram's civil rights work in Atlanta and New York brought him to the attention of the Johnson White House when it was looking for an appropriate figure to chair a much-anticipated White House Conference on Civil Rights. The conference had its genesis in a major address the president had given at Howard University at its 1965 June graduation in the wake of the Civil Rights Act of 1964 and with Congress on the verge of passing the Voting Rights Act of 1965.

In the address, Johnson noted that as the barriers to freedom were being knocked down, the next phase of the struggle would be "to give twenty million Negroes the same chance as every other American to learn and grow, to work and share in society, to develop their abilities—physical, mental and spiritual, and to pursue their individual happiness." He continued, "To this end, equal opportunity is essential, but not enough, not enough. Men and women of all races are born with the same range of abilities. But ability is not just the product of birth. Ability is stretched or stunted by the family that you live with, and the neighborhood you live in—by the school you go to and the poverty or the richness of your surroundings. It is the product of a hundred unseen forces playing upon the little infant, the child, and finally, the man."[14]

Johnson announced his intention to convene a high-level group of scholars of both races, black leaders, and government officials whose object would be "to help the American Negro fulfill the rights which, after the long time of injustice, he is finally about to secure."[15] The reaction to the Howard University speech was highly positive among black civil rights leaders. It had been read to Martin Luther King Jr., Roy Wilkins, and Whitney Young in advance and all had responded enthusiastically.[16]

In the spirit of bringing together an integrated group of scholars, leaders, and officials, the White House organizers decided the conference "To Fulfill These Rights" would be led by one black and one white co-chairman. For the former, they chose William Coleman, the first black to serve as a clerk to a Supreme Court justice, coauthor of the plaintiff's brief in the historic *Brown v. Board of Education* case, and partner in a distinguished Philadelphia firm. For his counterpart, Vice President Humphrey proposed three candidates, Father Theodore Hesburgh, President of Notre Dame; Bronson LaFollette, the attorney general of Wisconsin; and Morris Abram, whom he described as "a southerner with an excellent reputation as a leader in the broader field of human rights."[17]

In a meeting of Johnson's domestic advisors in late September, which included the attorney general, presidential assistant Lee White, who was given the major staff responsibility for the conference, reported that "there was a strong sentiment for Morris Abrams [*sic*], as a can-do fellow with the best credentials and a fast starter."[18] Abram was selected to serve with William Coleman as co-chair of the conference.

The most venerated veteran of the civil rights movement, A. Philip Randolph, agreed to serve as honorary chair. The executive committee read like a "Who's Who" of the national civil rights leadership, including Roy Wilkins of the NAACP, Whitney Young of the Urban League, Martin Luther King Jr. of the Southern Christian Leadership Conference, James Farmer of the Congress of Racial Equality, Dorothy Height of the National Council of Negro Women, John Lewis of the Student Nonviolent Coordinating Committee, and Jack Greenberg of the NAACP Legal Education and Defense Fund.

To say that President Johnson had high hopes for the conference would be an understatement. As planning got underway, he met with Abram and the conference's executive director Berl Bernhard. Bernhard asked the president what kind of conference he desired. He answered this way:

> In the hill country in the spring, the sun comes up earlier, and the ground gets warmer, and you can see the steam rising and the sap dripping. And in his pen, you can see my prize bull. He's the biggest, best-hung bull in the hill country. In the spring he gets a hankering for those

cows, and he starts pawing the ground and getting restless. So, I open the pen and he goes down the hill, looking for a cow, with his pecker hanging hard and swinging. Those cows get so Goddamn excited, they get more and more moist to receive him, and their asses just start quivering and then they start quivering all over, every one of them is quivering, as that bull struts into their pasture. . . . Well, I want a quivering conference . . . I want every damn delegate quivering with excitement and anticipation about the future of civil rights and their future opportunities in this country.[19]

A quivering conference planning session was pretty much what the president got several months later, but it was far from what he expected or desired. Warning signs were already on the horizon. That summer the Watts neighborhood of Los Angeles exploded over allegations of police brutality. For six days beginning on August 11, looting and arson resulted in thirty-four deaths and over $40 million in property damage. Nearly four thousand members of the California National Guard had to be called out to quell the rioting.

The White House looked to the established civil rights organizations to help it deal with riots that would later spread to northern cities. But none of these organizations had much of a base in northern or western ghettos.[20] And the established civil rights groups were now fighting a growing militancy within the ranks of the black community, including young leaders calling for black separatism. Complicating those divisions were two additional factors. One was the escalating costs of the war in Vietnam, which was beginning to limit expenditures for social purposes. The other was a growing controversy over the underlying obstacles to black advancement.

The controversy was stimulated by a report that had been drafted by Daniel Patrick Moynihan, then an assistant secretary of labor, and sent to the president by his boss Labor Secretary Willard Wirtz, in March 1965.[21] The nine-page document, which soon became known simply as "the Moynihan report," pointed out that the next phase of the black's struggle for equality would need to take it beyond the realm of political and legal equality to the achievement of more equal results in the areas of education, housing, and employment.

At the center of the report was the assertion that the single greatest impediment to achieving these results was the breakdown of the black family. Far from "blaming the victim," as many of Moynihan's fiercest critics later charged, the author of the report attributed the breakdown to the consequence of four primary historical factors: slavery, reconstruction, urbanization, and mass unemployment. The report included many grim statistics, among them the reality that over a third of black children were living in families with one or both parents missing, over half were receiving welfare under the Aid to Dependent Children program, and "probably not much more than a third of Negro youth reach eighteen having lived all their lives with both parents."[22]

The reaction to the report after its release that summer was mixed: liberals were pleased with its calls for eliminating economic inequality; conservatives approved of its implications of the need for self-help.[23] But critics on the left, including civil rights activists, were vocally hostile, many arguing that the report was fueling a new racism by focusing on the victims rather than the system that fostered it.[24]

Typical was James Farmer, cofounder of the Congress of Racial Equality, who wrote in his syndicated column, "We are sick unto death of being analyzed, mesmerized, bought, sold, and slobbered over. . . . Moynihan has provided a massive academic copout for the white conscience and clearly implied that Negroes in this nation will never secure a substantial measure of freedom until we stop sleeping with our wife's sister and buying Cadillacs instead of bread."[25]

The New Left also took strong issue with the Moynihan Report. Marcus Raskin, cofounder of the Institute for Policy Studies, questioned why adopting middle class values was the solution to the problem of the black family: "It is only the foolish who would think that the middle-class is the be-all and end-all of existence. It is hardly something that has to be emulated." Raskin objected to the notion that blacks should "run that rat race of opportunism which [their] white American brethren had become so adept at running."[26]

The Moynihan Report heavily influenced the president's graduation address at Howard. Moynihan himself had collaborated closely on it with White House speechwriter Richard Goodwin, working right up to the time it was delivered.[27] The original idea for the White House conference called for in the address was to make the report its centerpiece. Now, with the controversy over the report, White House officials were forced to change their strategy. They decided to make the conference planned for November a planning meeting of several hundred activists for a much larger conference to take place the following year, and to reduce the family issue to one seminar among many others.[28]

Abram later noted how radical black nationalists who saw themselves as the new leaders of the movement viewed the conference as an opportunity to attack the government and to heap scorn upon Randolph, Wilkins, and other members of the "old guard." He was particularly troubled by the fact that it took his persistent intervention to get the author of the Moynihan report invited to the planning session in the face of resistance from many black leaders. Abram recalled Moynihan's reaction after he finally got the approval of the White House to call him with the invitation: "Goddamn it, it's about time! Hell, there wouldn't be any conference had I not written that into the Howard University speech."[29]

As Abram recalled two decades later, "Pat came, and was thoroughly trashed." When asked his own reaction to the controversy, he replied,

> I guess that created a certain disenchantment in me. I tend to want to go about as far as logic will take me, and logically I thought the man was dead right, irrefutable. And the fact that he had opened a Pandora's box, exposed a nest of worms, I thought was absolutely significant and important. . . . Now as long as you will not listen to Pat in what he's saying about the figures and the dire consequences, I think you just repeat and repeat and repeat the tragedy. That was beginning to surface at the White House conference. But I'm going to say I was too naive to realize it was part of the issue.[30]

Although the Executive Committee for the conference were all integrationists, "out in the wings, "Abram later pointed out, "unnoted by us, this Black Power movement was beginning, and the Black Power movement is a separationist movement." Abram believed there are two schools of thought in this country on civil rights, one integrationist, the other, separationist. He left no doubt with which side he identified. "These young kids now were assailing the old titans of the movement who had created the revolution."[31]

In his opening remarks to the planning session, Abram offered a realistic assessment of what the participants faced in addressing the problems of black America:

> We meet at a time when long overdue legislative advances have opened not only the gates of opportunity but also the floodgates of expectancy. And we seek the means of matching opportunity with achievement before hope turns to despair. Already the signals from Harlem, Bedford-Stuyvesant, Chicago and Watts tell us that the time is short. Our task is enormous. Though we deal with the problems of fellow citizens whose ancestors came to these shores before 1808 and who thus should be amongst our first families, they came without family and until now, in the main, never even enjoyed the equalizing opportunity of attending a truly American school system. . . . We are not here to discuss merely the symptoms of America's gravest national problem, but also the causes and cures. We will deal not only with the pathologies of some families, but with some of the pathologies of the total society.[32]

Much of the rhetoric of the planning meeting was filled with anger directed at the government and its efforts to date. The planners, according to White House domestic policy advisor Harry McPherson, "vied with one another in demanding more and more extreme reparations."[33] The White House became alarmed that the actual conference to be held the following summer would be overrun by the militants, which would have the effect of setting back the movement from those achievements that had already been made. By the time the conference "To Fulfill These Rights" was held in June 1966, Abram and Coleman had been replaced as conference chairs by Ben Heineman, a Chicago-based businessman. Abram believed that their relegation to the Executive Committee had resulted from the frustration of the president in not receiving the praise he had expected for his civil rights achievements. A team of corporate and labor leaders were brought in to serve on the committee.[34]

During the conference, SNCC supporters and New York activists carried signs outside Washington's Sheraton-Park Hotel that read, "Save us from our Negro Leaders, Uncle Toms!"[35] John Lewis, who as SNCC chairman led the celebrated march in Selma, Alabama the previous year in what became known as "Bloody Sunday," was one of the conference's most prominent casualties. As he recalled,

> there were individuals, activists in SNCC and other civil rights groups that were opposed to my being part of this conference. They said Lyndon Johnson is trying to coopt the movement. And it was not a good time for me. Stokely Carmichael and a small group had what I call a coup. They said I was not "black enough" and they needed to tell Lyndon Johnson where to go. And there was a picture of President Johnson when he presented me with one of the pens that he had used to sign the Voter Rights Act on August 6, 1965. I was too close to Lyndon Johnson; too close to Dr. King. And I loved Dr. King, and I admired President Johnson. I had a problem with the war, but I admired him. And I thought the speech he gave on March 15, 1965 when he said "We Shall Overcome" was one of the great speeches. And I quote from time to time what he said.[36]

When John Lewis was expelled from his position as the chairman of SNCC and replaced by the black nationalist Stokely Carmichael, he moved to New York to work for the Field Foundation's director, Leslie Dunbar, and its chairman, Morris Abram.

Abram recalled the White House conference as "my first experience with raw black militance, my wound from black colleagues in the struggle for racial equality in which I had been engaged for twenty years." The task, he later described, would turn out to be an unhappy experience, "one that would permanently influence my attitudes toward radicalism and unbridled social expectations." Even so, "I was still unwilling to do the black man the honor of examining his conduct as critically as that of whites."[37]

The replacement of John Lewis with Stokely Carmichael to head the Student Nonviolent Coordinating Committee was symptomatic of a growing split within the ranks of the larger civil rights movement. Establishment figures such as Roy Wilkins, Whitney Young, and King himself were being challenged by younger, more militant blacks impatient with fighting for gains by working through a political system where the pace of change was not to their liking.

One important turning point in the alienation of black radicals from the civil rights movement had occurred during the Democratic National Convention of 1964, where an integrated delegation of "Freedom Democrats" from Mississippi sought to be seated in place of the all-white party regulars. While Martin Luther King Jr. and white liberal allies of the freedom delegation including Allard Lowenstein and Joseph Rauh reluctantly supported a compromise, many SNCC activists believed they had been sold out.[38]

One later wrote that the struggle was now one "not for civil rights but rather for liberation." The term "white liberal," formerly one of praise, was now an epithet used by those blacks challenging the established civil rights leadership, and those using it were now reaching out to the New Left, rather than to longtime liberal allies.[39] Like Morris Abram, a high percentage of those allies were Jewish. Jews and organizations working on their behalf had played a major role in lobbying for the Civil Rights Acts, in organizing and participating in freedom marches in Southern states, and in providing funding for the activities of groups such as the NAACP and the Student Nonviolent Coordinating Committee. But now tensions were running high between the new generation of black activists and their onetime allies in the Jewish community.

Riots in the ghettos of major U.S. cities, which began in Harlem in 1964 and spread across the country, frequently targeted small businesses, many of them owned and operated by Jews. According to longtime civil rights strategist Bayard Rustin, attacks on Jewish merchants were part of a psychology that blamed not the enemies of black advancement but rather those who had worked over the years for civil rights.[40] In the late 1960s, Rustin, who had organized the 1963 March on Washington, found himself fighting a losing battle in his argument that the black community could achieve basic educational and economic goals only by working with the liberal white majority.[41]

Blacks who favored separatism and who sought to turn the civil rights movement into a racial revolution found their hero in Nation of Islam follower Malcolm X. A charismatic figure who gave voice to the frustrations of many blacks in northern ghettos, Malcolm portrayed Jews as exploiters of blacks. In his autobiography, released after his assassination in February 1965, he depicted Jews as hypocrites who claimed friendship with blacks to further their own purposes.[42] Within just a few years, the book sold millions of copies and was adopted by hundreds of colleges nationwide.

Israel's victory in the Six-Day War of 1967 furthered the friction between Jews and black activists. Malcolm, who had converted to Islam while serving a prison sentence early in his life, had adopted the line that the Jews had established the state of Israel by stealing Muslim-owned land. When the war broke out, SNCC's newsletter commented that Zionist imperialists had been responsible for the unrest in Palestine since the late nineteenth century. The article included antisemitic drawings and cartoons.[43]

Over the Labor Day weekend of 1967 a group of political activists on the left convened in Chicago to build a new biracial coalition that would challenge President Johnson in 1968. A militant black group led by SNCC activist James Forman presented thirteen resolutions, one of them condemning the "imperialist-Zionist war" in the Middle East. When the press reported that Martin Luther King Jr. had given the keynote address, Morris Abram reached out to his friend to inquire why he and his organization, the Southern Christian Leadership Conference, had participated in a conference with antisemitic overtones.

On September 20, 1967, King sent Abram a four-page reply. The letter began with a complete denial of SCLC support for an anti-Israel resolution at the Chicago conference. In fact, said King, it was members of his organization who were the most vigorous opponents of the "simplistic" resolution on the Middle East and who pressed for the elimination of its reference to Zionism. Writing that he had attended the conference only to give a speech and leave immediately afterward, had he been present for the debate, "I would have made it crystal clear that I could not have supported any resolution calling for black separatism or calling for a condemnation of Israel and an unqualified endorsement of the Arab powers."[44]

King asserted that at the heart of the problems in the Middle East are "oil interests," and the solution would have to be based upon "statesmanship by Israel and progressive Arab forces who in concert with the great powers recognize that fair and peaceful solutions are the concern of all humanity." According to King, "Israel's right to exist as a state in security is uncontestable."[45]

Regarding antisemitism, which King insisted the SCLC had denounced "expressly, frequently, and vigorously," he wrote that it is not only immoral but is used to separate blacks and Jews, partners in the struggle for justice. Quoting from his recent book, *Where Do We Go from Here?* King noted that what little antisemitism existed in the black community was entirely a product of northern ghettos. While the urban black is associated with Jews as partners in the struggle for civil rights, he also meets them daily "as some of his most direct exploiters in the ghetto." Although those in the latter group operate as marginal businessmen, not according to Jewish ethics, the distinction is lost on some blacks who are mistreated by them. "It would be a tragic and moral mistake," he wrote, "to identify the mass of Negroes with the very small number who succumb to cheap and dishonest slogans." King assured his friend that he would continue to oppose antisemitism "because it is immoral and self-destructive."[46]

During this period of growing tension between the two communities, the American Jewish Committee sought to convince Jews living in the inner city that it was in their interest that integration succeed. AJC historian Marianne Sanua notes that Abram was openly critical of Jews who tried to escape integration by moving away to the suburbs, where he himself lived, or by not sending their children to public schools.[47] At AJC's annual meeting in 1965, after hearing reports of rioting in Philadelphia that targeted hundreds of Jewish establishments, Abram said, "You can't expect these people to reach a responsible maturity until they have developed self-respect and a feeling of self-worth. And in the growing up process there are going to be these tensions, these confrontations and these times of trouble."[48]

At a meeting the following year of AJC's executive board, Abram was critical of those who were not prepared to support the radical reforms needed to make white and black America one nation. As he exhorted his colleagues, "We in AJC must not, shall not, and do not intend to withdraw from this struggle. Rather, we shall intensify all our efforts to create fair and full housing, full employment, and integrated quality schools."[49]

By the fall of 1967 it had been a mere five years since Morris Abram had cast aside his doubts and moved with his family from Atlanta to New York. If it was visibility he sought, he could not have been more in the public eye than he was, given his partnership at one of the country's leading law firms and his national positions at the American Jewish Committee and the United Nations.

Given this visibility, which included taking public positions on important policy issues, Abram began to hear from prominent figures in the Democratic Party that he should consider a run for its nomination to oppose incumbent Senator Jacob Javits, then looking forward to his election to a third term in November 1968. It had been fourteen years since his unsuccessful campaign for a congressional seat in Georgia, a state then still dominated by the undemocratic county unit system.

Javits's record as a liberal Republican allied with popular governor Nelson Rockefeller made the prospect of defeating him in 1968 a formidable challenge. He had entered the Senate in 1956 after defeating popular New York City Mayor Robert Wagner Jr. by a half million votes and was reelected six years later in a landslide victory. A year before the election, leading figures in the state Democratic Party considered Abram their top candidate.[50] In an interview for *Women's Wear Daily*, Abram said that he had been a Democrat "since I could breathe," adding that he intended to become more and more active in the party. He told his interviewer that growing up in a small town and hanging around the courthouse had given him the opportunity to see government "at an intimate level." He related how he had lost his one bid for electoral office running against a segregationist and spending a mere $30,000 on his campaign because of the discriminatory unit voting system.[51]

In late October Abram served as toastmaster at the most successful Manhattan Democratic organization fundraising dinner in a decade, to which he brought his entire family. At the dinner, Senator Robert Kennedy quipped, "Some people are speaking of him for statewide office. I can't personally see how you could send a carpetbagger to the Senate—someone who doesn't even speak with a New York accent."[52]

But Abram soon found himself trapped politically in the fierce divisions within the national Democratic Party over the increasingly unpopular war in Vietnam. A group of representatives of the American Jewish Committee and the Jewish Joint Distribution Committee had recently come together to form the American Jewish Service Committee on Civilian Relief in Vietnam. As chair of the committee, Abram traveled to Vietnam in January 1968 to visit refugee camps and explore the feasibility of setting up a program there.[53]

Abram's dilemma was reinforced by what he saw during his visit: an unwinnable war absent a much larger commitment in blood and treasure, one he knew would be wholly unacceptable to the American people. Along with Robert Kennedy, Abram believed that distancing himself from the White House position would be highly problematic, since he needed its support to raise enough funds to run a credible campaign. When key Johnson associates read a memorandum he drafted recommending a negotiated settlement that adequately protected our South Vietnamese allies, they deemed it to be unacceptable, effectively quashing his plans to run against Javits.[54]

As Abram approached the end of his four-year term as president of the American Jewish Committee, tensions between blacks and Jews once again began to erupt. This time the scene was New York City, and the occasion a teachers' strike called in the spring of 1968 by the predominantly Jewish United Federation of Teachers (UFT). The strike kept one million students, a heavy percentage of them black and Hispanic, out of class for thirty-six days.

Working with the Ford Foundation, Mayor John Lindsay had sought ways to give parents more control over their children's education by decentralizing the city's vast school system. One of those designated for a pilot project was based in the Ocean-Hill Brownsville section of Brooklyn. The superintendent chosen, a follower of Malcolm X, began his tenure by dismissing a mostly Jewish group of supervisors and replacing them with 350 substitutes. This was followed by antisemitic flyers appearing in the mailboxes of school-teachers that the UFT leader, Albert Shanker, exposed by distributing them more widely, further enflaming tensions. Following the strike, the school district's board was suspended.[55]

The animosity between blacks and Jews, much of it attributable to the strike and the events surrounding it, lingered on well after its conclusion. Murray Friedman cites a major art exhibit at the famed Metropolitan Museum of Art that opened in January 1969 entitled "Harlem on my Mind." The catalog declared that "behind every hurdle that the Afro-American has to jump stands the Jew who has already cleared it."[56]

In a guest address to AJC's Executive Committee following the New York teachers' strike, Morris Abram asserted, "There will be many black-white confrontations and much friction between Negro and Jew—but we must pay the price of past wrongs. . . . We must recognize that not every conflict and confrontation signifies anti-Semitism." And in his final annual address to the organization as he was stepping down as its president, Abram distinguished between two cries for separatism this way, "One is a racist cry which I reject totally; but the cry of identity and pride is something I accept and applaud."[57]

SEVEN

Brandeis

When he left Paul, Weiss to go to that school, Morris thought he
had arrived at one of the pivotal points of his life.

Sometime in the early 1960s Morris Abram was asked by an executive of the American Jewish Committee what he would most
want to do if not practicing law. It did not take him long to reply.
He said he would want to be a university president and, if he had a
choice, it would be Brandeis, an institution for which he believed
he would be especially qualified.

Brandeis University, the only nonsectarian institution of higher
learning sponsored by the American Jewish community, was founded
in 1948 at a time when Jewish students were still facing discrimination in college admissions. Located in Waltham, Massachusetts,
ten miles west of Boston, and named for the first Jewish Supreme
Court Justice, Brandeis was the vision of largely one man, the historian Abram Sachar. It was Sachar who raised the money and developed a first-rate faculty that quickly lifted the university into the top
ranks of American higher education.

As Sachar was contemplating retirement, Morris Abram was considering the possibility of a second run for political office. While
still deliberating his decision to enter the Senate race against the
incumbent Jacob Javits, Abram received a phone call from Lawrence
Wien, the board chairman of Brandeis, with the news that he had
been selected from 120 candidates to succeed President Sachar as

the university's second president. Abram was thrilled. He believed that his resume up to that point had been compiled for precisely that purpose.[1]

When he learned that his position on the war in Vietnam would preclude support from the White House, Abram discarded his plans to run for the Javits seat. His acceptance of the Brandeis offer followed soon thereafter.[2] Letters of congratulation on his appointment poured in from friends and associates from around the country, including HEW secretary Wilbur Cohen, New York mayor John Lindsay, University of Chicago president Edward Levi, and his old college friend Bobby Troutman.[3]

As he prepared to take over the presidency of Brandeis, Abram could not have been unaware of many of the challenges he faced. As the year 1968 was quickly becoming one of the most divisive since the civil war, universities around the country were becoming centers of unrest, given both the growing unpopularity of the war and the rapid social and cultural changes taking place in the society at large. Many of the students and faculty at elite universities such as Brandeis were vigorously and sometimes violently challenging traditional conceptions of the role of the university. In the end, Abram's appointment marked a turning point in his career, though certainly not in any of the ways he had anticipated when his tenure began. Before taking on his new role, Abram's law partner Lloyd Garrison cautioned him that universities could be intensely political and petty. Garrison spoke from his experience as former dean of the University of Wisconsin Law School.

Kenneth Sweder, soon to graduate from New York University Law School, first met Morris Abram during an interview for an associate position at Paul, Weiss in the spring of 1968. Abram had a better idea and asked if he would like to be his personal assistant at Brandeis. Sweder spent the summer of 1968 on campus getting the lay of the land and reporting back to Abram in New York.[4]

Abram's inaugural, held over the first weekend in October, brought together for a series of addresses and panel discussions many people from his past, including labor leader Gus Tyler and the civil rights strategist Bayard Rustin, organizer of the 1963 March on Washington. Abram's period in Atlanta was represented by Jacob Rothschild, rabbi of Abram's synagogue that had been bombed by white supremacists in 1958, and Coretta Scott King, Abram's former client, whose husband's assassination six months earlier had reverberated throughout colleges and universities around the country, including Brandeis.

In her speech at the spiritual service entitled "Can there be One America?" Mrs. King declared that what happened to her husband had not shattered her belief in his vision of a united society. "The question now, as we move into this last third of the present century," she remarked, "is not whether there can be one America. Our very survival depends upon how rapidly we can overcome the forces which separate us from one another and alienate us from ourselves. Integration, personal and social, is the key to a healthier and happier America. If we can quickly learn to think anew and act anew, the dangerous, bloody future which looms on our horizon can be, instead, a liberating and exhilarating dawn of a new day."[5]

In Abram's inaugural address, he advanced the liberal philosophy that had defined his career. While acknowledging as a "compliment to education" the fact that the university was becoming a focal point for many of those seeking to reform society, any such institution that purported to be more than "a community of scholars or a commonwealth of learning" was putting at risk its central mission.

Universities, he believed, faced additional risks as well. While they continued to be threatened from the outside, today "the danger to dissent within the university comes also from a new direction. It comes from within." Abram related the story of a recent conversation with a professor who voiced agreement with those who thought that certain points of view were so wrong that they should not be tolerated within the university. Abram concluded the story by countering, "I do not believe that in the academy as well as in society as a whole, the majority has the right to stifle the voice of the minority."

Abram made it clear that he was not prepared to abandon the philosophy that formed the essence of his worldview. "I know that it has become fashionable in some liberal political circles to downgrade the liberal political creed. I am willing to examine and reexamine every substantive opinion, including those to which I am most committed. However, I am not prepared to reject the liberal methodology of fair play, civil liberty, and due process as the only way in which a civilized society can pursue truth, prevent the encrustation of error, and insure the fulfillment of one's creative talents and inclinations." The new president of Brandeis also voiced his strong objection to efforts to politicize the university. "A university politicized," he said, "is a university doomed, as the lessons of the German universities under the Nazis proved."[6]

The lofty rhetoric of inaugural weekend was interrupted by an episode that foreshadowed the difficulties Abram would soon encounter. During one of the panel discussions, Phyllis Raynor of Roxbury, a Brandeis senior representing the Brandeis Afro-American Society, accused the university of "institutional racism" by reneging on its promise to institute African and Afro-American Studies with major status in the curriculum. When Abram rose to defend Brandeis by attributing the problem to "procedural delays," Raynor shot back that there would be no progress as long as "men like you" were in charge. She then proceeded to lead a walkout of some twenty-five black students.[7]

To Kenneth Sweder, Abram was "ready for the challenge, and enthusiastic about taking it on. He seemed to be the perfect guy for that spot at that moment."[8] But for Abram, it would not be long before encountering the harsh realities of running the university. Topping the list was its weak financial position. As a young ambitious university, Brandeis's endowment was meager in comparison with its established peer institutions. When he accepted the position, Abram had little inkling of just how fragile the university's finances were, and therefore how much time would have to be devoted to fundraising just to maintain its operations. In one month during his first year as president, Abram spent a total of nine nights sleeping in his own bed, spending the remainder on the road raising money.[9]

There was also the question of what to do about the looming presence of Abe Sachar. While considering whether to take the Brandeis job, Abram's law partner Arthur Goldberg had advised him to "get rid of Sachar; get him off the campus."[10] But this was easier said than done. Sachar was a legend at Brandeis and was not going anywhere else. After Abram's inauguration, Sachar took the title of chancellor, which included an office on campus, his old presidential residence, and full secretarial assistance, indicating to the new president that he was not about to step down gracefully.

David Squire, who had worked with Abram at the United Nations and whom Abram brought to Brandeis at the end of the first student semester as vice president of student affairs, believed that "it was a mistake to allow Sachar to have an office on campus after he retired, looking over his shoulder and keeping all his contacts. I mean, he would have various faculty members come to his office and they were undermining Morris. It was a terrible situation."[11]

According to longtime Brandeis American studies professor Jacob Cohen, Abram was not alone in this treatment by the man who, he said, "turned this place overnight into the greatest success story in the history of American higher education." Sachar, with whom Cohen became close in the 70s and 80s, "made every subsequent president's life a living hell."[12]

In the wake of the Martin Luther King assassination that spring, Sachar had made several promises to a group of black students, including establishment of a black studies concentration that Abram, long after he left Brandeis, believed to be a means by which blacks would be segregated once again in a two-tiered system. After Abram assumed the presidency, he learned that Sachar had left it to his successor to deal with these promises.

A mere three months after he was inaugurated, all the skills that Abram had acquired as a courtroom lawyer and a liberal civil rights advocate were tested by one of the country's first student occupations of a university building. On the evening of January 9, 1969, the CBS *Evening News* with Walter Cronkite reported that a group of black students had taken over Ford Hall, a three-story red brick building that housed Brandeis's central communications network, the computer that serviced the university's administration, and other facilities.

The students in Ford Hall sealed themselves behind mattresses, desks, and steel lockers, barricading themselves behind the three building entrances. A large banner of Malcolm X was draped from the second story window, and calls to the university were answered with the greeting "Malcolm X University." Some two hundred white students marched around the building to demonstrate their support.[13]

The sixty-five students in Ford Hall sent the administration a tape-recorded message articulating a series of ten demands that included the awarding of full scholarships designated exclusively for black students and the creation of a Black Studies Department in which students would play a major role in selecting the chairman, faculty, and curriculum. In addition to these demands, the students insisted upon "total amnesty" from any punishment for their actions.

Returning to the Boston area from a fundraising speech, Abram held a press conference in which he said the students "have acted without prior complaint to the administration and even now refuse all discussions regarding the ten demands which they have made upon the university." He asserted that the university would use "sufficient force to clear the building if necessary."[14]

Although Abram felt blindsided by the takeover, he couldn't have been completely surprised by it. Several weeks earlier he had received a call from William Sullivan, deputy director of the FBI, warning him that black radicals were on their way to Brandeis from Canada where they were seeking to stimulate a takeover at Sir George Williams University (now known as Concordia). According to Sullivan, they regarded Brandeis as an easy target because of the liberalism of its predominantly Jewish student body, which was likely to sympathize with the demands of black students.[15]

Abram was skeptical. But in fact, only days before the occupation, two activists from San Francisco State University, a junior faculty member and a graduate student, had met on the Brandeis campus with a group of black students. Students at San Francisco State were then three-and-a-half months into a strike. Other than the assistant sociology professor who had issued the invitation, the only other Brandeis faculty member present was Jacob Cohen.

In addition to his position in the American Studies Department, Cohen was director of the Transitional Year Program (TYP), an innovative project established in the aftermath of the King assassination to prepare disadvantaged students for college. In the early 1960s,

Cohen had taken off two years from Brandeis to work for the Congress of Racial Equality (CORE). As he recalled,

> San Francisco State was a notorious example of the exercise of student power. Quite violent, with stories about graduate student teachers who were bringing guns into their classrooms and putting them right in front of the students during the lectures. I'm listening and I'm writing down what the speaker [from San Francisco State] is saying. All the black students who are there are in the front rows. And he looked at them and he said, "If you have any balls, you will take over this place tomorrow." And they rose, and they walked out together as a group and went into one of the classrooms on the first floor which at the time had glass walls. And it was that night that they cobbled together the ten demands. And put together this thing. Under the pressure of that meeting.[16]

The black students later denied that they developed their plan that night, insisting that initial planning had begun the previous November and a course of action decided upon three days prior to the forum.[17] One of the leaders of the group in Ford Hall, student council representative Ricardo Millett, said that any police sent to evict his group would have "to crack heads, and when they start to crack heads, we will fight them."[18]

Herbert Teitelbaum, a Brandeis alumnus, was then a young lawyer starting his career in the Boston area while his wife Ruth Abram was studying at the university's Florence Heller School for Social Welfare. He arrived on the scene to provide his father-in-law with legal and moral support. As Teitelbaum recalled,

> it was a pretty tense time for Morris and his family. You know, Morris came out of an experience down South where he was heralded as a leader of progressive politics, civil rights. When he got to Brandeis, there were kids there who were calling him "cracker." So, it was a lack of civility, and Morris was a person for whom that was not part of his culture, it was not part of his background. I think it was very distressing for him. Morris went to Brandeis with the idea that he would be able to become involved in reshaping the intellectual life on campus, maybe having it become more akin to what he had experienced at Oxford. He

wasn't able to do that because so much of his time was spent raising money, dealing with faculty issues, and Abe Sachar was not helpful.[19]

Abram's daughter Ruth explained, "Here he had been a Southern white taking stands that put him in some danger and were in opposition to the main tenor of the time, and he comes to Brandeis, a Jewish institution and to be told he is a racist, it was just so upsetting to him."[20]

Abram moved quickly to obtain the support of the faculty. In an emergency meeting he convened, it voted overwhelmingly (153–18) for the following resolution: "We utterly condemn the forcible takeover of the University's premises. We believe we cannot confront problems of a University under threats of coercion. The faculty demands that the students involved vacate Ford Hall and enter negotiations of any grievance with the University Administration." The faculty rejected an amendment proposed by assistant sociology professor Gordon Fellman expressing sympathy for the students in Ford Hall and voicing support for the students and faculty at San Francisco State.[21]

Fellman recalled sitting in that meeting, where President Abram was exhorting faculty members to "fan out to the dormitories, tell the students just cool it, do your homework, go to the library, the administration is on top of this whole thing." He and three colleagues walked over to Ford Hall that evening. The building was blockaded with chains and a padlock, so "we knocked on a window and they opened it. We said we're faculty and we want to hear your story." He continued:

> They went into a huddle for a while and then they let us come in. We climbed through the window. One of the women had on a very tight skirt and we hoisted her up. So, we go into this classroom in Ford Hall and then I think it was Randy Bailey [the group's spokesman] who was in that situation and Jewish at that point and wore a kippah. I think it was Randy who told us Sachar made some promises to black students when they came to Brandeis and Abram had not honored them. That's what was behind it.[22]

The charge was not without merit. Indeed, one of the university's harshest critics of campus radicalism, professor of politics and former LBJ advisor John Roche, noted after the crisis that the faculty committee set up after the King assassination to plan the concentration in Afro and Afro-American studies had failed to meet and when nothing happened, "they became invisible and let the president carry the can."[23]

To Kenneth Sweder, Abram's personal assistant who dealt primarily with student relations, the group in Ford Hall was for the most part not as radical as their counterparts in other parts of the country. "I'm one of those who never felt this was one of the more militant of the student protests or takeovers in those years," he said. "These were students, many of them who became doctors, lawyers, and businessmen who I still see from time to time. These were not militants in the most extreme." One of them was successfully ordered by his mother to leave Ford Hall.[24]

The most contentious issue presented by the students in Ford Hall was the demand involving black studies. Abram and most faculty members regarded the idea of students selecting the chairman of a department as a clear violation of fundamental academic principles. While expressing sympathy for the students, Lawrence Fuchs, professor of American civilization and former Peace Corps director for the Philippines, said that they simply did not understand what a university is and how it runs. "No distinguished black professor in the country which this faculty would want . . . would allow himself to be chosen chair on such a basis. He would almost certainly feel that his academic freedom had been compromised."[25]

Several days into the crisis, Abram received praise both in the local and national press for the way in which he was handling it. Typical was this commentary by John Fenton of the *New York Times*: "In the face of a series of tense situations in the last few days, Mr. Abram has impressed observers with his flexibility, his endurance, and his ability to keep the rest of the university functioning smoothly."[26] The students in Ford Hall were clearly frustrated by the coverage. In the first bulletin they issued, they accused Abram of negotiating in bad faith and playing politics with the press. In their second, they referred to him as a "fork-tongued Georgia cracker."[27]

Although Abram publicly expressed his support for a Black Studies Department, believing that he could not renege on Sachar's commitment, the concept was fundamentally at odds with his belief that ghettoizing black students in this way would only work to the detriment of all students, both white and black. As he argued during a 1982 appearance on William F. Buckley's syndicated public television program *Firing Line*, he did not believe that the black experience was being taught properly in American universities. To the contrary, the blacks in Ford Hall were correct that the teaching of American history either ignored or distorted the impact of racial discrimination.

He continued, "And I think there's an enormous amount of American history and American sociology and American politics and American economics—the loss to our country from the economic production of black people who are unemployed or underemployed, this has an economic impact. I never learned any of this in college. I wanted that introduced into the standard curriculum that blacks and whites would take, not put off in some segregated hole and taught as black studies, which only blacks would go to, which would qualify them for nothing."[28]

During the occupation, up to several hundred white student supporters sat in the corridor between the two administration buildings. At one point they sent a delegation to the administration to request amnesty for the black students and to seek assurances that the police not be called in. When the delegation was not met by Abram, they voted overwhelmingly to call a strike. Its effects were minimal, as most students were preparing to take their first semester exams.[29] Several days later, five black women wearing bandannas entered the reserve room at Goldfarb Library and scattered over two thousand books and periodicals. Guarding the door, one of them ripped out a telephone.[30]

Shortly after the students began their occupation of Ford Hall, Abram convened a group of advisors consisting of administrators and faculty who would meet periodically in the university's boardroom to assess the situation and consider their options. One of those present at these meetings was Jacob Cohen, whose Transitional Year Program was the subject of one of the ten demands. Cohen recalls the first meeting between the students in Ford Hall and Abram's negotiating team:

> In this first meeting, a student who, by the way, had very well-off parents and was outstanding academically, that student put a bull whip onto the table between himself and his group which had come on one side, and the representatives of the administration of which I am one, since I am the TYP Director, on the other side around Abram. And he said, "You listen to me mother-phile—though it was a little less alien than that—we're going to burn this place down if you don't give us what we want." Very soon after these meetings between the student leaders and Abram began, the black students were accompanied by elements in the Boston community: extremely radical, in very good condition by the way, really ripped, who came in and stood behind the students, very little sense of humor, in which they said to our students, the black community of Boston is behind you.[31]

The one student invited into the group of faculty members and administrators was Eric Yoffie, president of Brandeis's student council. Yoffie would later become the leader of the congregational arm of the movement of Reform Judaism in North America. According to Rabbi Yoffie, the main debate within the group from the beginning was between those who said the police should be called in and those who were opposed to that course of action, although both sides recognized that ultimately, if negotiation broke down, outside authorities would have to be called in. Yoffie believed that the black students had some legitimate concerns and seemed to be negotiating in good faith. He strongly believed that if the administration called in the police, "the campus would blow up, taking a bad situation, a dangerous situation, and making it much worse."[32]

Yoffie convened a group of student leaders with whom he conferred during the occupation and to the person, they agreed with that assessment, and believed that calling the police should be avoided virtually at all costs. But President Abram, who was receiving advice from some in his inner circle to call in the police, was himself ambivalent. As Yoffie recalled,

> the thing about Morris Abram is that he was someone who had fought the civil rights wars, based on the legal end of it. On the other hand, he was sort of a Southern gentleman, and there was part of him that reacted strongly that they were taking over these buildings. And he found something offensive in that. To some extent it was a generational thing between students and the older generation that was playing out all across America. So, he was a new president. He had a certain feeling that here I just came in. I'm someone who knows something about struggles of African Americans. I have a record here. I've done something on the ground, certainly in the legal world. And all of a sudden there's this hostility. There was a part of [Abram] that went along with that element of the negotiating group that said, you know, we need to call in the police. They've taken over a building, they've done so illegally.[33]

At a faculty meeting held the evening before the students left Ford Hall, politics professor Roche offered a motion directing the president to inform the students that the faculty would proceed with establishment of a legitimate Department of African and Afro-American Studies as soon as they withdrew from the building. The motion passed by a vote of 132–52–30.[34]

By then, the students in Ford Hall were beginning to realize that they were close to achieving virtually all their demands. One of the older TYP students, concerned that the whole episode might well end up badly for the group, proposed that they declare victory and end the occupation.[35] Eleven days after the takeover of Ford Hall, the slightly reduced contingent of occupiers walked out, greeted warmly by student supporters. In the end, Abram was hailed in the national media for mediating the crisis without calling in the police.

Morton Keller, the American historian who was chairman of the History Department at the time, recalled Abram's judicious handling of the occupation. "I thought he handled it well," Keller said, "very much in the tradition of a smart, reasonable, level-headed liberal lawyer, and I thought that was the right tone to take. It was not going to make the two sides very happy. There was criticism from the conservative side as well as the left, but that is often a good sign when someone ends up that way. I thought he did well."[36] Others, such as the sociologist Gordon Fellman, disagreed: "He certainly wasn't up for understanding why the blacks had taken over Ford Hall, what it was all about. There was a larger picture: this was going on nationally, it wasn't just Brandeis."[37]

Less than a month after the black students departed Ford Hall, Abram published a lengthy article in the *New York Times* magazine, a kind of "how to handle a campus crisis."[38] Eric Yoffie thought it ironic that Abram was offering his colleagues advice to favor negotiation over force:

> In addition to the article in the *Times*, he went on the Today Show and his central claim was, negotiate this out. And I was a hero because I listened to the students and I heard their concerns. Ultimately, what he was saying was "smart, sensitive negotiators such as myself can reach an understanding here," and he was presenting his negotiating model as a model for other universities. And I remember my strong reaction as the only student participant was it wasn't an entirely honest picture because repeatedly, he had been close to doing the exact opposite of what he said he did in the article. And he had repeatedly been close to bowing to those who took the opposite view and said, "Let's call in the police." And had seemed sympathetic. When we got through this, my view was whew, my God, we made it. But look, ultimately, he deserved the credit. Ultimately, the decision was his, ultimately it was the right decision for Brandeis, but he presents himself as much more of a dove than he actually was during the negotiations.[39]

Kenneth Sweder disputes the notion that Abram was ever on the verge of calling in law enforcement to end the occupation of Ford Hall. "We certainly discussed it, but I don't believe that he was ever really that close. It was the kind of situation where if it was floated by him it was more of a testing out of the ideas among [his advisors] to hear our arguments. But I don't remember that he was close to calling the police."[40]

Many on campus perceived the article in the *Times* as a personal public relations tool for Abram that students found offensive and which, according to Professor Jonathan Krasner, "contributed to the undoing of his presidency."[41] Ten days before Abram's article appeared in the *Times*, he sent a copy to Abe Sachar. To it he attached a message that read, "One thing more: there are revolutionary forces on the campus—not necessarily at Brandeis. Yet the enclosed material from President Gloster of Morehouse makes the point."

Abram had served on the Morehouse College board of trustees since his days in Atlanta. The enclosure was a memorandum from its president to the board noting that during the last week in January, "a group of black revolutionaries, including Black Panthers from California, came to Atlanta for the purpose of leading our students in a takeover of the Atlanta University Center." The platform proposed by the group included the renaming of the university ("The University of New Africa"), student control over all courses, and cessation of the term "predominantly Negro" ("We are African People.") The platform failed for lack of student support.[42]

Soon Abram regretted the fact that he had agreed to grant the students amnesty before they left the building, particularly for those who had damaged university property. He envied his old law professor Edward Levi who, as president of the University of Chicago, had expelled a group of students who were part of a larger group that had occupied the administration building shortly after the end of the Brandeis takeover to protest the firing of a sociology professor.[43]

When Abram discussed this with Levi during the latter's tenure as attorney general under President Ford, Levi pointed out that, unlike the situation at Brandeis, in Chicago the student protesters were white, the university was more or less unified against their actions, and Chicago was not a Jewish-sponsored university, where an expulsion of the students would have been regarded, albeit mistakenly, as a clash between blacks and Jews. As Abram told William F. Buckley Jr., "I felt a little better and relieved, but still I feel very keenly that it would have been good for those students to be punished."[44]

One day after the students left Ford Hall, the day of Richard Nixon's first inauguration as president, David Squire assumed his new position as vice president for Student Affairs. His job, Abram told him, was to see to it that the ten demands coming from Ford Hall were implemented. "You take care of it," Abram told his new vice president, but, according to Squire, "the crisis really continued. It wasn't just with a takeover. There was pressure every day and there were student sit-ins all over the place. The faculty senate ended up in my office every day practically, because they were still working on trying to be helpful in resolving these ten black student demands. I was trying to work with the faculty and the students to get out of this thing without any further danger and without any occupation and without any cops."[45]

But problems persisted. On the night of February 25, 1969, two offices in the building housing the Politics Department were severely damaged by a clear case of arson. Authorities discovered eight separate fires, and damages totaled between $40,000 and $50,000. The targets were Professors Roche and I. Milton Sacks, two unapologetic supporters of the war in Vietnam. Benzine jars that had been stolen from a chemistry lab supply closet in Ford Hall were discovered at the scene. Although the Waltham police suspected students who had been involved in the Ford Hall occupation, the case was dropped in March of the following year.[46]

Six weeks after the end of the occupation of Ford Hall, a racially mixed group of students, including some who had been involved in the occupation, held a sit-in outside of the president's office to protest what they regarded as a delay in the implementation of the ten demands. Declaring that they would be subject to disciplinary action, Abram organized a judicial committee to handle the matter that was void of student representation. After additional protests, including a condemnation from the student council, he backed down and the resulting adjudication allowed the group involved in the sit-in to avoid punishment. For Abram, it affirmed his belief that the decision not to act against the occupiers of Ford Hall had been a mistake.[47] Abram's discomfort was reinforced by new demands related to the use of quotas in the future admission of black students that included full financial aid. He regarded it as "their most outrageous demand to date, but tragically, the most obtainable."[48]

Abram's skill in handling the Ford Hall crisis soon became overshadowed by his growing inability to relate well with Brandeis's faculty and students. According to Squire, "He didn't really listen to and respect the students. I think that was the main thing, students more than faculty. And he pretty much talked down to the faculty. In meetings with the faculty Senate, he did some lecturing about what should be and about the students' terrible performance and the faculty wasn't really doing anything about it. They weren't showing any resistance, any discipline in any way or another to students for doing this. Too many were sympathetic. Soft, he called them, soft."[49]

Recalling her father's experience at Brandeis, Ruth Abram related what he had described to her as the "éclair" story: "He invited some deans to have a discussion one day and I guess there were six deans and he had expected five. He had ordered his favorite dessert, eclairs, and the deans started fussing about how to divide them. And he felt that this was a metaphor for the pettiness of academic life."[50]

Later that year, Abram received an offer from an unnamed donor to fund the establishment of a law school, something he was promoting as a logical tribute to the university's namesake. Many on the faculty and board of trustees believed that it was particularly unwise to start a law school at a time when Brandeis was under enormous financial pressure. When he shared with a reporter plans for the law school, it infuriated many on campus, including members of the board who had not been consulted.

Among those surprised by the announcement was his advisor David Squire:

> One day in January I picked up the *New York Times* and lo and behold I read an article entitled "Brandeis to Have a Law School." Now, mind you, I was with the president every day. Never heard that. Never heard anything; we never talked about it. He loved to be with the press, he loved to have news conferences and get the press in. And evidently, I wasn't in the room, but he said something like "we're going to have a law school." Mind you, you know how universities work, the faculty are the most important thing and he hadn't ever discussed it or even offered it or mentioned it to the faculty, never mind his colleagues like me.[51]

In an article published in the journal *Daedalus* in the winter of 1970, Abram voiced the frustrations of administrators trying their best to deal with both external and internal challenges, given the constraints under which they operated:

> The basic problem of most administrations is that they have great responsibility without the accompanying power over the causes of discontent in the university community. These causes originate largely in the outside world; the university president can rail against them, but seldom has the capacity to change them. . . . Moreover, disciplinary action from the administration is likely to be perceived, often unjustifiably, as an infringement on academic freedom. Nevertheless, administrations have a large role. The president who does not regard himself as a leader of the faculty, as a problem-solver, and as a source of innovation and renewal in academic matters is failing both faculty and students.[52]

In the end, Abram's ambitions exceeded both what he could accomplish and what was expected of him, leading to his downfall. While praising his ability as a fundraiser, Squire attributed many of his difficulties to a lack of acceptance of his role: "He didn't understand at all about how a university governs itself, the role of the faculty and how important it is, and the role of the president how unimportant it is, except for fundraising. He never understood that nor accepted it."[53]

Eric Yoffie's take on his tenure was similar if a bit more sympathetic:

> He was a guy of great personal charm, somebody who knew how to work a room. He knew how to talk to people. He saw himself and rightly so as somebody who could be convincing in a debate or in a personal argument. He was somebody who was used to bringing folks over to his side. And he walked into a university situation in the 1960s. So first of all, there are all these constituencies in the university. He thought that in short order he was going to win them all over and charm them as only he could do. So, my sense is this smart, charming accomplished attorney coming out of the South all of a sudden found that his particular skills really didn't work terribly well in this environment. And it was going to be a struggle for him to succeed here and that the satisfactions that he hoped to get from life were not going to be forthcoming from a university setting.[54]

To Kenneth Sweder, Abram was simply not a good fit with the

world of the academy. "With its prerogatives and protocols of the administration, faculty, and students, it was too cumbersome for him. He was an activist lawyer. And I don't think trying to function in the way he had to in the academy was something that worked for him."[55] Jacob Cohen said, "[Abram] saw this university in some idyllic college president way that was totally unsuitable for the times, and for the situation, and for Brandeis."[56]

When Hubert Humphrey, then a Brandeis trustee, suggested that Abram enter the wide-open Democratic primary for the Senate seat in New York held by Republican Charles Goodell, he seized the opportunity, saying goodbye to what he had once considered his dream job after less than a year and a half. In a final act of humiliation, when he announced his resignation from the Brandeis presidential residence in the town of Weston, he faced a group of student protestors who blamed Abram for abandoning the university in the middle of a financial crisis. Many there and on the campus charged that he had used his brief tenure at the university to further his political career.[57]

Abram's tenure at Brandeis was deeply demoralizing. Ambassador Alfred Moses, who knew Abram well at the American Jewish Committee and later at UN Watch, said "He never really recovered from it. It tarnished him. Up to then, he was the golden boy."[58] To his Atlanta law partner Robert Hicks, who stayed in touch with Abram throughout the rest of his life, "It was one of the turning points in Morris's life. A terrible blow. It rattled his fundamentals. When he left Paul, Weiss to go to that school, Morris thought he had arrived at one of the pivotal points of his life. Instead, it was a critical disappointment. It really crushed him."[59]

Although Abram's tenure at Brandeis was short, his immediate experience with political radicalization contributed significantly to his political education and, as he later wrote, toughened him for his subsequent battle with leukemia.[60] He had spent the first two decades of his career championing the cause of racial integration. Now, as in the case of the aftermath of the Six-Day War, he was seeing the old coalition of Jews, liberal Protestants, and blacks breaking apart in a new political climate, one in which the New Left was attacking fundamental values that had informed his worldview.

When Abram consulted students and faculty about punishing the students, particularly those who had damaged university property, he was advised against doing so. "The law," he said, "for me the hallmark of civilized life, would have to be ignored." Recalling Martin Luther King's respect for the law, the contrast between his expectation to suffer the consequences of breaking it, including time in jail, could not be more different from that of the black students on campus and their supporters.[61] While demoralizing to him personally, Abram's Brandeis experience fortified his commitment to the liberal principles that had guided his actions and beliefs since his early days.

EIGHT

Values

When he sat down to talk to you, you felt as if you were at the center of his orbit.

When they met in 1943, Morris Abram saw in Jane Maguire everything he was looking for in a wife: she was elegant, intelligent, and comfortable in social settings. Abram said that he always felt more at ease going to parties with her: "She knew what to wear and she knew what to do, and she had been properly trained and she knew how to entertain, she furnished what I thought were the keys that opened all the locks."[1] As Ruth Abram put it, "My mother certainly wasn't an outsider. I think he was marrying someone who knew how to act inside."[2]

Abram was particularly impressed with his wife's compassionate identification with the underdog. From the beginning of their time in Atlanta, Jane Abram supported her husband's involvement in liberal causes. And following their divorce, she spearheaded fundraising efforts to make possible the archiving of the papers of Grace Towns Hamilton, the first black woman to serve in the Georgia legislature.[3]

For a young lawyer starting his career in the big city, taking on unpopular causes was not the clearest path to financial security. That was particularly true for a growing family. Between 1948 and 1962, the year the Abrams left Atlanta, their daughter Ruth acquired four siblings: Ann, Morris Jr., Adam, and Joshua. Abram was deeply devoted to each of them. When an interviewer asked what provided him the most happiness in his life, he mentioned his children first. Abram would frequently take them with him, one at a time, while working on projects. And until they were all grown into adulthood, he would leave his office early enough to have dinner with them. These dinner discussions became the model for those he conducted later in his life on Cape Cod and in Geneva.

Hamilton Fish, the future publisher of *The Nation* magazine who spent a lot of time with the family during the early 1970s, said that Abram "had a style of interrogating his children with the overt goal of encouraging them to frame an insight or some kind of factual response or to be implicated in some way in the topic at hand."[4] Abram's youngest son Joshua said that he always looked forward to participating in these discussions, but even as a youngster, "you had to come to dinner ready to ask questions." The happiest place for his father, he noted, was with a curious child.[5] "Ham" Fish had met Abram's son Morris Jr. during his sophomore year at Harvard in 1971. According to Fish, "B," as he was called, then a senior, was "an astonishingly versatile and skillful young guy, the most talented political mind I've ever encountered of anyone at that age."[6]

In July 1971, the Twenty-Sixth Amendment to the U.S. Constitution guaranteeing the right to vote at age eighteen was ratified and signed into law by President Nixon. Morris Jr. and Fish believed that without a concerted effort to register young voters, they would be stymied by local officials, particularly in college towns where they might be subject to strict residence requirements. Together they created an organization called the National Movement for the Student Vote.

According to Fish, their campaign struck a chord among the liberal establishment, many of its members parents of radical students from whom they had become alienated as the result of political, cultural, and social changes that were rocking the country. Fish was aware that B's father was working behind the scenes, enlisting some of the leading figures in New York's legal community and national political affairs who signed on and joined the group's board of directors.[7] (The group's New England director was Billy Keyserling, a member of a South Carolina family prominent in both state and national Democratic Party politics who knew the senior Abram as a student at Brandeis.)

The Abrams invited Fish to move in with them and their three sons—Ruth and Ann were no longer living at home—in the Dakota apartment building in Manhattan. As Fish recalled, "When I met Morris (senior), he was charismatic, extremely charming, accessible, extremely generous, fatherly, solicitous of his children's friends in the same manner as he was with his own children." He found Jane to be extraordinarily welcoming and unquestioning in making a place for him in the household. The senior Abram included his son's friend in the dinner discussion. "The experience," he said, "wasn't quite as if you were having breakfast with the litigator, but it had this mix of intellectual formality and southern informality always. It was very seductive."[8]

Fish remembers another frequent guest at the Abrams's breakfast and dinner tables. When the family left Atlanta for New York, they brought with them their housekeeper and her husband who did their gardening and performed additional household chores. But this vastly understates Ed Brown's value to the family, which regarded him as a revered figure. Joshua remembers as a child being given rides by Brown in the family's wheelbarrow. But his value to Morris Abram was both more significant and intangible. The two had a special bond, and Abram would refer to Brown as his "psychiatrist."[9]

Brown had come from a sharecropping family in Wilcox County, Georgia, adjacent to Abram's home county of Ben Hill. There he grew up picking cotton and fighting to survive the hardships of grinding poverty and relentless mistreatment. His story, told in a voice that is both poignant and humorous, was faithfully recorded by Jane Abram for a book published shortly after the Abrams's divorce.[10]

Fish recalled that during a discussion at the dining room table, Abram would suddenly turn to Ed Brown and break into a monologue, describing what the two of them shared from their Georgia experience. Often, he would explain how whatever was being discussed was something Ed would certainly understand, or something "he could tell you more than anyone alive."[11] To Fish, there was a powerful bond between the two, and Brown seemed to respond positively to the attention he received. "I didn't feel Morris treated Ed Brown inappropriately," he said. "He spoke lovingly, tenderly, and truthfully about him, often more so than about a wide range of people he was very close to."[12]

Although Abram's feelings for Brown were genuine, Fish, among many others, could not help but notice his penchant for hyperbole, a practice that was aimed at overdramatizing the circumstances of those he was describing. Reflecting on this style, Fish believes that Abram was "a little out of water" in New York, by which he meant that "the manner and style that worked for him in the South probably didn't work so well in the North. And there probably was a Northern prejudice toward Southerners that he ran into without it being overt."[13]

According to Ruth, her mother had to teach her father how to act in formal environments. "And that served him very well," she said,

> because he found himself in a lot of them. But at the same time, he wanted his Cool Whip and his ketchup on his everything. His favorite thing was to go to a dive and eat barbeque and he wasn't into trying fancy dishes. He had his country ways, and he enjoyed them and in some cases my mother found them inappropriate. But mainly, the real fact is that he gained a lot by learning how to use your forks and knives, not to drink the finger bowl and all that kind of thing. And how to conduct himself in social situations.[14]

But Abram's unsophisticated down-home style was deeply ingrained in him and destined to survive the many advances in his life. Growing up in South Georgia, Abram recalled with affection the fish fries he attended as a child with his family, the catfish brought in by local fisherman and placed on a giant skillet made from the boiler of a steam locomotive.[15] Many years later guests at the dinner parties he and his second wife Carlyn held at their home on Cape Cod would be greeted in the kitchen by the host in the middle of frying the fish that would soon be served.[16]

Joseph Lefkoff said that Abram would find many excuses to return to Atlanta after leaving for New York, mainly to experience authentic Southern cooking once again. Receiving the call from the airport, Lefkoff would pick up Abram's friend Osgood Williams and the three headed straight to Harold's Bar-B-Que.[17] Abram's tastes extended to cheap eats and fast food. Jeh Johnson remembered the morning Abram was about to make a presentation to the partners of Paul, Weiss about a case he was trying on behalf of the board of directors of the global services firm Marsh and McClennan. When Johnson, who was serving as his associate on the case, arrived at Abram's office that morning to pick him up on the way to the meeting, he saw him sitting in the rocking chair he used instead of a desk eating junk food. "It was like Yodels or Twinkies or Ring Dings," Johnson recalled. "I'm addicted to those things. I was twenty-seven years old at the time. It was a validation for me to see the great Morris Abram eating junk food. I continued it for years after that, figuring if it was good enough for Morris, it was good enough for me."[18]

At the end of a vacation with his father in England, where Abram would take his family to show them the sights of his and Jane's days in Oxford, Joshua remembers his father, now the U.S. ambassador at the UN in Geneva, getting his newlywed wife Bruna out of a meeting to say he would be picking her up upon his arrival to take her to lunch. No doubt the patrons of the McDonald's in Geneva were surprised to see the U.S. ambassador's limousine pull up in front of the fast food restaurant.[19]

While living in Geneva, Abram would appeal to his former law partner Bob Hicks, who also grew up in rural Georgia, to visit him. Hicks would ask, "Why do you want me to come all the way there, Abram? We'll have breakfast together and you'll just go off on all your business and I'll have nothing to do." But Abram was desperate, he said, to hear someone who could speak the English language properly. And while he was at it, he asked his old partner to bring him two South Georgia delicacies, Agrirama grits and Claxton fruit cakes.[20]

It was his frugality that impressed Abram's young executive director of UN Watch Michael Colson when they were working together in Geneva. Toward the end of his life, a frail Abram would cut off a conversation to tell Colson he had to leave to do his grocery shopping in France. When Colson asked why he couldn't simply let his housekeeper take care of it, "he looked at me like I was crazy. He said, 'Michael, she will buy Swiss eggs which are four times the price of French eggs!'" Colson told a reporter covering Abram's funeral on Cape Cod that his favorite place to eat in Geneva had been the self-service counter at the local supermarket.[21]

During his extended time spent as a guest in the Abram's home at the Dakota, Hamilton Fish did not sense any tension between Morris and Jane. "They were always impeccably gracious to one another," he recalled, though she did exhibit some unease at the grilling of their children at the dinner table. But during the time Fish was a guest of the family, the relationship between Morris and Jane was in fact deteriorating. For all his admiration for her intellect, character, and devotion to her children, Abram found his wife of thirty years domineering, much like his mother, and felt himself ultimately stifled by the relationship. Shortly after his divorce, Abram told Eli Evans, "The older I become the more I feel that touching is the most important thing in the world. I think you get strength and sustenance from touching, and Jane was not a toucher."[22]

But there was also the fact that he had begun to rekindle a relationship with a woman he had known many years earlier in Atlanta. When Abram met Carlyn Feldman in 1940, she was a high school senior. Struck by her extraordinary physical beauty, Abram courted her for three years, but because she was so young, they were not thinking of marriage. There was also the matter of their diverging interests, his in law and politics and hers in the visual arts. She was also reluctant to be drawn into the world of someone so ambitious. But as his marriage to Jane was ending, Abram began seeing his long-lost love during business trips to Atlanta.

In the summer of 1973, only six weeks after separating from his wife, Abram contracted acute myelocytic leukemia, thought widely at the time to be a death sentence. The agony of his treatment was compounded not only by his uncertainty of whether he would survive the illness, but also by the guilt he felt over the breakup of his marriage to Jane, his concern about the well-being of his children, and his strong desire to marry Carlyn, who had been divorced the previous year. During that period, he later said, he was more preoccupied by his marital problems than with his medical condition.[23]

The two were married in January 1976, three years before his treatments were ended. From the beginning of his illness, Carlyn Abram played a key role in her husband's physical and psychological recovery. But their marriage was fraught with complications almost from the beginning. For one, there were the differences in their interests that had played a role in keeping them apart after they had begun dating many years before. By the time of their marriage, Carlyn Fisher had established a solid reputation in Atlanta as an accomplished painter who had been a cofounder of the city's annual arts festival.

Although she was able to practice her craft in New York and on Cape Cod, where she developed her skills as a landscape painter, Carlyn Abram resented her husband's preoccupation with his career and the lack of interest he showed in her daughter from her first marriage as compared with his own children. There was also the matter of his infidelity. In a letter she wrote to Abram after discovering it, Carlyn Abram said, "I hoped and believed that I was high on your list of priorities. I discovered unmistakably, on the contrary, I was low on the list."[24]

Two years later, Abram informed his siblings and their spouses that he and Carlyn would no longer be living together. "She is a fine woman," he wrote, "a beautiful one too, vivacious, spiritual, articulate, and ever so meaningful to me for years particularly in the terrible crisis of my illness. Not that she had not been loved by me since then; far from it. Yet we grew apart and except for times, wonderful times, at the Cape we found it hard to mesh." He continued, "However, Carlyn and I differed profoundly in so many ways. Once, I did see this fact for so long as an intriguing, complementary circumstance. These differences, however, developed, I fear, into a situation in which each had unfulfilled needs."[25] By the time of their divorce two years later, Carlyn Abram had returned to Atlanta.

Deborah Forman, an artist on Cape Cod, had become friendly with Carlyn in the early 1980s when the two were exhibiting their work at the same gallery in the town of Orleans. Soon they began working together on a documentary about the artist colony in Provincetown, Massachusetts that was later shown on PBS. In addition to her career as an artist, Forman was then a feature writer for the

Cape Cod Times. When she found out who her friend's husband was, she thought it would make a great feature story for the newspaper. When she went to interview him at the Abrams's home in Dennis, "he started, as he always did, asking questions. And I kind of felt like I was at Brandeis for an admission interview."

Although it made her a bit uncomfortable at first, Forman was flattered that he was interested in her opinions. Thus began a friendship between the two, along with her husband Jerry, that would last until Abram's death. She remembers the many dinner parties that began with Abram in the kitchen frying fish. "And then we'd sit down to dinner. He would present an issue and then everyone else would talk. Morris was a great listener."[26]

He was also an effective flatterer. Michael Colson vividly remembers the dinner parties he and his third wife Bruna Molina hosted for ambassadors and other dignitaries in Geneva. Typically, the dinner began with a welcome by Abram, presenting the guest of honor and offering brief introductions of everyone sitting around the table. This he did entirely from memory that, according to Colson, managed to be flattering without being obsequious. (Once he saw tears coming from the eyes of a leading international banker while the host was saying nice things about him.) When dessert was served, Abram would present an issue in the form of a question, turn to the guest of honor for his or her reaction, and then sit back and listen to the discussion.[27]

In the appreciation she wrote for the newspaper after his death, Forman noted that while Abram was passionate about his beliefs, "he always wanted to hear what others thought. He asked a lot of questions and listened intently. He was always curious, always exploring, always learning. . . . When he sat down to talk to you, you felt as if you were at the center of his orbit."[28]

This trait was also observed by Abram's law partner Max Gitter, whose wife reminded him that

> if you spoke to him, regardless of who you were, you were the only person in the world. He never started to look around the room for people more important. You know, he continued, you go to a cocktail party

with a lot of big shots and the first thing you notice is that they'll be looking around the room for somebody more important. Morris had this trait. It's a fabulous quality. Not many important people have it. You have to have self-confidence and you have to be genuinely interested in people.[29]

Amid the political turmoil and divisions of the late 1960s and 1970s, Abram frequently found himself at odds with longtime friends and associates. But despite his intensely held convictions, he continued to engage with those who disagreed strongly with his views, winning their respect in the process. Abram's Paul, Weiss partner Sidney Rosdeitcher recalled, "Morris was a very open-minded, liberal person, but the thing I remember most was how easy it was to talk to Morris about these issues." Although the attorneys in the firm were usually too busy to talk about the issues of the day, Abram frequently found the time to walk into Rosdeitcher's office to engage with him on something he had read in the *New York Times* that morning that had caught his attention. "Morris was a very publicly interested figure," he said, "an admirable trait whether you agreed with his views or not. And he discussed them in a very reasonable way. I treasured the relationship I had with him, which was one of intellectual give and take." Although the two often disagreed, "he was never hostile. I never ceased enjoying those discussions."[30]

Not that he liked to be criticized. According to Mark Levin, who worked with Abram as a young professional in the Washington DC office of the National Conference on Soviet Jewry in the mid-1980s, "Morris, as many great men or women, had quite a large ego. And he didn't like to be questioned or criticized. He really didn't like it when people questioned whether he was listening to what they had to say. He'd look up and say, 'of course I've heard everything you had to say,' and in the most polite, southern way, he'd say, 'but I disagree with everything you had to say.'"[31]

Levin recalls the first time he heard that Abram had been named to chair the National Conference on Soviet Jewry in 1983. Then a young professional in its lobbying shop in Washington, he knew little about Abram's background, but vividly remembers the eager anticipation in the office of what this would mean for the organization. He marks that period as the most significant in his professional development: "Morris always liked to be a teacher and he provided me ample lessons on how to do my work better as an advocate, how to look at the big picture and the big issues that confronted not just the Soviet Jewry movement but how the movement fit into the larger picture of U.S.-Soviet relations, human rights, how one defines human rights, how one defined universal human rights. He remains one of the great influences in my life."[32]

Jonathan Tepperman was a twenty-three-year-old graduate of Yale when he received a one-year fellowship to work with Abram at UN Watch in Geneva in the mid-1990s. Growing up in a provincial Canadian town and majoring in English at Yale, Tepperman had not taken a single course in political science or international relations. His assignment was to write speeches and op-ed pieces, and he was terrified. At first, he found his boss intimidating, a "huge personality" who projected the aura of "a big player."[33] Tepperman recalled, "From the beginning what struck me was the way he engaged with me as a real person the moment I walked in, despite the fact that I was not a real person. I was a baby, and I didn't know shit from Shinola, especially in this area. And he treated me like a serious professional."[34]

Tepperman, who today is the editor of the magazine *Foreign Policy*, will never forget the first op-ed he drafted for Abram. The two of them sat at a table in Abram's apartment and "he took a red pin and stuck out his tongue at the corner of his mouth and then started redlining everything I had written. And in his southern drawl he said, 'Jonathan, this is terrible. I mean, this is awful! I would never write such purple prose. I can't use this; this is just awful.'" Abram's demanding approach paid off for the young writer. "I quickly came to realize that it was an enormous gift of respect that I actually didn't deserve, but by treating me like I was a serious professional, Morris helped make me into that kind of a person as well as goading me into trying to become that kind of a person."[35]

The two began arguing politics, which Abram indicated to Tepperman he loved to do, whether the topic related to the work they were doing or not. "And he never did what I would have done if I were in his shoes," Tepperman says, "which would have been to say 'Kid, you don't know what you're talking about. Just shut up and take notes.' But he would engage with me on the merits no matter what the issue was. And I didn't appreciate at the time just how extraordinary it was and how lucky I was. And so, it was an enormous education for me."[36] Tepperman says there is no way he would be in the position he is in today were it not for the year he spent working for Morris Abram.

All of the Abram children built rewarding careers. His oldest daughter Ruth, in addition to founding the Lower East Side Tenement Museum, got deeply involved in women's rights issues. Ann Abram, who played an important role in her father's recovery from leukemia, became a therapist specializing in depression, anxiety, and family relationships. Morris Jr., after studying art history at Oxford University and spending years abroad, settled into the California art world, founding a gallery in Los Angeles. Adam, from his base in North Carolina, has built substantial companies in real estate, insurance, and banking, taking some of them public. Joshua is an entrepreneur and early stage investor in New York who has founded several successful technology companies. Before he left the United States for Geneva, Abram told a reporter that one of his greatest disappointments was that he was not going to finish his life with Jane, "the mother of my children."[37]

In 1972, Morris Abram admitted to the graduating seniors of Emory University that he did not know the answer to many questions, but he nonetheless held onto several beliefs. One was not to be too certain of anything. There was, however, one exception—namely, that love is the one thing in life that is an unmixed blessing, and that in the case of children, love "is as necessary as food and water. So, too, is education." And while few can say, in the end, that they left the world any better, "One who leaves behind children who are questioning and actuated by a thirst for knowledge has accomplished one of the most difficult modern feats. He or she shall have gained in the process great satisfaction."[38]

NINE

New York Lawyer

I was a young guy just getting started, and I was watching him not only from the perspective of what an expert does, but here's how he operates.

Jacob Cohen attended the February 1970 press conference in Manhattan where Morris Abram announced his candidacy for the Democratic nomination to oppose New York senator Charles Goodell that fall. As Cohen recalled, "To me, the central line of that speech and the one which brought the audience to its feet—although they may have been cued to do this, including many black leaders in New York City—was that he did not agree to premature death notices of the civil rights movement. As far as he was concerned, there was still much to do, and he was not going to join that chorus of people who say it's all over."[1]

But to Cohen, who had worked on the speech, Abram's candidacy was little more than a pipe dream. Others, including his friend Vernon Jordan, who tried to talk him out of running, were also skeptical. When Arthur Goldberg announced his candidacy to oppose Nelson Rockefeller for governor, an action he had personally assured Abram his status as a former Supreme Court Justice precluded, it was clear to Abram that they would be competing for the same donors. The problem was compounded by questions that had been raised about Abram's ability to meet the residency requirement for the New York Democratic primary. Although the requirement was ultimately waived, by that time

Abram had little choice but to drop out of the race, which he did only two months after the February announcement.[2] Despite working on the Goldberg campaign that fall, he later told Eli Evans that his law partner "never apologized to anybody for entering the race because he thought he was God's gift to the state of New York. Naturally, he turned out to be the world's worst candidate who ever lived."[3]

Shortly after his return to New York from the Boston area, Abram sought and gained reelection to the firm he had left to pursue the presidency of Brandeis. After all, he had a large family to support. The law firm of Paul, Weiss, Rifkind, Wharton and Garrison, stocked with political celebrities past and present, among them Adlai Stevenson, Arthur Goldberg, Willard Wirtz, Theodore Sorenson, and Ramsay Clark, was at the time among the largest two dozen law firms in the United States. But it was not so much its partners who accounted for its fame but rather the importance of its clients, which included government agencies and high-level government officials. Although it had departments specializing in bread-and-butter legal matters including trusts, corporate law, and taxation, its specialty was in the more volatile litigation area.[4]

The firm's leading partner was a short, mustachioed man named Simon Rifkind, the son of Russian Jewish immigrants who had been a classmate of William Douglas at Columbia Law School. Appointed to a federal judgeship by President Franklin Roosevelt, Rifkind left the bench in 1950 to join what was then a fledgling law firm. Considered by many to be the best trial lawyer in the country, Rifkind provided Paul, Weiss the leadership it needed to prosper.[5]

Judge Rifkind (as he would always be known), who was awarded the Presidential Medal of Freedom by President Truman for his work with uprooted Holocaust survivors after World War II, had brought into the client base of the firm a substantial number of wealthy entrepreneurs, including many in the Jewish community.[6] When Rifkind sustained a heart attack in the late 1950s, there was a great deal of concern about the prospect of losing many of its connections to the Jewish community earlier than expected. Abram's presidency of the American Jewish Committee beginning in the early 1960s made him an attractive candidate to fill that expected void.[7]

Abram told Eli Evans in the mid-1970s that his move to New York had been prompted by his curiosity to see if he could "swat in the big leagues." But reflecting on his New York practice, he was less than enthusiastic: "If the truth be known, I'd rather practice law in Atlanta or even Fitzgerald than practice in New York. I've had all the legal experiences and all the courts I want."[8] Several years earlier, he had turned down a federal judgeship in New York that Senator Kennedy had offered him. "I didn't want to sit in court on my fanny and listen to lawyers argue and try to pass out sentences on narcotics cases," he said. "That just wasn't my idea of life."[9]

During his early days in the firm, Abram had his work at the American Jewish Committee and the United Nations to stimulate his intellectual and political interests. When Abram's autobiography was published in 1982, some of his partners were irritated by the fact that he had given unusually scant recognition to the firm, choosing to highlight the other aspects of his career. This complaint was echoed in a review of the book by legal journalist Lyle Denniston. Describing Abram as "one of the heroes of American law" and "a leader in the cause of human dignity," he concluded that Abram must believe that the powerhouse firm where he spent the previous twenty years was simply "a way station" on a path to "livelier or more important missions elsewhere."[10]

According to Jeh Johnson, who entered the firm as an associate in the mid 1980s and became its first African American partner, "Morris was kind of aloof. He was sort of an independent actor. Since he did a lot of his own stuff, he wasn't a part of the central fabric of the firm. I don't mean that in a negative way. I don't mean to say he was an outcast; he was kind of like me in a way, he had a lot of things going on in addition to his practice."[11]

Although Abram's work at Paul, Weiss was as challenging as anything else he faced during his career, it could not match the satisfaction he derived from his mission-driven activity outside the firm. Nor could it match the sheer joy and educational value he had derived from his early years practicing law. Many of the cases he argued in Atlanta went before juries where Abram relied on his charm and rhetorical skills to succeed. In fact, it was during his early career in

Georgia that he gained an abiding respect for the men and women of the jury. Even in the one case in which he lost what he believed was an open-and-shut case due to the local prejudice in an Appalachian town in the northern part of the state, "I cherished the very opportunity to experience such a case. I would never have been content in a large firm whose principal clients were banks or insurance companies."[12]

Max Gitter, a longtime partner at Paul, Weiss, recalled the time as an associate in the firm when he went with Abram to argue a case before the Georgia Court of Appeals:

> In southern courtrooms there was a wonderful custom where the justices came down to shake hands with the lawyers. Twice I experienced this in the 4th Circuit in Virginia. And it was really gracious and nice. Morris would tell the story of when he argued some important case early in his career. In the course of the argument, he used "dayenu," Hebrew for "it would have been enough," to say, *a fortiori*, my client is innocent. He kept repeating "dayenu" [i.e., even this would have been enough to acquit]. He ran into the chief judge at some function after the argument and the judge said to him in a very deep southern accent, "DA-EINU!" So, he obviously made an impression on that judge.[13]

Abram handled a wide range of corporate litigation for the firm, including cases dealing with antitrust, taxes, securities, and real estate. His reputation in the New York legal community was, according to Gitter, "very high. He was a very devoted lawyer to his clients, and very protective of them." In 1977 Abram was described in *New York* magazine as "one of New York's most respected lawyers."[14]

Sidney Rosdeitcher, who had accompanied Abram to Americus, Georgia in 1963 as an associate at Paul, Weiss, recalled Abram's courtroom style: "He was a very persistent cross-examiner. And he had an enormous presence in court. It was very difficult to resist his cross-examination. I'll never forget Morris's cross-examination of the plaintiff who had sued an insurance company he was defending. It was terrifying; I can't tell you exactly what made it so terrifying, but it was so relentless, and he was so forceful and yet smooth. You know, he had this Southern accent which sugarcoated some of the things he was saying. But it was terribly intimidating to a witness."[15]

Abram reflected on his courtroom style in his conversations with Eli Evans: "A mild man," he said, referring to himself, "in the courtroom my adversaries think I'm a terror. There it's a different situation. Aggression, which is the hallmark of a trial lawyer, every one of them who's successful is a very aggressive person, but aggression in a controlled environment. Nobody's going to hit you for what you say in a courtroom."[16]

Success in the courtroom, Abram believed, required not only an instinct for the jugular but also enormous powers of concentration with respect to both the laws and the evidence. It also required an ability to improvise in situations in which a witness hesitates or offers a surprising answer. Abram told young lawyers in his firm not to follow a script or read to a witness during cross examination. Instead, he suggested, "Talk to him, watch him, see what's making him nervous."[17] When Abram knew a witness was lying, he would pull out some papers and review them slowly to make that person think he was reading something incriminating. This technique, he said, "will turn liars into truth tellers."[18]

In the fall of 1963, Abram was invited back to the University of Chicago where he had received his law degree nearly a quarter of a century earlier to deliver a lecture on the first day of class to its first year law students and the board of its alumni association. The lecture was entitled, "The Challenge of the Courtroom: Reflections on the Adversary System," and was reproduced in the school's publication. Abrams told the students, "The reason I choose that of the advocate in the adversarial system is the plain truth that I would find any other practice a bore." He did not, he said, want to advise clients in the intricacies of corporate law but rather enjoyed studying legal issues at the point of controversy. "I am a generalist in the law," he declared, "and a specialist only in procedure and drama. The principles of my branch of the profession are drawn not only from the cases but from Machiavelli and Clausewitz."[19]

Robert Destro, who later served on the U.S. Commission on Civil Rights with Abram, first encountered him as an adversary in a 1977 civil rights case. This time Abram was on the side of a law firm charged with discriminating against an Italian Catholic graduate of Notre Dame law school by turning him down for a partnership. According to plaintiff John Lucido's complaint, the firm Cravath, Swain and Moore, described by the *New York Times* as "the Rolls Royce of Law Firms," had a history of favoring white Protestant males in its promotions.[20]

Fresh out of law school, Destro was the general counsel of the Catholic League for Religious and Civil Rights, which weighed in on behalf of Lucido. Cravath hired Paul, Weiss, with Abram as the lead counsel, to defend it in the first big lawsuit brought against a prestigious New York law firm under Title VII of the 1964 Civil Rights Act. The Cravath and Paul, Weiss position was that Title VII did not apply to legal partnerships.

Destro believed Lucido's case was a solid one: "There was a certain disdain for the idea that an associate, even a senior one with a stellar record like John's, would have the temerity to challenge a big white stocking firm like that." Abram, Destro pointed out, was defending a group of people who stood at the apex of the legal profession and who regard law firms as private clubs.[21]

The Harvard Law professor Alan Dershowitz was outraged that a "Jewish firm" such as Paul, Weiss would be taking the position that anti-discrimination laws did not apply to the same law firms that once kept Jews out of their boardrooms. "I thought it was extremely cynical. My view is that discrimination against anyone is discrimination against everyone. I thought I was on the right side and Morris was on the wrong side. I mean, this was not a criminal case. He did not have to defend Cravath."[22]

Not surprisingly, Robert Rifkind, a partner at Cravath and the son of Paul, Weiss's leading partner, saw things differently: "We weighed the issues of what defense we should rely on," said Rifkind. "We desperately wanted to bring the case to an early halt. There was a view that as a technical matter, the statute didn't apply. That is to say, that a partnership is not a position of employment. It's a position of ownership, and that therefore, the statute didn't apply."[23]

Dershowitz took on the first part of the Lucido case, winning the argument that his client had the right to take legal action against the law firm. The next phase of the case involved the question of whether the firm actually discriminated against John Lucido by denying him a partnership.[24] Rifkind, who started as an associate at Cravath the year before Lucido and knew him well, pleaded with him to drop the suit and get on with his life. "It had never occurred to me that the firm had discriminated against him on the grounds that his family had been Italian. 'Oh yes, he said, that's what they were doing.' And of course, the charge that we were discriminating against Catholics was nonsense, because we had many Catholic partners at the time."[25]

When Destro joined the plaintiff's team, it was very much up in arms about the tactics Abram and his team were using, insisting that depositions be taken for thirty consecutive days:

> Now I can tell you everything from the day I was born in less than half that time, maybe if you said eight hours a day for ten days that would be just about it. But they wanted thirty. And I have to tell you, Morris could be pretty theatrical. I was a young guy just getting started, and I was watching him not only from the perspective of what an expert does, but here's how he operates. Of course, Morris was doing his client thing. That's what he was supposed to do. There did come a time when we said, look, this is over. If you want, we will go down and see the judge. Some of that is lost in the fog of antiquity, but Morris did a very good job. He was very detail oriented; he didn't let one jot or tittle escape.[26]

In the summer of 1973, feeling some dizziness when standing up from the rocking chair he occupied while working in his office, Abram arranged to have a complete physical. He set the appointment with his longtime physician for June 19, the date of his fifty-fifth birthday. Within days he was diagnosed with acute myelocytic leukemia (AML), a type of cancer that starts in the blood-forming cells of the bone marrow.[27]

Abram met the news with a mixture of "terror and disbelief." Recently separated from his wife Jane, he was aware that just a year earlier, the wife of his Atlanta law partner Robert Hicks had died of the disease a mere five months after receiving the diagnosis. "When I heard that Morris had that horrible disease," Hicks recalled, "I really wrote him off. I thought I might see him only one more time when I went to New York."[28] But Abram's determination to face his disease was steadfast. Hicks wrote to Abram telling him how upset he was, saying how he wished there was something he could do. Abram later recalled that he had received a letter from a friend assuming he was going to die "that made him so mad," Hicks said, "he said he would not die to spite me."[29]

But in fact, the odds were significantly stacked against him. As of 1973, survival rates for patients with AML were fifteen percent for five years, lower for someone Abram's age. Abram's treatment at Mount Sinai Hospital in New York City began that September under a new protocol that doubled these odds, according to early statistics. The regimen included a particularly aggressive treatment of chemotherapy involving two agents, one administered for seven days and the other for three.[30] Abram's progress was checked with highly painful bone marrow extractions. Despite weakening with constant fever, by the end of the month, three weeks after his treatment began, he was being kept alive by the infusion of red cells, platelets, antibiotics, "and the blind luck that no infection had appeared."[31] Despite his weakness from both the illness and its treatment, Abram, a dedicated tennis player and swimmer, was determined to maintain as much physical activity as possible. Doctors, nurses, and patients could see him sprinting through the corridors of Mount Sinai holding on to one or even two tables containing his bottles and tubes attached to his forearm.[32]

Two months after being released from the hospital and placed on maintenance therapy, Abram contracted hepatitis, which put continued treatment for his AML on hold while he dealt with another debilitating disease. He faced the additional challenge of being scheduled to try a complicated tax case for Textron, the Providence, Rhode Island–based defense contractor, for which he had spent two years in preparation. At first, his doctors were adamant that he not attempt to brave the winter elements in Rhode Island while battling both his ailments and the pressures of high-stakes litigation. But when they saw the anxiety caused by the prospect of dropping out of the case, they relented. After a four-day trial, in which he won the case for his client, he returned to New York in a severely weakened state.[33]

By the spring of 1974 Abram was able to return to chemotherapy, this time leaving him with bouts of nausea and chills. Abram's determination to beat the disease was reinforced by his deep involvement in every detail of his therapy. As an undergraduate at the University of Georgia, he had seriously considered a career in medicine before turning to law. His renewed interest in the subject served him well during his consultations with his medical team about proposed treatments. On at least one occasion, he believed his spotting of a deviation from his prescribed treatment may have saved his life.[34]

While Abram considered himself fortunate to be at a hospital he described as "a wonder of modern science," he was less impressed with its day-to-day operations. He was outraged, he later wrote, to see "elementary principles of hygiene and nursing care violated." He registered constant complaints and "never surrendered to the system."[35]

During his early days at Mount Sinai, Abram became aware of new and promising treatments for leukemia, one in Israel involving an immunological agent with the acronym MER, the other in England involving the injection of radiation treated leukemic cells. Since the former had not received FDA approval, Abram was prepared to fly to Israel to receive the treatment. Such a radical step was avoided when he received the necessary permission to use it with the intervention of Senators Henry Jackson and Hubert Humphrey.[36]

Abram's hematologist, Dr. James Holland, an internationally renowned cancer researcher, initially was not sanguine about Abram's chances for survival. For an adult, he told the *New York Times*, AML was the most malignant of tumors.[37] Holland was just beginning an experimental treatment using leukemia cells treated with an enzyme much like the radiation treated cells being used in England. The treatment required an elaborate effort to set up a team of physicians, nurses, and technicians to put together the program and equipment necessary to separate leukemia cells from diseased patients, treat them, and inject them back into patients. Holland decided to combine this treatment with the immunotherapy developed in Israel. Abram wrote, "During this period I never doubted that I had Dr. Holland's goodwill and sympathy. In fact, I had the sneaking suspicion that he wanted me as a patient as much as I wanted his novel therapy. I sensed that he saw in me a will to fight, a basically healthy constitution, and a willingness to take risks."[38]

A bone marrow test in June 1974 showed that Abram was still in remission when the administration of the combined injections commenced. Two years later he was taken off MER, with which he had become saturated, but the injections of leukemia cells continued monthly along with bimonthly chemotherapy that left Abram with chills, nausea, and fatigue.[39]

As he approached his fourth year in remission while continuing to receive aggressive monthly treatments to maintain it, Abram decided to go public with his story, giving a series of interviews over several weeks at his home and office to Pranay Gupte of the *New York Times*. Abram had met Gupte, a graduate of Brandeis, during his presidency. The result was a front-page article in which Abram attributed his survival, against very high odds, to the team of expert physicians who treated him, combined with his determination to defeat the disease. Up to that point, his illness was known only to family and close associates and friends. He hoped his story would give strength to others with the disease. "My devotion to the people I love and to my work is magnified," he told Gupte. "I am relishing every minute of this new lease on life."[40]

Shortly after the article appeared, and after Abram contracted hepatitis for the third time from blood contaminated products, the doctors discontinued his chemotherapy. The cell injections ended in January 1979 when they declared him cured. Abram's assertion that willpower can play a key role in curing an acute form of cancer was challenged years later by Barron Lerner, a professor of Medicine and Public Health at Columbia University. Still, Lerner concluded, "The idea that concrete steps can be taken in the face of a dreaded illness may serve as inspiration for those who become ill with cancer."[41]

In January 1975, during a particularly difficult period in Abram's battle with leukemia, he was called upon by New York Governor Hugh Carey to chair a Moreland Commission investigation of the state's nursing homes. The governor was acting in the aftermath of evidence uncovered by the Temporary State Commission on Living Costs, headed by Assemblyman Andrew Stein, looking into the mistreatment of elderly patients. The patients were residents of nursing homes owned by a large-scale operator in New York and New Jersey named Bernard Bergman, an Orthodox rabbi. Since leaving Brandeis five years earlier, Abram had felt deprived of the chance to "do the moral deed." And in addition to looking for an effective investigator, Carey had quite deliberately sought out a prominent member of the Jewish community to chair the commission.[42]

In New York, Jews were heavily involved in the nursing home industry. Abram knew that Jews tended to enter the untested businesses and from 1966 on the nursing home business was, in his words, "an untested field with a gush of federal money." Conditions in many of the state-subsidized homes were appallingly decrepit, and many New York politicians were implicated in the system either by reaping its benefits or simply looking the other way. By appointing someone with Abram's background, the governor believed he could limit his political risk that might accompany the implication of Jews, including religious leaders, in wrongdoing. Although Abram anticipated criticism, there was no backlash from the community, with every major Jewish leader saying to him to go after them, since "they are a disgrace."[43]

Abram also knew that the investigation was guaranteed to be rife with political implications involving the ways in which government favors had been doled out during Nelson Rockefeller's nearly fifteen year tenure as governor. Again, the issue involved members of the Jewish community, since the governor's closest link to the Jewish community, Samuel Hausman, had ties to Rabbi Bergman.

The hearings, held at the New York County Lawyers Association Building at 13 Vesey Street in Lower Manhattan, were televised on New York's Channel 13, the local public television station. They reached a dramatic pitch with the testimony of Nelson Rockefeller. By the time Abram had the opportunity to question him, Rockefeller had left the governor's chair to become the vice president of the United States under Gerald Ford.

Rockefeller requested to have his testimony taken in private, but Abram insisted otherwise. He and the commission staff prepared extensively over a period of several days for the questioning of the former governor. Having studied Rockefeller's performance before the U.S. Senate during his vice presidential confirmation hearings, where he was able to outmatch the committee's undisciplined questioning, Abram and his staff concluded that he alone should conduct the interrogation.[44]

Abram spent the day before his encounter with the vice president scrawling pages of questions on a legal pad. On the day Rockefeller appeared, the commission's staffers handed out to the press and to the witness incriminating documents. By comparison, Rockefeller was not prepared, having spent the previous two days on a campaign swing through the South.

For the next five hours, Abram, with his family looking on, pursued the ex-governor relentlessly. He established that Rockefeller could have saved the state millions of dollars by hiring auditors his health department had requested. He demonstrated that the state's nonprofit nursing homes had a vastly higher cost per bed than privately built ones. He showed that the state lacked a plan to deal with patients released from state mental hospitals, a charge Rockefeller himself had leveled against New York Mayor Lindsay while accusing him of mismanagement. And above all, Abram was able to remove any doubt that the vice president had been made aware of the conditions in his state's nursing homes while doing little, if anything, to address them.[45]

Ken Auletta, covering the hearing for the *Village Voice*, was mesmerized by the former governor's "dazzling" performance: "He was alternately: Funny. Bored. Impatient. Angry. Sincere. Incredulous. Hostile. Charming." He even managed to play the role of host, "acting as if he had invited them to the hearing and rewarding his guests with 'I think that your commission is offering tremendous service.'" Rockefeller's position was that he had left his appointees to take care of operational matters while he concentrated on the bigger picture.[46]

The commission had deliberately waited months before calling Rockefeller to testify to build a case against him. His testimony had followed hearings on a Bergman-owned nursing home in the Concord section of Staten Island built several years earlier without the prior approval of the State Department of Health and that had subsequently failed to receive an operating license. Bergman built the home with the confidence his political connections would get him the required approval. Those connections included Rockefeller's key link to the Jewish community, Samuel Hausman.

As Abram pursued this line of inquiry, which included the revelation that Hausman had a relative with an interest in the nursing home, Rockefeller, abandoning for the moment his earnestness and charm, tried to turn the tables on his inquisitor by asking Abram if he had never himself tried to intervene on behalf of a family member with a public official. It was not an empty gesture. He was on the verge of revealing that Abram had tried to do that very thing with respect to relatives bidding on a Port Authority concession. But as Abram later pointed out, even though there was no conflict of interest involved, he had withdrawn the request after accepting the Moreland Commission position. In the end Rockefeller decided not to pursue the gambit.[47]

The vice president claimed that the interest of his staff in the Bergman matter, which included no fewer than eight meetings his chief of staff had held with either Bergman or Hausman on his behalf, had arisen from the rabbi's charge that he was being discriminated against. But as Abram pointed out, the governor's chief of staff had spent two and a half years on the Bergman matter after finding out that the charge of discrimination was bogus.[48]

His testimony concluded, it was time for the vice president to depart, but not before demonstrating his legendary political agility. He shook hands with each commissioner, including Chairman Abram, to whom he brought up his upcoming speech before a dinner of the United Negro College Fund that Abram chaired. He answered questions from the press, thanked the reporters present for their patience, and, when asked if the hearing would affect his campaign to stay on President Ford's reelection ticket, insisted that there was no such campaign. After being congratulated by the commission's public relations counsel and shaking the hands of several policemen and others on the street, he departed. Abram wrote, "though I had a duty to discharge in exposing his responsibility in a great human tragedy, even I admired what he himself would have called his 'chutzpah.'"[49]

Following the report of the commission, Rabbi Bergman was convicted of Medicaid fraud and bribery and sentenced to four months in federal prison and eight months in state prison. He was also ordered to repay $2.5 million that New York State auditors said he had stolen from the Medicaid program.

In its 218-page report, issued on February 25, 1976, the commission pulled no punches, implicating over a dozen major public figures—including Vice President Rockefeller, his successor as governor, Malcolm Wilson, New York Attorney General Louis Lefkowitz, Assembly Speaker Stanley Steingut, Assembly Majority Leader Albert Blumenthal, Mayor Abraham Beame, and former mayor John Lindsay—in negligence, interference, and/or impropriety.

Abram told a press conference that the commission had turned over thousands of instances of larceny "or worse" to a special prosecutor. The report quoted Lindsay saying that he had no knowledge of the poor conditions in the nursing homes. Regarding that comment, Abram remarked, "That's what happens when you govern a city of eight million people by the six o'clock news." Sixty-eight nursing homes were closed in the aftermath of the commission's report. Ten of eleven bills recommended by the commission to strengthen regulation of the nursing home industry were soon passed into law in Albany.[50]

In a speech before the National Retired Teachers Association the following month, Abram commented on what he had learned from the experience. As long as care is paid by third parties, especially the government, he told the group, "an increasing number of hands will be available to receive the handout." The only possible control over the accelerating costs of service to the elderly is a requirement that in every possible case, some portion of the cost be privately born.[51]

In November 1978 Congress created a Commission for the Study of Ethical Problems in Medicine and Biomedical and Behavioral Research (PL 95–622). The commission's mandate was to study issues such as the definition of death, genetic testing and counseling, and the differences in the availability of health services depending on income or residence.[52] When White House staff proposed that Abram be selected to serve as chairman of the Commission, Health, Education and Welfare (HEW) Secretary Joseph Califano sent a memo to President Carter making the case for another choice. Although he agreed that Abram, whom he knew well, was "an excellent and dedicated lawyer," he preferred Dr. Maurice Lazarus, who was already serving on HEW's ethics advisory board and would be much better received in the community that is most interested in the work of the commission. Lazarus, he added, "supported you early on and continues to be a strong supporter."[53]

But the White House staff held firm to its first choice. In their memorandum to Carter, senior presidential aides Tim Kraft and Arnie Miller cited Abram's national reputation, his early support for the president, his interest in working with the administration, and the credibility he would bring to the commission's recommendations. In addition to his partnership in a prestigious law firm, his UN credentials, and his presidency of Brandeis, they also cited his service since the previous year as a lay member of the Human Subjects Review Panel at Mt. Sinai Hospital and his authorship of "Living with Leukemia," the lead article in the 1979 edition of the *Encyclopedia Britannica Health Annual*.

When he received the call from the White House, Abram was hesitant. He had, after all, given up the idea of pursuing a medical career over forty years earlier. On the other hand, he did have first-hand experience as a leukemia patient who had personal experience with issues the commission was authorized to pursue, among them informed consent, protection for human research subjects, and doctor-patient relations.[54]

Abram also had to overcome his concern that a government commission would naturally be drawn to recommending a host of new laws and regulations to deal with matters that he believed, in this case, called more for ethical guidelines than legal prescriptions. After he agreed to serve, the president announced the membership of the panel on July 18, 1979. In addition to the chairman, it included a high-level group of experts on the medical aspects of research, law, ethics, economics, and genetics.[55]

Abram's nomination was confirmed by the Senate at the end of September. For four years beginning in January 1980, the commission met nearly thirty times and issued reports dealing with subjects as varied as genetic engineering, defining death, protecting human subjects, securing access to health care, and deciding to forego life-sustaining treatment.[56] The commission's recommendations included guidance to relevant federal agencies, government support to ongoing initiatives, and a few targeted legal and statutory reforms.[57]

Abram realized early on the importance of achieving consensus among the commission's members, given the heavy emphasis it would be placing on ethical guidelines. With such consensus, he believed, the commission "could lay the cornerstone of a national moral structure for handling biomedical issues." As it turned out, even with a turnover of the Carter-appointed members after their term expired and their replacement with Reagan appointees, there was only a single dissent on a single report of the eleven the commission issued. And Abram was particularly proud that the panel's work was completed over 80 percent below its authorized budget of $20 million.[58]

1. With daughter Ruth at Oxford, ca. 1947. Courtesy of the Cuba Family Archives for Southern Jewish History at the Breman Museum.

2. Campaigning for Congress with family in Rockdale County, 1954. Courtesy of the Cuba Family Archives for Southern Jewish History at the Breman Museum.

3. Abram with Pope Paul VI during AJC delegation to the Vatican, May 1964. With the permission of the AJC Archives. All rights reserved.

4. Abram with Israeli Prime Minister Levi Eshkol, June 1964. With the permission of the AJC Archives. All rights reserved.

5. Abram with Vice President Hubert Humphrey and Dr. Martin Luther King Jr. at the Annual Meeting of the American Jewish Committee, 1965. With the permission of the AJC Archives. All rights reserved.

6. Abram introduces President Lyndon B. Johnson to the 60th Anniversary meeting of the American Jewish Committee, 1966. With the permission of the AJC Archives. All rights reserved.

7. Abram addressing a rally of the National Emergency Leadership Conference for Israel during the Six-Day War at Lafayette Park, Washington DC, June 1967. With the permission of the AJC Archives. All rights reserved.

8. Author meets the new president of Brandeis University, September 1968. Courtesy of the Robert D. Farber University Archives & Special Collections Department, Brandeis University.

9. With mother, Irene Abram, and Romanian relatives, Vaslui, Romania, 1969. Courtesy of the Cuba Family Archives for Southern Jewish History at the Breman Museum.

10. Abram with author Eli Evans and National Urban League President Vernon Jordan, Atlanta, 1977. With the permission of the AJC Archives. All rights reserved.

11. Abram receives American Jewish Committee's National Distinguished Leadership Award, New York, December 1999. *Pictured*: Ambassador Richard Holbrooke, UN Secretary-General Kofi Annan, Abram, World Jewish Congress Chairman Edgar Bronfman, and AJC President Bruce Ramer. With the permission of the AJC Archives. All rights reserved.

12. Morris B. Abram. Courtesy of the *Cape Cod Times*. Photo credit: Arnold Miller.

13. Portrait of Morris Abram sitting in his New York law office. Artist: Anne Green. Courtesy of Max Green and Joshua Abram.

TEN

Transition

It is a mistake to perceive the struggle entirely in the context of race.

Vernon Jordan had met Morris Abram before he left Atlanta for New York in 1970 to become President of the United Negro College Fund (UNCF). Jordan was then heading the Southern Regional Council's Voter Education Project, the highly successful effort to raise and distribute funding to civil rights organizations in their registration and education campaigns in the South during the 1960s. Nearly two decades younger than Abram, the two did not become friends until after Jordan's move to New York, since during their years in Atlanta, "I was not big enough, or known enough to be considered a peer or anything like that."[1]

Jordan saw a lot of Abram after moving to New York. The two met frequently in the morning to play tennis at a court located near 42nd Street and 10th Avenue, followed by breakfast at the University Club at 54th and Fifth. When Jordan asked Abram to be the UNCF's chairman, he readily agreed and was voted in unanimously by the fund's board. Jordan wrote, "Morris, needless to say, I am personally elated that you will render this service to the Fund. I look forward to the closer working relationship that the Fund brings us."[2] Over the next year, the two spent much of their time together on the tennis court or at the club discussing projects the fund was undertaking.[3]

Incorporated in 1944, the UNCF provides scholarships for black students and contributes to the general scholarship pool of thirty-seven historically black colleges and universities around the country. During his brief tenure, Jordan transformed it from a mom-and-pop operation into a highly respected organization.[4] But when National Urban League President Whitney Young died unexpectedly the year after Jordan assumed the top position at UNCF, he was offered the highly prestigious position and, after much soul searching, left the fund at the beginning of 1972.

Morris Abram saw the fostering of a sense of black consciousness in young adults as central to the mission of historically black colleges. In a speech he gave in 1970 during the first year of his chairmanship of the fund, Abram said that liberals, including himself, had been slow to recognize the need for black institutional power. UNCF colleges, he said, had excelled at nurturing black awareness, "the pride of black men in their heritage and accomplishments, which he contended was essential to the development of black leadership."[5] Abram would stay on as chairman of the UNCF for the remainder of the decade.

There is no question that the country's upheavals of the 1960s had made a deep impact on his political thinking, including on matters related to race. For all his life Abram had considered himself a liberal, certainly as it was defined as an unwillingness to accept the segregationist milieu in which he spent the first forty-five years of his life. But with the growing impact of the New Left on major political and cultural institutions, including foundations, elite universities, and media outlets, combined with the growing militancy of groups preaching black nationalism, Abram was finding himself clinging to a liberalism that was being redefined in ways that were at odds with many of his most fundamental beliefs.

David Harris, the longtime CEO of the American Jewish Committee, believes that Abrams's personal, political, and ideological viewpoints were deeply affected by three related developments of the late 1960s:

> One was how many old friends and allies of Morris turned against Israel after the Six-Day War, and I think this shocked and dismayed him. The people he thought were our natural partners flipped and turned against

Israel. The second was how a number of people, particularly in the civil rights community, had left the Jews behind in places like Ocean-Hill Brownsville. Wait a second—the African American community had no better ally and partner than the Jewish community and within the Jewish community there were few people who were more front-line and outspoken and courageous than Morris Abram, and now we are reinvented as the enemy, as the other side? How can this be? Now I think the third thing was his experience as president of Brandeis. It was a short stint, but there were protesters, demonstrators, trying to take over the president's office. I know from subsequent conversations that in Morris's mind that kind of breakdown of the norms of civility, of inquiry, of open discussion replaced instead by the mob, by intimidation, by occupation, I think really shook him to his core, because at heart he was a liberal in the best sense of the western term. People would disagree with each other, they would do it civilly, they would listen to each other, they would form their own opinions, but there wasn't the thuggish quality to what was experienced on the college campuses in the late 60s. I think those three events, which in some ways drew on each other, were all very formative in Morris's later political evolution.[6]

In 1972 Abram returned to his native state to deliver the commencement address at Emory University. Before preparing his remarks, he consulted with his son Morris, who was graduating from Harvard later that week, about what he should say. Morris Jr. recommended that he speak about what he had learned since his own college graduation in 1938, a period, Abram told the graduates, that encompassed "depression, war, political and cultural revolutions, the civil rights revolution, the development of the United Nations, the growth of megalopolis, the degradation of our cities, the emergence of a distinct American underclass, and the challenge to conventional mores and institutions." Abram said that he had been connected to several of these changes "in some small way," but touched by all of them.[7] The address provides a window into much of Abram's thinking at the time about large questions, including his evolving political philosophy.

At the time of his own college graduation, Abram told the graduates, he viewed things in black and white. Today, he no longer saw them in such absolute terms, his preference running "to the greys." Dogmatism, he said, is "a bar to learning."[8] Describing advances in science and economics, he decried the worship of technology, noting that science had not, as previously hoped, been able to overcome the laws of nature, as attested to by the environmental crisis and the resulting rise of the ecology movement. Although democracies need to do everything possible to improve the condition of their deprived groups, even the one man, one vote principle established in the county unit case has its flaws, since dependents of working age who are either unemployed or unemployable "are naturally more likely to respond to the pangs of their stomachs rather than constructs of Cartesian logic."

Turning to civil rights, Abram described the deplorable conditions for blacks in the South at the time of his graduation and for many years thereafter. And although their political and civil rights had finally been achieved, these victories had been relatively costless. The next phase of the struggle, which would come with a higher price tag, would come over economic, educational, and housing rights: "The problem arises because with the doors of opportunity now pried open, larger masses of economically and socially crippled blacks have not been able to cross over the threshold. However, the problem exists for an even larger number of whites, and in that sense, it is a mistake to perceive the struggle entirely in the context of race."

From the time of his graduation until the year 1965, Abram said, his liberal faith led him to believe that these problems could be resolved through the passage of legislation granting civil and political rights. But after these victories had been won, they had hardly any impact on the conditions of the underclass in major U.S. cities, which, if anything, had worsened. Civil service reforms had only entrenched inefficient and insensitive bureaucracies. Trade unions had prevented entry to skilled jobs and adopted restrictive practices in contradiction of their stated goal of improving the lot of the common man.

In perhaps the greatest challenge to his previous beliefs, Abram had come to the realization that "government cannot rectify the most glaring defects in the society. Childhood mirrors manhood and the damaged child becomes the destructive man. The chain of causation is continuous from generation to generation, time without end. The primary environment of the child is the home, and it is pure self-deception to assume as we have that the school can make up for the home's deficiencies. The alienation and violence in our society are a reflection of what has happened to the American home of all classes and races."[9]

During the campaign for the 1972 Democratic Party nomination for president, Abram aligned himself with the heavily favored senator from Maine Edmund Muskie. Muskie had been widely praised for the balancing act he played as Hubert Humphrey's running mate during the unsuccessful presidential campaign of 1968, when the party was torn apart by the divisions over the war in Vietnam. Coming out of that campaign as the prohibitive favorite for the nomination four years later, he and others in the "establishment" wing of the party were blindsided by the growing voices on the left for a "New Politics" that empowered those who favored a break with policies the party had championed dating back to the Truman administration.

Abram headed a task force for Senator Muskie on domestic policy and was already proposing cabinet choices for a future administration.[10] But he would later fault himself for authoring a policy paper whose pessimistic tone reflected the dark mood growing about America, primarily on the left. As Abram later put it, he was following the same ideology that had led to the takeover of the party by its most extreme forces, "which downplayed America's virtues and magnified its flaws."[11] It was these forces that Senator George McGovern rode to secure the Democrats' disastrous nomination, paving the way for the landslide reelection of Richard Nixon in November.

Abram's relationship with Jimmy Carter began in 1971, when he shared a platform with the future president the year after he became Georgia's governor. He thought it was odd that the two, who had grown up so close to one another in Georgia six years apart in age, had never met up to that point. But as a Georgia state senator, Carter had not involved himself in the civil rights battles of the 1960s. Running a campaign designed to appeal to segregationists, his landslide victory over former Governor Carl Sanders for the Democratic nomination for governor in 1970 had yielded him only seven percent of the black vote in the head-to-head primary runoff.[12] Still, the new governor's assertion during his inaugural address that "the days of segregation are over" propelled him into the national spotlight as one of the new voices of moderation among southern office holders.

Shortly after Carter's inaugural speech, he received a letter from Abram saying how pleased he was with it: "Your speech set a new standard of official discourse and your candor was so refreshing. As a native Georgian I have always felt that the South would lead the way in terms of a human solution to the problems of race and that the initiatives would come from a new breed of Southern public officials."[13]

When Carter began his campaign for president two years before the 1976 election, he reached out to Abram, inviting him and Carlyn to join him and Roslyn at their home in Plains. There he asked Abram if he would help him meet members of the U.S. Jewish community outside of the state of Georgia. Following their breakfast together, Carter sent a handwritten note expressing how pleased he was with the discussion: "We enjoyed being with you and Carlyn this morning, and I appreciate your giving me this much of your precious time in Georgia. Your help and advice will be very valuable to me, and I'll do my best never to disappoint you." Carter added that his new friend should not hesitate "to load [him] down with information and suggestions."[14]

In fact, Abram had already committed to supporting Washington senator Henry Jackson for the 1976 Democratic presidential nomination. Jackson, a liberal on civil rights and other domestic issues, had become the leading spokesman in the Democratic Party for increasing military spending and taking a hard line against the Soviet Union. He stood in the tradition of Harry Truman, John F. Kennedy, and Lyndon Johnson as Cold War liberals ready to intervene internationally in the cause of freedom, as JFK expressed it in his inaugural address.

The leading critic of the Nixon-Kissinger policy of détente with the Soviet Union, Jackson had played the key role in the congressional initiative tying trade preferences for countries in the Soviet bloc to the lifting of restrictions to freedom of emigration and other

human rights. The amendment that came to be known by the sur-
names of its sponsors, Henry Jackson and Congressman Charles
Vanik (D-OH), targeted most specifically the Soviet persecution of
Jews applying for exit visas to leave the country.

Abram agreed to serve as Jackson's New York campaign chairman for a variety of reasons. For one, he believed Jackson to be "a
thoroughly honest guy loyal to his principles." Although Abram did
not agree with all the senator's positions, Jackson was prepared to
argue them, "as I have done with him." A less than dynamic figure,
Jackson was not considered by Abram to be "an imperial president
type" and "I don't believe in all this charisma crap."[15]

But there were more personal reasons as well. Jackson had called
him twice during the early stages of Abram's illness to cheer him up
and had helped him secure the drug treatment developed in Israel
that had not yet received FDA approval. And Abram believed that
with a President Jackson, he had a realistic chance of a U.S. Supreme
Court appointment.[16] Although Jackson did manage to win the New
York Primary, his loss to Jimmy Carter in Pennsylvania in April 1976
all but ended his campaign.

When Abram turned his focus and support to the all but guaranteed nominee Carter, it did not seem to be much of an ideological
stretch. As Georgia's governor Carter had put Henry Jackson's name
into nomination at the 1972 Democratic National Convention. In an
interview with *Time* magazine shortly after he became the prohibitive favorite for the Democratic nomination, Carter named Harry
Truman as his favorite modern president, listing as one of his most
admired attributes Truman's vision on foreign policy. Carter also
considered Winston Churchill the preeminent leader of our time.[17]

During the fall campaign, Abram became more than a lukewarm
supporter of his fellow Georgian. Setting aside whatever misgivings
he had about Carter's absence from the civil rights struggles of the
past, Abram jumped on the bandwagon to promote him as the best
governor Georgia ever had, "and the first who truly felt, and more
important acted, as if he were the chief executive of and for all the
people—blacks and whites."[18]

In June, Abram took to the pages of the *New York Times* to defend

Carter against suspicions that his convictions as a religious Southern Baptist were incompatible with America's political system. Abram told the story of his father's friend Sheriff Elijah Dorminy of Ben Hill County, a "hardshell Primitive Baptist," who warned a visiting Klansman who tried to recruit him that he would be run out of town if he disobeyed the law. Abram also mentioned that when Carter had asked him to help introduce him to Jews outside Georgia, he had readily complied, knowing that the governor had appointed a Jewish friend of Abram's to head the state Board of Regents. It was a body he himself had aspired to serve on during his days in the state, knowing that, as a Jewish liberal, this was simply out of reach under any governor at that time. "I do not claim," Abram wrote, "that Jimmy Carter knows all the nuances of American pluralism. But on his record, and knowing him, I believe he wants to learn. Nothing that has happened in the months of his presidential campaign has changed my mind."[19]

In another op-ed written on the eve of the 1976 Democratic convention in New York's Madison Square Garden that July, Abram pointed out that Carter's ascendancy represented a turning point in American politics. While LBJ had to ride to prominence in national politics in a "western saddle," Carter had no need to hide his "Southernness," since Southern politicians were no longer captive to the segregationist demands of their constituents.

Abram described Carter as the best of the new breed: "Gifted with raw courage, monumental physical endurance, and sparkling intelligence," he had overcome opponent and media attacks on his credibility by demonstrating to audiences around the country who saw him as someone "who truly believes in himself." And though Abram confessed that he didn't know him well, "we share the same roots and perceive the world through the values of a common generation."[20]

Characterizing him as a "Southern liberal," Abram said that like his cultural opposite FDR, Carter combined the two major strains of the Democratic Party: Jeffersonian theory and Jacksonian pragmatism. During the fall campaign, Abram's support for the Democratic nominee turned from defending his background to offering advice. As the race, which had begun with a large lead by Carter, began to tighten, Abram sent a memorandum to the candidate saying that he had not come into focus and, as a result, "The fundamental differences between yourself and Ford are not perceived." He reminded Carter of his distinguishing features: "integrity grounded on religious faith; a toughness born of self-confidence; a compassion derived from being an outsider."[21]

His career, he pointed out to Carter, was more miraculous and more of a credit to himself than FDR at this stage. He proposed, as he had advised close Carter aide Charles Kirbo, that in the final debate he should remind himself of what he has become in contrast to Ford, who was still essentially the congressman from Grand Rapids. Carter should propose reform of the United Nations to emphasize human rights and not giving a pass to our friends on their abuses. For good measure he offered the text for an opinion piece that *Newsday* had agreed to run.[22]

Carter's election that November proved a disappointment for Abram almost from the start. On a personal level, he was offered a midlevel position in the White House that he saw no reason to accept. As his friend Vernon Jordan put it, "Morris thought, and I agree with him, that the offer was not what Morris was up to."[23]

And it was not long before policy disagreements would set in. By early summer, Abram was writing to the White House to express concern over the administration's Middle East diplomacy.[24] But what had started with early disappointments would soon bring Abram a strong measure of buyer's remorse. Much of his advice to Carter as a candidate centered around the opportunity the presidency offered to emphasize human rights and the prospect of using the UN as a forum for articulating its importance. When early in his administration the president went before the General Assembly to announce his human rights initiatives, Abram joined him as his guest.

But while Abram had advocated calling out friendly regimes as well as foes for their human rights abuses, he still believed distinctions needed to be made between allies who were sensitive to Western criticism and completely unaccountable antagonists. And though human rights advocacy should be an important component of U.S. foreign policy, it should never be allowed to supersede a nation's vital interests. Abram also believed that a human rights policy could benefit from emphasizing America's recent advances in addressing our own historical shortcomings.[25] In his choice for UN Ambassador, Carter selected someone Abram had known from his days in Atlanta. Andrew Young had been a close confidante of Dr. King as executive director of the Southern Christian Leadership Conference. Following King's assassination, Abram had organized and co-chaired a fundraiser that raised several hundred thousand dollars for the SCLC.[26]

Young, who had represented Atlanta's Fifth Congressional District in Congress, had been regarded as a political moderate. For example, he had been the only member of the Congressional Black Caucus to confirm Gerald Ford as vice president in 1973.

It came as a surprise to Abram and others to see Ambassador Young making use of his new platform to praise Third World dictators, underplay Soviet threats, and atone for America's sins past and present, the latter in his view giving us little standing to criticize Communist regimes. While it is true, Young said, that the Soviet Union represses its dissidents, "many of our own students were shot down on their own campuses" as a result of their political activities against the war in Vietnam. And even if we do not go in for literal torture, as some other countries do, the United States "still has subtle but very strong systems of intimidation at work that inhibit the possibilities of our poor, our discriminated against, and our dissidents, from speaking fully to address themselves." During the trial of Soviet dissident Anatoly Sharansky, he said that there are "hundreds, perhaps even thousands of people whom I would call political prisoners" in the United States.[27]

President Carter offered lavish praise for his UN Ambassador, saying that he "has a great sensitivity about the yearnings" of Third World peoples, as well as an understanding of the reasons for their "animosities and hatred" toward the United States. "I think," said the president, "he's made great strides in repairing [the] damage that [has] been done." For his part, Young returned the favor, saying that Carter "has the capacity as president of the United States to do more to put an end to racism than anybody since Martin Luther King."[28]

In a speech he delivered at Columbia University in 1978 on the

thirtieth anniversary of the UN Declaration of Human Rights, Abram
referenced the president's emphasis on the linkage between freedom and bread: "I reject the idea that freedom of speech and press,
indeed all political civil rights, are somehow to be tied to the impre-
cise and newly discovered rights such as that to development and a
New Economic Order. These are but smokescreens blown by those
who fear clear and well recognized rights such as those of speech,
religion, and emigration."[29]

Young resigned from his position in August 1979 following a secret
meeting with the UN representative of the Palestine Liberation Organization in violation of U.S. policy about which, it was claimed, he
deliberately misled the Department of State. His dismissal resulted
in an uproar among black leaders, many blaming what was to them
clearly the result of pressure they alleged President Carter faced
from the Jewish community.[30]

In an op-ed submitted to the *New York Times* (approved by two
editors before being spiked by a third), Abram sought to ring the
alarm bells of growing black hostility to Jews and Israel in the wake
of the Young resignation. Black anguish is understandable, he wrote,
"But the venting of this by wholesale anger at another group con-
verts a very human reaction into the unfair and dangerous public
malignancy of bigotry of the type which has afflicted blacks as well
as Jews for centuries."

While noting honest differences between black and Jewish organizations over the issue of racial quotas, Abram pointed out that
many other American organizations oppose quotas without being
the targets of abuse. He referenced a raucous meeting held in New
York with two hundred black leaders where moderate voices were
shouted down and others called for turning to Middle Eastern oil
money for financial support. He contrasted these voices with that of
Dr. King, whose "treasured" letter sent to him in 1967 condemned
antisemitism as something that hurts blacks as well as Jews, since it
endorses the doctrine of racism "which they have the greatest stake
in destroying."[31]

But these events, Abram pointed out, were not occurring in a
vacuum. When the Young matter broke, "the dikes which hold the

polluted stream of anti-Semitism were leaking badly." From what? From the failure of President Carter to rebuke offensive remarks by the chairman of the Joint Chiefs of Staff, from his close friend Bert Lance, and from his brother Billy. He had maintained silence in the aftermath of the Young resignation when he could have set the record straight on the reasons his dismissal had created "a serious threat to public harmony."[32]

Abram had other problems with the president as well. Racial preferences were becoming "a hallmark" of an administration that was getting "further and further ensnared in the competing demands for preference" by aggrieved groups. "There would not be enough of America," he wrote, "to satisfy the insatiable grievances, real or imagined, in this country whose first and last settlers were refugees."[33]

Despite his appointment toward the end of the Carter administration as chairman of the Commission for the Study of Ethical Problems in Medicine and Biomedical and Behavioral Research, Abram had so soured on his adopted friend's presidency that he could not see supporting his reelection. He set forth his reasons in a signed four-page document dated October 15, 1980. They included Carter's "limited view of the moral obligations of the presidency; his dangerous vacillations on foreign affairs; and his disastrous domestic record." Abram renewed his complaint about Carter's "inadequate" response to the overt antisemitism of friends, relatives, and colleagues. Calling his domestic policy "appalling," he criticized the president's inconsistency in foreign policy and closed with the regret that a man from his native state who grew up so close to him "disappointed so many who expected perhaps too much."[34] In an interview with the Jewish newspaper *Forward* in 1982, Abram went several steps further, calling Carter "a feckless, hopeless leader of this country who was leading the country into a psychological depression."[35]

Abram had voted for Democratic challenger Edward Kennedy in the 1980 New York primary. But voting in his party's primary was one thing; now he was prepared to give his support to a Republican for the first time in his voting age life. In a move reminiscent of his jump aboard the Carter bandwagon when his candidate Henry Jackson pulled out in 1976, Abram reached out quietly to senior advisors of Ronald Reagan before the final 1980 presidential debate to provide them with information they could use against Carter if the president resorted to personal attacks on his opponent. They related to his lack of public support for the Civil Rights Act of 1964 and his appeal to segregationists in his successful run for governor in 1970.[36]

Abram agonized over whether to make his presidential choice public. He made his decision to do so after consulting with his friend Theodore White, author of the Making of the President series dating back to Kennedy's slim victory over Nixon in 1960, who assured him that Reagan was "a decent man."[37] Abram announced his decision in a joint statement with his law partner Edward Costykian, the man credited with reforming Tammany Hall while serving as the leader of Manhattan's Democratic Party. Abram's endorsement, he later said, was "the only honest way of voting against Jimmy Carter." A second Carter administration, he believed, would continue to diminish U.S. support for Israel and erode the concept of equal treatment for all Americans.[38] Abram told an interviewer around the halfway point of Reagan's first term that despite some misgivings, the president demonstrated an ability to lead. His projection of authority was something he had found lacking in President Carter.

In addition to cutting ties with his party, it was time for Abram to say goodbye to an institution that had influenced his decision to move to New York nearly two decades earlier. By the mid-1970s, Abram and some other board members of the Field Foundation he chaired had begun to express their lack of enthusiasm for several key projects supported by its executive director, Leslie Dunbar. Abram had known and worked with Dunbar, the former head of the Southern Regional Council, since their civil rights days in Atlanta. Dunbar's strong opposition to the war in Vietnam had led him to take a more critical look at the international as well as the domestic policies of the United States in the 1960s and 1970s.

In the mid-1970s the foundation awarded grants to the left-leaning Center for Defense Information and the Center for National Security Studies. Things came to a head in 1980 when Dunbar recommended grants to support an anti-draft organization and the continuation of a study by the Institute for Policy Studies (IPS) on the role of the

United States in armaments transfers. Abram played the major role in blocking the two grants, saying that the board did not share Dunbar's concerns over American foreign policy. The United States, he said, was "one of the most moral nation states." This triggered Dunbar's resignation.[39]

Following Dunbar's departure, Abram was unsuccessful in blocking another grant to IPS. Although it didn't immediately result in his resignation, as it did one board colleague, it was clear that he and most of the foundation's board members were moving in different directions in their political thinking. There had been "deep rumblings" when Abram's vote for Reagan had been made public. Now, when he tried to redirect the focus of the foundation to poverty in single-parent families, a problem that had only grown since the Moynihan report, the board was unreceptive. Abram's formal departure from the Field Foundation took place on October 12, 1981, sixteen years after succeeding Adlai Stevenson as its chairman.[40]

ELEVEN

Challenging New Definitions of Civil Rights

Civil rights laws belong to all Americans.

On June 23, 1982, Morris Abram appeared on William F. Buckley's *Firing Line* program to discuss his recently published autobiography. The episode was titled "Odyssey of a Southern Liberal." Two decades had passed since the two had faced off in debate at Emory. As Buckley recalled that evening:

> Twenty-odd years ago I was engaged by Emory College in Atlanta to debate with a local liberal about whom, now I confess, I knew very little, other than that he was defiantly Jewish, defiantly liberal, anti-segregationist, and a lawyer. The auditorium was crowded, and I found myself facing one of the most ferocious advocates in my experience, even then extensive. It transpired that he had spent days in the library researching everything I had done and, more importantly, not done. It was a high-pitched evening, and the next day I visited his offices where he showed me a blueprint for a serene and integrated, happy America.[1]

This time the atmosphere was much more congenial. Buckley began his questioning by asking Abram about the case of Allan Bakke, a white applicant denied admission to the Davis Medical School of the University of California, whose lawsuit against the school had been ruled upon by the U.S. Supreme Court four years earlier. The medical school had set aside sixteen of its one hundred slots for black applicants, and Bakke contended that in the absence of this program, he would have been admitted based upon his qualifications.[2]

The court ruled that while racial quotas are unconstitutional, race could be considered in college admissions for purposes of achieving a more diverse student body. Abram told Buckley that he believed the Bakke decision was "a muddle," since it didn't come down on either side of the controversy over racial preference. His view, as it was at the time of the Emory debate twenty years earlier, was that the constitution was intended to be color-blind, drawing no distinctions between people on the basis of race, ethnic origin, religion, or sex. Although the civil rights movement, he pointed out, had taken the same position during the desegregation cases, "the movement by and large has departed and now wants racial preferences."[3]

Abram was even more disturbed, he said, by the more recent Supreme Court decision, *Fullilove v. Klutznick*, upholding the federal appropriation setting aside for minority contractors a certain percentage of public works funding. Not only was this law discriminatory against struggling contractors not of Hispanic or black origin, it opened the door to corruption through "all kinds of fabrications and falsifications and maneuvers and devices to give contractors a black or Hispanic front behind which whites or other majority elements could operate."[4] Both the *Bakke* and *Fullilove* opinions reflected divisions among the justices, even among those who agreed on their outcomes.

This was not the first time Abram had challenged the direction in which his old allies in the civil rights movement had moved. In a symposium appearing in *Commentary* magazine in January 1980, he noted that liberals, Jews notably among them, had traditionally supported reforms designed to help those who were disadvantaged either by prejudice or by educational and economic disparity. Although "wise men" understood that absolute equality could never be achieved, "equality before the law, neutrality as to ethnicity, religion, or sex, were the proper goals of the advocates of equal opportunity."[5]

During the 1960s, his views on this subject were entirely consistent with those of virtually all civil rights activists. After all, these were the views advanced by those civil rights organizations arguing for a color-blind interpretation of the Constitution that, in the landmark *Brown* case, sought to bring an end to the practice of classifying and legislating based on race. But beginning in the late 1960s came a demand that government "should classify and treat Americans on a basis which liberals had denounced for one hundred years as contemptible and invidious." This view was now regarded as liberalism, and "those who resisted were branded as conservatives, neo-conservatives, or reactionaries."[6]

This turn of events, in Abram's view, represented a reversal of the progress in the law, as described by the renowned nineteenth-century jurist Sir Henry Maine. Maine held that what distinguished the modern world from the ancient one was that individuals had become autonomous agents, no longer tied to their status at birth. And to Abram, the new version of civil rights represented a complete inversion of what distinguished liberalism from conservatism, since "the liberal thrust throughout history has always been against these conservative-sponsored rigidities in which one's place in society was ascribed at birth."[7]

In May 1981, Abram appeared before the Senate Judiciary Committee's Subcommittee on the Constitution studying the constitutionality of affirmative action programs. He warned the panel of the potentially negative consequences of allowing discrimination based on birth to take precedence over the rule of law. A color-conscious interpretation of the Constitution, he argued, provides a loaded weapon for those who would use it for some other urgent purpose." Furthermore, the Balkanization of ethnic groups, if allowed to proceed very far, will lead to problems here similar to those currently wracking Lebanon and Ireland, "duplicated, triplicated to the tenth exponential power."[8]

In an op-ed that appeared in the *New York Times* the following month, Abram noted his support for affirmative action as it was originally intended—namely, an effort designed to reach out broadly to disadvantaged persons on behalf of equality of opportunity. Unfortunately, he argued, this policy had become "skewed into a program of quotas, goals, and timetables," to further equality of result, a turn that "has been grafted into our conscience and consciousness by imaginative legal craftsmanship."

The fundamental principle of addressing the problem of discrimination, he wrote, is that a person should be treated as an individual, "with due regard for his or her distinctive abilities and character." By contrast, the practice of preferential treatment deals with that person "as a member of a group with a person's merit counting for little or nothing as compared to one's gender or skin color." Furthermore, insofar as the policies of preferential treatment are aimed at the skilled, the educated, and the middle class, "they leave those in direct need in the pit."

Abram also took on the argument that these policies should be regarded as temporary: "An ethnic spoils system, once introduced, is bound to become entrenched and requires a suspension of the Fourteenth Amendment, a step no less hazardous than the suspension for a time of free speech and press."[9]

Responding to an earlier piece in the *Times* on the decline of black political power in New York, Abram had placed much of the blame at the feet of black leadership itself. In a letter entitled "Misguided Black Political Strategy," Abram described the strategy of black leaders in advocating racial preferences in housing, education, hiring, and promotion as "ill-conceived," and having the effect of breaking up the coalition politics that had served the civil rights movement well during the 1950s and 1960s. "It is particularly distressing," he wrote, "that the coalition that had gained so much ground during the years of Truman, Kennedy, and Johnson should be in such total disarray now when it may be needed more than ever."[10]

Abram attributed much of the decline in black voting strength to an increase in the number of female-headed households fostering a black underclass that not only doesn't vote but also cannot do useful work in a service economy. He took both the *Times* and black leadership to task, the former for excluding this issue as if it weren't relevant to the issue of black political decline, and the latter for not addressing it.[11] In a handwritten note to his son-in-law Steven Novak that he attached to the published letter, Abram wrote that it marked his departure "from the main thrust of the civil rights establishment."[12]

Abram's association with the Lawyers Committee for Civil Rights Under Law had gone back to its founding when President Kennedy summoned a group of leading attorneys to the White House and appealed to them to offer their expertise and advocacy skills in the battle for civil rights. Since that time, he had served on the organization's executive committee. But his stand on the use of hiring quotas now put him on the opposite side of his committee colleagues.

In 1981 a lawsuit was brought against the U.S. government alleging that the Professional and Administrative Careers Examination (PACE), a written test used by the Civil Service Commission to fill positions in federal agencies, had an adverse impact on African Americans and Hispanics. Since the failure rate for black and Hispanic applicants was higher than for whites, the charge was that this disparate impact constituted de facto discrimination.

When the committee entered the suit on behalf of the plaintiffs, Abram registered a strong complaint. In a letter to Norman Redlich, dean of New York University's School of Law and co-chairman of the committee, Abram objected to the committee's participation in a lawsuit unrelated to the discrimination addressed by Title VII of the Civil Rights Act and its predecessor statutes dating back to the late nineteenth century. In a wide variety of circumstances, Abram noted, discrimination can be supported by the kind of disparate impact charged in the suit. Literacy tests, such as the one in Georgia Abram attacked in his 1949 *amicus* brief, was one such example, "the purpose of which was to put a screen around the discrimination rather than to set neutral tests for voter qualification."[13]

But Abram doubted that any fair-minded member of the executive committee believed that the PACE exam was designed to bar blacks and Hispanics from working for the federal government rather than to provide for a qualified civil service. The Civil Service Reform Act of 1978 and its legislative history, he wrote, made clear that its minority recruitment program was intended solely as a recruitment program and not a program governing actual appointments. He continued, "It is because I believe so passionately in the principle of equality and non-discrimination that I now so strongly oppose efforts to traduce these principles by misapplication."

Abram's objections went unheeded, and the Lawyers Committee entered the case on the side of the plaintiffs. In early 1981, the two sides signed a consent decree approved by a federal court later in the year phasing out the PACE exam over a three-year period and replacing it with alternative examining procedures "which will eliminate adverse impact against blacks and Hispanics as much as feasible, and which will validly and fairly test the relative capacity of applicants to perform PACE occupations."[14]

By 1983, with the closing down of the President's Commission on Bio-Ethics, a restless Morris Abram began a personal lobbying campaign aimed at attaching himself to the Reagan administration at a time when it was looking to reshape the U.S. Commission on Civil Rights. Established by the Civil Rights Act of 1957, the commission was tasked with the mission "to inform the development of national civil rights policy and enhance enforcement of federal civil rights laws."[15]

But as reflected in the *Bakke* and *Fullilove* cases, the very definition of what should constitute civil rights policy was now a matter of bitter debate and deep national division. Was it to make sure that the hard-won battles over the legislation of the 1960s were followed up with vigorous enforcement against racial and other forms of discrimination? Or was it to ensure that preferences be extended by law to those minorities, particularly blacks, who had suffered historical injustice?

In rejecting the latter definition, the Reagan administration was accused by its critics in the civil rights movement of undermining the very mission of the Civil Rights Commission. "Don't tell me that cuts in food stamps aren't a civil rights issue," argued Joseph Rauh Jr., a veteran of many civil rights battles, now serving as the general counsel of the Leadership Conference on Civil Rights. "Food stamps are a form of recompense for past discrimination against minorities, blacks, Hispanics, whose parents didn't get enough to eat, whose parents did not have the chance to grow and learn like white children. That is a racial issue."[16]

To the commission's critics, it had become a body guilty of conflating civil rights with interest group advocacy. Others objected to its intervention in issues beyond its mandate. One example they offered was the letter the commission sent to the president complaining that the administration was keeping the Equal Employment Opportunity Commission from taking a position in favor of racial quotas in a case involving the New Orleans Police Department.[17]

The first time Linda Chavez met Morris Abram was when the two, along with former San Jose State University President John Bunzel and Catholic University Law Professor Robert Destro, were brought together at a press conference in the Treaty Room of the Old Executive Office Building by President Reagan to announce their appointment to the Civil Rights Commission in May of 1983. All were registered Democrats.

Chavez had been assistant to American Federation of Teachers president Albert Shanker and editor of the federation's publications. Although she was offered a position on the commission, she opted to accept the vacant position of staff director. She knew that Abram was outspoken on the issues that had brought the two of them to the attention of the White House and "were bona fide liberals on many issues but were disturbed by the idea of race preferences."[18]

The appointments were made possible by the replacement of three of the most outspoken critics of the administration's civil rights record. In response to questions raised at the press conference about whether the administration was violating the commission's independence, Abram noted that the Carter administration had dropped its intention to appoint him to the commission when he informed officials of his opposition to racial quotas, a position that he agreed it had every right to take. He remarked, "I have not been asked with respect to this appointment what I may or may not do. And I will tell you this, I will follow the dictates of my conscience and the decisions of the Supreme Court."[19]

Catholic University Law professor Marshall Breger was a senior fellow at the conservative Heritage Foundation when he was asked to help prepare Morris Abram for his upcoming hearing before the Senate Judiciary Committee. He recalled, "I don't think anyone had anything against the other nominees. But he was the big one, you might say." Breger said that he tried to sensitize Abram to the political situation he faced, because "this was still when he was, how should I phrase this, crossing the aisle. That was a bigger deal than I think he quite realized, because he saw it as a matter of principle." They spent about three hours one day on potential lines of questioning, and one more hour the following day. "To me," Breger said, "he was an iconic legal hero. So, there's no doubt that when they asked me to prepare Morris Abram, I was a little, even in my arrogant youth, awestruck and humbled just by the thought of it."[20]

The question of the independence of the commission became the line of attack against the Reagan appointees when they came before the Senate Judiciary Committee for their confirmation hearing. The committee convened on the morning of July 13, 1983, in a spacious hearing room of the Dirksen Senate Office Building. The irony of Chairman J. Strom Thurmond, who built his lengthy political career in support of racial segregation, offering a warm welcome to one of the South's most tenacious fighters against the old system could easily have been lost on the audience about to witness a heated partisan battle. Of the many letters the committee received in support of the four nominees, the one Thurmond chose to read was a lengthy one from Rev. Martin Luther King Sr. in support of the Abram nomination. The letter read, "Morris Abram, from the time he arrived in Atlanta in 1948, was in the forefront of the public battle against racial discrimination. . . . I do not believe that any southern white people have had a longer experience in support of civil rights than Mr. Abram and whatever he does on the commission, he will do so on the basis of principle and conscience."[21]

This was followed by the oral statements of the three senators who had attended the hearing to speak in Abram's behalf: the two from his adopted state, Moynihan and D'Amato, and his longtime friend Henry Jackson. Pointing out that Abram stood in the tradition of Thurgood Marshall and Dr. Martin Luther King, Jackson quoted from a 1978 article the nominee had written for the *Atlanta Constitution*, in which he pointed out that the country cannot solve its problems by dividing Americans into competing ethnic and religious groups.[22]

The nominees received unqualified backing at the hearing from its first outside witness, the American Federation of Teachers' leader, Albert Shanker, who had been Chavez's boss at the union federation. Shanker, a foe of the Reagan administration on a host of issues, including civil rights, had fought against school systems in Boston and Jackson, Mississippi that had used racial quotas to determine teacher layoffs against the teacher federation's position that seniority was the only fair way to manage them.[23] In arguing for the Reagan nominees, Shanker characterized them as "Democrats of the JFK–Hubert Humphrey stripe with strong pro–civil rights positions." Pointing out that most Americans were opposed to racial quotas, he asked whether the Democratic Party was really going to make the support of them a litmus test.[24]

But at the hearing, the committee's Democrats were determined to fight the nominations not on the qualifications of the nominees or even directly on the question of racial preference. Rather, they contended that by replacing sitting commissioners with these appointments, President Reagan was undermining the independence of the commission. Senator Joseph Biden compared this action to President Roosevelt's plan to pack the Supreme Court with those who supported his policies. The Judiciary Committee's ranking Democrat Howard Metzenbaum remarked that up to this point, no president had sought "to chill the Commission's independent voice."[25]

What Linda Chavez thought most striking about the hearing was the unwillingness of those opposing all four nominees to acknowledge their records on civil rights and their genuine commitment to improving the social and economic conditions of blacks and other minorities. Dismissing the independence argument as "nonsense," she added,

> no, they really didn't want to admit that what they were really worried about was having someone like Morris Abram, who was in his own right a civil rights champion, who had been there early in the civil rights movement in the sixties and marching alongside other great figures. They didn't want a person with those credentials to come in and question the scheme in place at the time which was frankly to be lazy about trying to improve conditions for African Americans by simply imposing preferences, if not outright quotas, in college admissions. I just thought they were very disingenuous.[26]

Abram himself was not an uncritical supporter of the Reagan administration's record on civil rights. He criticized it for not getting behind the extension of the Voting Rights Act and for favoring restoration of the tax-exempt status of Bob Jones University, a segregated institution. He said that on some issues such as these, the administration had "shot itself in the foot."[27]

But to appointee Robert Destro, who would become a swing vote on the commission on some issues,

> the idea was, you guys are taking one of our institutions. I was only thirty-two at the time, but when you bring in someone like Morris, and Bunzel, and add them to [black conservative chairman] Clarence Pendleton, all of a sudden you get a major threat to the normal way of looking at things The whole idea was that anyone like Morris who had been in this from the beginning was somehow anti-civil rights, I mean he and the civil rights establishment didn't get along, but this was much more establishment versus interloper.[28]

Letters of support for Abram's nomination came from other important civil rights figures from his past. While taking the opportunity to criticize the Reagan administration for mishandling the nominating process, Bayard Rustin wrote, "Morris Abram's credentials in the struggle for civil rights need not be defended, for they are written with bold letters into American history."[29]

Others whose experience with Abram dated back to his early days in Atlanta were equally emphatic. Grace Towns Hamilton pointed out that "For the thirty-five years I have known Morris Abram, he has not varied in his principles. He believes in human equality and he practiced his beliefs when very few southern whites surfaced in our struggle."[30] And according to Charles Weltner, one of only a handful of Southern congressmen to vote for the Civil Rights Act of 1964 and now a justice of the Georgia Supreme Court, "How soon some people forget how it was down here twenty years ago. The idea that Morris Abram's appointment would frustrate the work of the commission is ridiculous."[31]

The committee also received supportive letters from two prominent liberals, former Supreme Court Justice Arthur Goldberg and longtime ACLU leader Charles Morgan Jr. Noting that for three decades Abram had struggled to obtain the rights for all to be subjected to equal justice, Morgan pointed out that "unlike some of his critics, he has done that in tough times and hard places, without fear and hope of reward." Noting that he had differed with Abram on a number of issues, including racial preference and school busing, he wrote, "these differences of opinion are insignificant when compared with our areas of agreement, and the president has the right to select those who agree with him."[32]

The national Jewish "defense" organizations were generally supportive of the nominees, the most enthusiastic among them the Anti-Defamation League (ADL), a strong critic of racial quotas. National director Nathan Perlmutter charged that "behind the assaults on the president's nominations, racial quotas and mandatory busing are being presented as a litmus test, a latter-day loyalty oath to determine one's fealty to civil rights."[33]

An exception was the United American Hebrew Congregations, the congregational arm of Reform Judaism in North America, which opposed the nominations, claiming they undermined the independence and integrity of the commission. Two years later, the Reform movement's chief lobbyist in Washington, Rabbi David Saperstein, told the NAACP's national convention that his million member organization's position on affirmative action was in sync with that of the NAACP. "It's cruelly unfair," he remarked, "to measure the entire Jewish community by the Morris Abrams and the Ed Koches."[34]

Shortly after the nominations were announced, Ralph Neas, executive director of the Leadership Conference on Civil Rights, released a statement opposing all the nominees. The statement was signed by the vast majority of member organizations, including the NAACP, AFL-CIO, ACLU, National Urban League, and League of Women Voters. Although the main reason cited was the independence issue, one of the founders of the conference said that the focus on that issue did not mean that many of the mainstream civil rights organizations were not also concerned with the nominees themselves and their opposition to affirmative action programs and court-ordered busing.[35]

In a letter to Neas, the ADL's Perlmutter wrote, "What concerns me, beyond this casting of a shadow over Morris Abram's reputation, is the seeming questioning of one's devotion to civil rights if that person opposes the quota system. Your statement as carried did not comment on this, but in the shrill chorus of criticism of the president's action, support for the quota system would seem to be the litmus test—an ironic 'loyalty test'—for being considered as pro civil rights. This, of course, is demagogic and hypocritical."[36] The most extreme reaction in opposition to the nominees came from the NAACP's executive director Benjamin Hooks: "I don't know how we could have any more incompetent people anywhere in this nation, unless they openly wore Ku Klux Klan robes."[37]

Regarding the nominee himself, Andrew Young, now the mayor of Atlanta, denied that Abram had ever been directly involved in the civil rights movement. He told reporters that Abram had gotten Martin Luther King Jr. out of jail "on a traffic ticket," adding, "it didn't require a great deal of courage."[38] Julian Bond wrote, "But, did Morris Abram get Martin Luther King Jr. out of jail? Whether he did or didn't matters less today than whether his supporters believe that questionable credential overshadows Abram's opposition to legal and time-tested remedies for racial discrimination. Even if [the account] is true, the decent acts of yesterday cannot excuse hostility to civil rights today."[39]

In his testimony before the committee, Abram summed up his civil rights creed in one phrase, to which he said he hoped to die faithful: "Equal opportunity for all, with no guaranteed results for any." He refused to believe that the country should proceed with proportionate representation in education and the workforce, as well as in the medical and legal professions, an idea rejected only recently by Justice Thurgood Marshall in a case involving discrimination against women with respect to financial annuities.[40]

Later in the hearing Abram elaborated on his position on racial and ethnic preference. One problem with the concept of proportional representation, he said, is that it is entirely divorced from the pool of talent. The reason our nation has flourished is that "we have permitted people who are immigrants and who are underprivileged to come forth in this nation of free enterprise and freedom, to flower."

And while his Georgia background made him particularly sensitive to the fact that many require assistance, need, not color or some other classification, should determine how that assistance is provided.

He continued, "The only reason, Mr. Chairman, that an America of such diverse creeds has not been torn apart by religious strife, as in Ireland and countries of the Middle East, is because the government is neutral on this question of religion. If government continues on a path of being unneutral as to jobs and food, on the basis of blood, can't you see how we will be at each other's throats?"[41]

The fight over President Reagan's dismissal of commissioners continued into the fall and threatened the renewal of the commission's authorization to operate. Just before its statutory expiration date, a compromise was reached between the White House and the Senate that restored two of the three dismissed commissioners by splitting the appointment between the administration and the Congress. The president was given the selection of the chairman, vice-chairman, and staff director with the consent not of the Senate but rather a majority of commissioners. Reagan reappointed black conservative Clarence Pendleton as chairman and for the other two slots selected Morris Abram and Linda Chavez, respectively. Mary Frances Berry and Blandina Cardenas Ramirez were brought back to the commission by the Senate and House Democratic leadership, respectively.[42]

But civil rights activists alleged they were double-crossed when congressional Republicans failed to renominate the two Republican women, supporters of affirmative action programs, they believed were part of the compromise. Throughout the remainder of the Reagan administration they continued to charge that the commission had lost its independence by lining up with the administration on such hot topic issues as busing and racial preference.[43]

Chavez's goal as staff director was to restore the commission's dual roles of overseeing federal civil rights programs and producing studies to guide public policy on matters related to race, ethnicity, and gender. For example, she initiated studies of social and economic indicators for blacks to try to explain why there were still disparities. She noted that the previous commission would look at the aggregate numbers and say there's a gap in earnings, there's a gap in education, so it must be the result of discrimination. "We tried to do a better job of disaggregating the numbers while looking at all the factors that went into determining such things as wages."[44]

The two commissioners Chavez worked most closely with were Abram and John Bunzel, both of whom she would speak to about the commission's work on a regular basis. She found Abram easy to work with, notable given the fact that "he was such a powerful alpha male personality."[45] Chavez was particularly proud of the commission's work on "comparable worth," an issue raised by those who contend that gender discrimination is the principal cause of the disparity in the earnings of men and women. Bunzel had been reluctant to see the commission take on this hot button issue, but the staff director found a strong ally in Abram. He played the role of getting his colleague not to object to the study, which Chavez said he was able to do because the two of them had a strong peer relationship as former college presidents: "Morris was very willing to play that role, which you sort of think of him coming in and wanting to take over. He was, of course, the vice-chairman, but Clarence Pendleton was the chairman. And he didn't seem to have a problem with that, which I thought was remarkable for a man of his stature."[46]

The issue of comparable worth had not been on commissioner Robert Destro's radar screen. The midwestern son of a policeman, Destro was much more interested in the question of comparable police protection. Acknowledging discrimination in the workplace, he saw the issue of comparable worth as one fraught with danger to trade unions: "If you're telling me a bunch of pointy-headed intellectuals should decide what jobs are worth in the workplace, you're going to destroy the unions."[47]

According to Destro, comparable worth is a form of affirmative action. "And Morris went after it the way he normally did." In a *New York Times* op-ed Abram warned of dangers ahead if the country went down the path of equating jobs "that have entirely different market values."[48] Abram pointed out that the wage gap narrowed when other factors, such as schooling, education, marital status, and job choice were taken into consideration. By putting wage and salary decisions in the hands of bureaucrats and other "experts," any deviations would result in lawsuits where employers would bear the burden of proof. And many women would suffer, since by raising wages in jobs to non-market levels, employers would seek ways to eliminate them through automation.

Abram left himself open to criticism through his provocative observation that comparable worth marked a departure from the civil rights revolution by moving us "from the assertion of civil and political equality, which we all support, to economic and social equality, which many of us do not support." It was not until the next sentence that he clarified the statement to mean "guaranteed" equality, which negatively impacts freedom "by making government the arbiter of the rewards of human effort."[49]

The response from the leadership of the Congressional Caucus for Women's Issues was scathing. Congresswomen Patricia Schroeder and Olympia Snowe wrote that the "shameful" statement by the vice-chairman of the U.S. Commission on Civil Rights had revealed the commission's agenda on this and other issues "with disgraceful clarity." They declared his comment that many Americans do not support economic and social equality as "utterly backward and entirely unsupportable," an observation that "flies in the face of our nation's history and its aspirations." Quoting President Reagan's most recent state of the union address that minorities would not have full power until they had full economic power, they said that for once, the Civil Rights Commissioner was taking a position independent of the president.[50]

The reconstituted commission continued to draw controversy as it tried, in the words of its vice-chairman, to replace polemics with serious academic work in determining the causes of inequality among blacks, whites, and other groups. Abram said the new commissioners favored what he called "a fair shake" for individuals as opposed to preferences for particular groups in order to foster equality of results.

In a statement issued by the commission in February 1985, Chairman Pendleton and Vice-Chairman Abram called upon the civil rights community to acknowledge the difference between what they called "nondiscriminatory" affirmative action and racial preferences, whether called a quota or a goal. A competing statement was issued by the two commission holdovers from the Carter administration, Berry and Cardenas, who contended that "civil rights laws were not passed to give civil rights protection to all Americans," but rather "out of a recognition that some Americans already had protection because they belong to a favored group; and others, including blacks, Hispanics, and women of all races, did not because they belonged to disfavored groups." Abram told the *New York Times* that, by contrast, a majority of the commission disagreed with this perception, believing that civil rights laws were meant to apply to all Americans.[51]

Abram expanded on his opposition to both quotas and goals in employment in a 1984 debate with Berry published in the Bureau of National Research's Employee Relations Weekly. Quotas and goals, he wrote, share the same root—namely, the mistaken assumption that the qualifications for any given job are distributed identically among groups, with the conclusion that each group must be represented proportionately in that job.[52] By contrast, he pointed favorably to a decision in a class action lawsuit brought in the Northern District of Georgia charging a trucking company with discrimination in which the court granted an injunction against the disparate treatment of women (*Kilgo v. Bowman*). In his opinion Judge Marvin Shoob rejected the plaintiffs' request for goals and quotas, requiring instead a detailed plan to prevent discrimination, the removal of all barriers impeding the hiring of women, and outreach and recruitment that included training and counseling programs to qualify them. The court ruled that "Preferential treatment on the grounds of sex, by means of a quota, is destructive of self-respect and merely substitutes one form of discrimination for another."[53]

All the major civil rights groups scheduled to testify before the Civil Rights Commission's two-day consultation and hearing on affirmative action the first week of March 1985 pulled out, claiming its majority had already made up its mind.[54] Abram continued to pay a personal price for his outspoken views, telling a *New York Times* reporter that old friendships had chilled over honest political differences, something for which he grieved. His longtime friend Vernon Jordan, whom he had called "my brother in every confidence and dream" in a major address a decade earlier, declared the reconstituted commission "useless." Because it had violated its historic mandate of independence, he said, it should be abolished.[55]

To Abram, his transformation from civil rights hero to civil rights villain over a period of two decades could be attributed to a misunderstanding of the difference in this country over the true meaning of the term. Abram believed that America's constitutional democracy was built not on the proposition that people are guaranteed a piece of the economic pie; rather, "it is up to each individual to compete for economic goods, constitutionally protected from interference by guarantees of equal protection under law, due process, the Bill of Rights, and most fundamentally, the ballot."[56] So, while society must provide for the poor or disadvantaged, there is no constitutional right to health care or housing subsidies, "any more than a farmer has a constitutional right to a tobacco subsidy or Chrysler a bailout."[57]

Abram believed that when economic and social goals became labelled "civil rights," the movement lost a measure of its moral force and therefore its unity. "Americans, who were persuaded to salute civil rights as they did the flag," he wrote, "were not willing to pledge allegiance to a certain level of food stamp spending."[58]

As for the argument that racial preferences were needed to compensate black citizens for past discrimination, he argued that the logic of that proposition would lead black voters to be rewarded additional votes or that white voter registration should be suspended until the proportion of registered blacks were equivalent to the number of registered whites.[59] The fact that no one would dare advocate such a measure demonstrated its absurdity. Abram's effectiveness in arguing the case against racial quotas was a function of not only his skills as an advocate but also the clarity and consistency of his argument. But just as his obligations as a lawyer complicated his pure commitment to principle in the case of *Lucido v. Cravath, Swain, and Moore* in the 1970s, another case emerged at the very end of the decade that raised questions about whether those principles had to give way to the imperatives of representing clients.

The controversy involved a massive housing project located near the poor black East New York section of Brooklyn. At the time, Starrett City was one of the largest subsidized housing projects in the country, with forty-six apartment buildings totaling nearly six thousand units. In an effort to maintain racial integration, the owners imposed a quota on black families applying for apartments in order to keep the project from "tipping" to a segregated community by being abandoned by white residents. Since the tipping point for white families was believed originally to be any number below 70 percent of occupancy, black families were placed on a waiting list until that level of white residency (eventually reduced to 65 percent) was reached.

When the quota was challenged at the end of 1979 under the Fair Housing Act of 1968 in a class action suit brought by the NAACP and other civil rights organizations on behalf of five black families waiting for a subsidized apartment, Starrett City engaged Morris Abram to defend it. In the spring of 1984, an agreement was reached between the corporation and the lawyers for the black families, along with the NAACP, which forced the alteration of racial rental policies in eighty-six projects subsidized by the state housing authority, affecting the residents of nearly seventy thousand apartments.[60]

Challenged to explain why he was defending a clearly race-conscious policy, Abram said that in addition to carrying out his obligation to his client, the policy was perfectly legitimate inasmuch as it was promulgated to achieve the objective of the Fair Housing Act, which was to achieve integrated housing. "No one can say that this project isn't superb," he said. "Nobody can suggest that it is anti-black. But if you're going to have integration, you have to respect the 'tipping' problem."[61] Abram said that the settlement the parties had agreed to "recognizes the need for a managed rent roll, managed occupancy, in order to preserve the principles of integration."[62]

Following the settlement, the Reagan Justice Department indicated its intention to bring a suit challenging the legality of the quota, one now supported not only by Abram but also by the NAACP and other civil rights groups. In a letter to his friend William Bradford Reynolds, the Department's civil rights chief, Abram argued that given the settlement agreement, it was not necessary for any court to determine what actions were authorized by the act. To Abram, the key points were not the difficult legal questions involved but rather the results of the policy. Why waste the scarce resources of the Civil

Rights Division, he argued, when as a result of the policy, "Starrett City is one of the nation's most successful, large integrated housing projects. For nearly ten years, persons of all races and a wide variety of ethnic groups have lived together in well-maintained moderate-low income housing built on a site reclaimed from a swamp and a garbage dump.... This progress should not be disrupted or disturbed."[63]

In response, Reynolds expressed his respect for the effort to resolve the dispute in a manner satisfactory to all the parties involved. But the fact remained that the Justice Department had a fundamental disagreement with Abram's interpretation of the act, the purpose of which was to prevent discrimination in housing on the basis of race. Discrimination to force a racial balance, Reynolds argued, was no more justified than one to force a racial imbalance.[64]

The lower courts agreed with the Justice Department's position. But Abram persisted. Although by 1988 he was in semi-retirement from his law firm and no longer the lead counsel on the case, Abram sought to sharpen his colleagues' petition to the Supreme Court for a hearing. He advised them to put up front the stark contrast between Reynolds's views and "what we know to be the purpose of the Act." He suggested the following language: "This petition for the writ asks the court to protect the largest, the most successful, integrated subsidized housing project in the United States from being turned into another large urban ghetto."[65] It was to no avail. The Supreme Court let the lower court decisions stand.

Not surprisingly, Abram came in for criticism from liberals who charged him with hypocrisy for his support of a discriminatory quota. According to the *New Republic*, Abram's defense of Starrett City "profoundly subverts the neo-conservative position on quotas." The *Village Voice* was less subtle, bestowing on Abram the "Let's Pull up the Ladder After I Get into the Lifeboat Award," which is "given to the New Yorker who does the most to diminish equal opportunity for blacks and Hispanics."[66]

Before he left the Civil Rights Commission in 1986, Abram contributed to a Harvard Law Review symposium on affirmative action in which he divided its two contrasting groups of advocates into "fair shakers" and "social engineers." While those in the former category believe that government should assure access to all spheres of public activity, be it social, economic, or political, those in the latter argue that it is the role of government to ensure that minorities are represented in all institutions and occupations in proportion to their percentage in the population, the absence of which would be proof of past and/or present discrimination.[67]

The first social engineers with whom Abram said he came into contact were those who devised the county unit system in his native state of Georgia. They justified assigning disproportionate power to rural interests in much the same way as their modern counterparts, arguing that they lacked not only the benefits of good schools, libraries, health services, and so forth, as in places like Atlanta, but also the potential power of the city's voting blocs. Of course, those earlier engineers had more in mind than boosting the fortunes of rural voters, knowing that by dominating state politics, they could maintain the segregationist system they were able to do locally through intimidation.

Abram wrote that these early experiences made him wary of those advocating "code-colored group rights" and other substantive notions of justice inconsistent with the equality of everyone before the law. "The role of securing racial justice," he came to believe, was best limited to "vigilant concern with equal opportunity, procedural regularity, and fair treatment of the individual."[68]

Abram debunked the notion that all unequal results must be the result of discrimination. The idea of advocating for proportionality in occupations, repudiated as far back as the nineteenth century by none other than the preeminent black leader Frederick Douglass, ignores the fact, he pointed out, that minority groups (as well as majorities, he might have added), "do not necessarily have the same distribution of, among other characteristics, skills, interest, motivation, and age."[69]

Abram cited the pronouncements of Justice William Douglas and constitutional scholar Alexander Bickel to debunk the idea that the U.S. Constitution can accommodate a color-conscious interpretation. In the case of *DeFunis v. Odegaard*, a forerunner of the *Bakke* case, Douglas noted that the Equal Protection clause of the Fourteenth Amendment "commands elimination of racial barriers, not their creation, in order to satisfy our theory as to how society should be organized." And to Bickel, "The great decisions of the Supreme Court and the lesson of contemporary history have been the same for at least a generation: discrimination on the basis of race is illegal, immoral, unconstitutional, inherently wrong, and destructive of democratic society."[70]

Returning to a theme he had written about a decade earlier and that Senator Jackson cited in his support for his nomination to the Civil Rights Commission, Abram noted the potential destructiveness of policies championed by the new social engineers to American society itself. Noting that this country is a highly pluralistic one where many have suffered discrimination, "how and by whom shall the varying grievances of different groups be weighed and judged in order to decide what varying levels of compensation society should pay?" Quoting Professor Paul Brest in a 1976 *Harvard Law Review* article reviewing the history of the anti-discrimination principle, most societies allocating power according to race and ethnicity "are strikingly oppressive, unequal, and unstable." And in the ultimate irony, color-conscious policies have done, in the words of Harvard sociologist Nathan Glazer, "just about nothing" to improve the progress of black Americans.[71]

Finally, Abram turned to the current debate over the very definition of civil rights, the way it was being waged, and his own role as someone who was being written out of the very movement in which he played a key role. The reason the civil rights movement triumphed, he said, was because it had a broad-based appeal to the American people who in the end acknowledged the justice of equal opportunity for all. In turning traditional civil rights to redistributionist rights, large segments of the civil rights lobby have made support for those policies a precondition for being part of the movement, and losing the support of many of those, black and white, "who sustained the movement from the outset." Abram ended the article by appealing to social engineers to refrain from masking their redistributionist goals as civil rights, since such rights belong to everyone, and are too important "to be captured by a set of special interests."[72]

The *Harvard Law Review* article represented a valedictory for

Abram's long career in the struggle for civil rights. That year he submitted his resignation to President Reagan as vice-chairman of the U.S. Commission on Civil Rights, writing that he believed the civil rights movement "should return to first principles—the zealous regard for equal opportunity and the promotion of colorblind law and social policy."[73] In a letter to his daughter Ann in February 2000, one month before his death, he told her he would never forget those days, "when the entire civil rights establishment appeared to praise me and then opposed my appointment to the Civil Rights Commission because I did not favor racial preferences."[74] By the mid-1980s Abram had already turned to a larger stage, returning to the cause of international human rights that would command his attention for the remainder of his life.

TWELVE

Leadership

There was something about Morris that was Jewish royalty.

The morning of December 6, 1987, could have been any typical Sunday on the National Mall in Washington DC, the sun burning through the freezing chill of an early winter day. But as the busloads of people began to arrive by the tens of thousands, it was clear that this day would be different, for it marked the climax of an international struggle that had begun two and a half decades earlier.

Morris Abram looked out over the crowd of nearly a quarter of a million people who had come from every region of the country to rally on behalf of those Elie Wiesel had famously called the "Jews of Silence" when he visited with them in the Soviet Union in the early 1960s. Abram had been skeptical when the idea of a mass rally was proposed to him by Natan Sharansky that summer. Believing that a large crowd could not be guaranteed, Abram had recommended instead the idea of bringing one hundred senators to the steps of the U.S. Capitol Building to greet Soviet leader Gorbachev with the declaration, "Let our people go!"[1]

As chairman of the principal organizing group of the Freedom Sunday rally, the National Conference on Soviet Jewry (NCSJ), as well as chairman of the Conference of Presidents of Major American Jewish Organizations, Abram opened the proceedings by reading a welcoming letter from President Reagan, whose highly anticipated meeting with Soviet leader Gorbachev the following day had been the impetus for organizing the demonstration. Speakers included Vice President Bush, civil rights hero John Lewis, and Wiesel himself, who contrasted the lively rally with that tragic period during the 1930s when the cries of Jews in peril went virtually unheeded.

And then it was time for the day's real celebrities: the refuseniks on whose behalf many in the crowd had devoted years of activism to get released: Sharansky, Nudel, Begun, Slepak, and Mendelevich. The latter had disrupted a Solidarity Day rally in New York earlier that year, voicing his anger at Abram for what he regarded as his and other American leaders' naivete in dealing with the Russians. But today, Mendelevich was willing to lock arms not only with his fellow refuseniks but also with Abram himself and join in the singing of Hatikvah, the national anthem of the Jewish state of Israel.[2]

For Morris Abram, the March for Soviet Jewry and its successful aftermath marked the culmination of a personal odyssey that began in a rural southern town and brought him to the pinnacle of the American Jewish community. The previous year he had been elevated to chair the Conference of Presidents, the principal umbrella group of the largest Jewish community in the world outside of Israel.

When Abram left Fitzgerald, Georgia, for the University of Georgia at age sixteen, he had entertained thoughts of becoming a rabbi, despite his lack of the most rudimentary Jewish education. And though he was quickly disabused of the idea, the experience a little over a decade later of spending a summer during his Rhodes Scholarship working with the American prosecuting team on the Nuremberg Trials had marked a major turning point in his life. "I would never be the same after Nuremburg," he wrote, "for I now understood that the veneer of civilization is thin, and that when it cracks, even in the twentieth century, the Jew is a first victim." As his involvement in the Jewish community grew, he recalled, "I found the essence of what it meant to me to be Jewish. That essence lies in the collective unconscious of the people from whom I spring; the linkage of ourselves one to another; the ties that we all feel, to a greater or lesser extent, to Zion; and the determination to survive as Jews, free men and women wherever we may live."[3]

Abram was delighted with the demonstration, describing it as "the largest gathering in Jewish history since Moses led the Jews out of Egypt" and remarking at a press conference afterward that the rally would enable the president to offer it as evidence in his meeting with Gorbachev of the deep commitment of the American people to human rights.[4] Still, he was not optimistic about the long-term outlook for Jewish emigration, regarding the release of the most well-known refuseniks as a ploy to improve the atmosphere of the meeting between the two presidents. On the eve of the meeting, he told a reporter that "we will feel the summit has failed if it does not make significant headway on human rights."[5]

Richard Schifter, who was the Reagan administration's point person on human rights, recalled what happened the next day, as told to him by one of the interpreters in the room where the summit took place:

> As soon as the meeting started the niceties had been taken care of, Reagan immediately said, "You know, there was this gathering in Washington on the issue of the refuseniks." And Gorbachev said, "Yes, I heard about it." And Reagan continued to talk about the emigration issue. Gorbachev wanted to move on to arms control. For about five minutes, I was told, Reagan stayed with the emigration question, told the Soviet leader how important it was to the American people, how important it was to the relationship between the U.S. and the Soviet Union, and how it needed to be resolved. And from then on emigration numbers really started moving.[6]

By the end of the 1980s, the large majority of Soviet Jews applying to emigrate were being permitted to do so.

When he was tapped to chair the National Conference three years earlier, Abram was no Johnny-come-lately to the cause of Soviet Jewry. After exposing Soviet antisemitism at the United Nations in February 1962, Abram, in his capacity as president of the American Jewish Committee, chaired the first major gathering of Jewish organizations to develop a public campaign on behalf of the Jews of the Soviet Union. Over two days in early April 1964, a packed crowd of over six hundred representatives from twenty-five sponsoring organizations at the famed Willard Hotel in Washington DC heard

addresses by Associate Supreme Court Justice Goldberg and Senators Ribicoff and Javits before getting down to the business of establishing the American Jewish Conference on Soviet Jewry (AJCSJ).
The conference would serve as a coordinating body of national and
local Jewish agencies, whose purpose was to mobilize public opinion into a worldwide force to expose "the deprivations, denials, and
oppressions to which the Jews of Russia are subjected" and to save
the Jewish community from "spiritual annihilation."[7]

The following year Abram shared a platform at one of the first U.S.
rallies for Soviet Jewry with a star-studded cast that included Senator
Robert Kennedy and labor and civil rights leader A. Philip Randolph.
He roused the crowd of twenty thousand at New York's Madison
Square Garden by telling them that until the Kremlin stopped discriminating against Soviet Jews or allowed them to emigrate, "we
shall protest, we shall march, we shall overcome."[8]

Less than a month after the establishment of the AJCSJ, a massive demonstration was held in front of the Soviet UN Mission in
New York, heralding the creation of the Student Struggle for Soviet
Jewry (SSSJ). By the early 1970s, The SSSJ had been joined by two
national organizations, the grassroots Union of Councils for Soviet
Jewry (UCSJ) and the National Conference on Soviet Jewry (NCSJ),
both of whose sole mission was to advocate on behalf of Soviet Jews.
The National Conference was a successor to the AJCSJ, consisting
of a coalition of local community relations councils and national
Jewish agencies.

From the beginning of the Soviet Jewry movement, the Israeli
government had been a key influence in the development of the
American Jewish community's organized effort. Israel regarded the
rescue of Jews behind the Iron Curtain not only as part of its sacred
mission as a Jewish state but also a potential demographic prize in
maintaining its democratic majority. During the 1950s it had established a secret operation known internally as the "Lishkat HaKeshar,"
or Liaison Bureau, that included a presence based in New York.[9]

During most of the 1970s, Shulamit Bahat, a former Captain in
the Israeli Defense Force and later an AJC official, headed the efforts
on American and Canadian university campuses on behalf of the

Israeli Students Organization, which became deeply involved in the Soviet Jewry movement. (The group's representative at MIT was a graduate student named Ben Nitay, who now calls himself Benjamin Netanyahu.) Bahat remembered an important demonstration the group organized at the UN on behalf of the cause in 1970: "Morris was there and of course he spoke. I saw him not as Morris, but as Moses. He had that aura about him. One of the most articulate speakers I have ever heard, in the same league as Abba Eban. When people hear a Southern accent, the speaker isn't usually considered intellectual, but when Morris opened his mouth, you knew you were standing next to a real orator."[10]

In New York, the Greater New York Conference on Soviet Jewry, under the leadership of Malcolm Hoenlein, a former student struggle activist from Philadelphia, became an important bridge between the young activists and the more established Jewish organizations.[11] Hoenlein said it was during that period that he first met Morris Abram. Given Abram's background on issues related to international human rights advocacy, it was only logical to turn to him for advice. "I know I looked at him with awe during that period," recalled Hoenlein, who became the longtime executive director of the Conference of Presidents of Major American Jewish Organizations in September 1986, the same month Abram became its chairman. "I would call on him if we had a legal forum, if we had anything where we needed that voice, with the recollections of the Nuremburg trials, the lessons of war crimes charges."[12]

Another Jewish leader who looked up to Abram was Jerry Goodman. Goodman, who became a leading spokesman on Soviet Jewry issues while serving as the NCSJ's executive director from its formative period in the early 1970s through most of the following decade, had met Abram after joining the staff of the American Jewish Committee out of graduate school in 1963, the year Abram was named its youngest ever national president.

When he approached Abram to serve as the NCSJ chairman two decades later, he knew he didn't have a significant position at that time in the Jewish world. And when he proposed his name to the board, they were quite aware of his track record on these issues and unanimously agreed.[13] According to Goodman, "Morris was very articulate and effective. He worked very closely with the Israeli operation that supervised Soviet Jewry. He developed a close tie with the Reagan administration. If we had to give testimony before a congressional committee, it was certainly better to have Morris B. Abram than Jerry Goodman testify. Clearly, his name was much more significant."[14]

But it was not only his name that mattered. Mark Talisman, who was the chief Washington lobbyist for the Council of Jewish Federations during that period, noted that "Morris was a much sought-after witness on the Hill. To have the head of a major organization who didn't need his staff sitting next to him whispering answers was a real find [for committee staff]. They knew he would be fully prepared and could handle questions on his own."[15]

The Soviet Jewry movement was notoriously split during those years. In addition to NCSJ, there was the Union of Councils for Soviet Jewry, composed of local organizations deeply committed to the cause; the National Jewish Community Relations Advisory Council (NJCRAC), a coalition of local Jewish federations dealing with issues across the board, including Soviet Jewry; and the pioneers of the movement, the Student Struggle for Soviet Jewry, some of whose members would turn to militant tactics to make their case.

Some of the fractures were over tactics, with the Union of Councils taking the position that the freeing of Soviet Jews could be achieved only by the application of relentless pressure from grassroots activists. By contrast, the more establishment National Conference led by Abram preferred diplomatic efforts to enlist the support of the Reagan administration and the State Department.[16]

Mark Levin, who later ascended to the leadership of both the NCSJ and, after the demise of the Soviet Union, its successor organization, saw Abram as a consensus builder who could effectively bring together the disparate elements that comprised the National Conference. He strongly believes the five years of Abram's chairmanship of the NCSJ were the most important for both the movement and the organization. "I've always believed that had Morris not been chairman during those years, it's not certain what type of organization we would have become, or even whether there would have been an organization at all." According to Levin, "because of the ways he could identify and articulate the mission of the organization, our credibility was so much greater when he became the chairman. Through those five years we became the voice in the U.S. and beyond on issues related to Soviet Jewry."[17]

Abram's chairmanship of the National Conference coincided with his selection to serve as vice-chair of the U.S. Civil Rights Commission by President Reagan, and he was able to parlay his increasingly friendly relations with the Republican administration in Washington with his work on Soviet Jewry and eventually the whole range of issues he faced as chairman of the Conference of Presidents. According to Levin, "The fact that Morris could pick up the phone and speak to the secretary of state, could arrange to meet the president, and almost anyone else in the federal government provided us more avenues to pursue our mission."

Levin recalls the first time Abram met as NCSJ chairman with Secretary of State George Shultz, who listened to him outline the challenges and what was needed from the U.S. government. "You could see there was an immediate connection." For his part, Shultz talked about leverage, what the U.S. government could leverage to try to get the Soviets to move.[18] In an interview with the former secretary of state, Shultz recounted how the Soviet Jewry issue was very much on the minds of the Jewish groups he met with both in the United States and abroad during his period as secretary of state. He struck up a personal friendship with Abram, with whom he exchanged ideas and to whom he would report following each trip to Moscow.[19]

Abram credited Shultz with placing the Soviet Jewry issue high on the list of administration priorities in his numerous meetings with Soviet foreign minister Eduard Shevardnadze, putting it even ahead of arms control. For his part, Shultz considered Abram his "rabbi," adding, "You might say he has taken me by the hand and led me around. . . . He is very gentle, and sort of suggests you do this and that."[20]

The agenda for the series of summits held between Reagan and Gorbachev in Geneva, Reykjavik, Washington, and Moscow encompassed the broad areas of détente, disarmament, and human rights. Included among the latter were issues related to emigration and the granting of cultural and religious rights for Soviet Jews.

Prior to the first meeting, which took place in 1985, the White House held a briefing for individuals and groups with interests in the Soviet Union. During a brief presentation, Abram raised the question of trust. As Abram saw it, many Americans wondered how they could trust a Soviet signature on a document related to nuclear disarmament when it had disregarded the provisions of the Helsinki accords it had signed guaranteeing emigration rights to its citizens. The president responded that he would convey that message to his summit partner. But the administration did not stop there. As Fred Lazin notes, the issue of emigration became a consistent agenda item not only at subsequent summit meetings but also in exchanges between U.S. officials and their Soviet counterparts.[21]

Herbert Teitelbaum, Abram's son-in-law who had assisted him during the Ford Hall crisis at Brandeis, became involved in the Soviet Jewry movement at the time he was involved in litigation against the Soviet travel agency Intourist. Now a New York–based civil rights lawyer, he believes that Abram's most lasting contribution to the movement was the credibility he brought to his work with the administration in Washington. This included his role in getting President Reagan to deliver a list of refuseniks to Soviet Chairman Gorbachev during their 1986 summit in Reykjavik. This was significant, since considerable progress was made behind the scenes of that meeting on how the two countries would deal with human rights issues.[22]

As Jerry Goodman put it, "We knew that in the end, to protect the status of Soviet Jews, the U.S. government had to be involved. And [Abram] was quite effective in helping us do that. Without the U.S. government, we could never have done it. We could stand there and protest all we liked, but it had to have some action quotient. And that quotient came in part with Morris."[23]

Abram said, in the early part of 1987, "I want to say this as strongly as I can, Soviet Jewry is not going to be freed by some internal Massada uprising among Soviet Jews to break their chains. It is not going to be freed by a sudden change of heart and change of direction of the Soviet state, a kind of disruption or coup." Only by the pressure of a great power, namely, the United States, he argued, would the desired result be achieved.[24]

Prior to the Reykjavik Summit in October 1986, Abram went to see President Reagan along with the refusenik Yuri Orlov. After the meeting, Reagan's national security advisor, John Poindexter, took him aside and asked for the names of the eleven thousand refuseniks he told the president he had. At a subsequent meeting Secretary of State Shultz told a large group of Jewish leaders that the administration was prepared to link its policies to this issue. Shultz asked Abram to prepare a graph substantiating his organization's assertion that there were three hundred and seventy thousand Jews who had not had their exit applications processed.[25]

In March 1987, ignoring his own assertion just months earlier that the liberation of Soviet Jewry depended upon the actions of the U.S. government alone, Abram was persuaded by Edgar Bronfman, the billionaire tycoon who headed the World Jewish Congress, to fly with him to Moscow to negotiate directly with the Soviets, an effort many in the movement thought ill-advised. Bronfman, whose business interests in Russia gave him access to the Kremlin, believed the time was right for direct negotiations at a time when emigration numbers were beginning to rise under the Gorbachev regime. Bronfman needed the legitimacy Abram's presence would give his mission.[26]

When they returned from three days of talks with Soviet officials, Abram told a *New York Times* reporter that authorities would soon permit a major increase in Jewish emigration in the form of direct flights through Romania, along with an improvement in religious education and practice. While he and Bronfman expressed caution, saying that they would await actual performance before declaring the glasnost policy real and inclusive of Jews, Abram said he had told Soviet officials that if Jewish emigration increased substantially, he and his colleagues would advocate a repeal of the two congressional amendments linking trade benefits to emigration.[27] Abram clarified his remarks about the amendments the next day, saying he had only suggested considering waivers for the time being based on a very substantial and sustained level of emigration.[28]

In the end, the mission accomplished very little beyond igniting controversy inside the movement, with both refuseniks and grassroots activists who had not been consulted in advance joining in the criticism, regarding the effort as both arrogant and naïve.[29] Moreover, the deals Abram and Bronfman were discussing on direct flights to Israel would violate the principle that émigrés should have freedom of choice on where to settle after gaining permission to leave, an issue that had been the source of tension between the Israeli government and U.S. grassroots advocates. By the summer, Abram came to regret the trip, doubting that Gorbachev's policy of glasnost would provide any significant benefit to Soviet Jews.

In October 1987 President Reagan announced that the Soviet leader would be arriving in Washington for talks with him in early December. According to David Harris, who organized the December rally, "we had only 36 or 37 days to plan the entire march because we had only that much notice that President Gorbachev would be coming to Washington and meeting with President Reagan on December 7. Where Morris was particularly helpful was his amazing network of relationships at the highest levels. Where we had to reach someone as a speaker or a resource and had to go through a battery of secretaries, we could turn to Morris Abram and he could go right to the top pretty quickly."[30]

Abram's close relationship with the Reagan administration had not developed overnight. On the day after seeing the president at a gathering of Jewish leaders at the Plaza Hotel in New York in 1984, Abram had written to him praising his denunciation of the UN's "Zionism is Racism" resolution to the group. He encouraged the president to use his bully pulpit to make a forceful public statement on this matter "which would meet with resounding public approval and put to shame those who will not respond to your moral affirmation." He added that as far as he knew, no Democratic presidential candidate in this election year had addressed the issue.[31]

When a controversy erupted the following year over the president's plan to make a ceremonial visit to a military cemetery in Bitburg, Germany, to commemorate the fortieth anniversary of the end of World War II, Abram went to the opinion pages of the *New*

York Times to defend the administration against charges that it was indifferent to the feelings of the Jewish community. While the president should have asked himself whether it was right to pay respects at the venue of the graves of nearly two thousand Nazi soldiers, including forty-nine SS troops, Abram wrote, he asked fellow Jews to consider the administration's overall record, including military cooperation with Israel that placed it in the front ranks of America's allies, its use of the U.S. Air Force to rescue Ethiopian Jews, and its demands at every high-level summit that Soviet Jews be allowed to emigrate. "Bitburg," he contended, "was the mistake of a friend, not the sin of an enemy."[32]

Abram's increasingly close relationship with the Reagan administration could not have been far from the minds of those advocating his chairmanship of the Conference of Presidents of Major American Jewish Organizations when a vacancy occurred in 1986. The Conference, composed of a cross-section of American-Jewish organizations, seeks to build consensus on issues of concern to the Jewish community that facilitates communications between the community and U.S. ambassadors. According to Abraham Foxman, the longtime national director of the Anti-Defamation League, "We were looking for leadership. I mean the community was starving."[33] The problem for those promoting Abram for chairmanship of the conference was that the organization he chaired was not a member. Thus, the only way that Abram could qualify to become its chairman was to admit the organization he chaired into it as a full member. "And we did," Foxman says, "and it was done quickly."

According to Foxman, "I know it was important for us because he provided a dimension of leadership and respect. He had to work his way in. I believe he was the first one the community recruited. He was a towering figure, respected, articulate, and he took us beyond Jewish issues. I think that made a big difference. He gave respect to the community being known so well outside it."[34] According to Billy Keyserling, who served as the Washington director of NCSJ during Abram's chairmanship before building a successful career in South Carolina politics, "I didn't know many people who didn't respect him from a substance point of view. . . . The Jewish community thought that with Morris Abram doing their bidding in Washington they were in pretty good shape."[35]

The beginning of Abram's chairmanship of the Conference of Presidents in the fall of 1986 coincided with the beginning of the tenure of Malcolm Hoenlein as its executive vice-chairman. Hoenlein had met Abram during his graduate school days and later, as noted, during the early days of the Soviet Jewry movement. Over the next three years, working closely on issues of major concern to the American Jewish community, they developed a particularly close relationship. As Hoenlein said, "I really loved him very much. I learned a lot from him. He had tremendous humility despite the status he enjoyed. There wasn't an issue that he didn't go into a meeting and you knew you were going to come out all right. Even if we didn't win our points, everyone gave him a fair hearing and I learned a lot about how you present and how you do certain things."

According to Hoenlein, "He would never brook any criticism of me without standing up for me. He would tell U.S. presidents, this is the guy you must deal with. We went together to see presidents and others. And having Morris there you knew you had your back stop for sure." Hoenlein noted that he was blessed with highly talented chairmen during his lengthy tenure. "And I say that all of them would agree that there was something about Morris that was Jewish royalty."[36]

Hoenlein recalled that his early tenure as executive director marked the formative years of the conference. His plan was, working closely with Abram, to refocus it to make it more activist in scope. What Abram could give the conference was what it most needed: credibility and stature.

As Hoenlein recalled, "He wasn't a billionaire. He didn't come in with a flashy presence. He wasn't a guy who showed off who he was. His quiet and powerful dignity, the respect that he earned from across the spectrum, I think he enabled us to start off this new phase of the conference."[37] Hoenlein continued, "His role was uniquely important, and we had a lot of support. Other past chairmen of the conference and current presidents [of constituent organizations] really rallied and helped, but all Morris had to do was ask. He could always make the case." Despite broad ideological differences among member organizations, "you could see that Morris was always able to sway them."[38] Mark Talisman called Abram "one of the most natural mediators I have ever known." His southern manner, lawyerly ability, and economical use of language enabled him to consistently win over the other side.[39]

According to Hoenlein, Abram's skill as an advocate and his long involvement in civil rights issues gave him credibility in many different communities with which the conference dealt. Hoenlein remembered occasional black-Jewish tensions that were addressed quietly. "Morris's record was clear. The majority of our chairmen have been lawyers. It does help in terms of advocacy, but I think Morris with that quiet southern drawl, he wasn't an aggressive advocate, he was much more laid back. But that didn't make him less effective and if he got angry, you saw a fire there, a spitfire that was very strong."[40]

Talisman, a veteran of Capitol Hill, noted how effectively he operated in that environment. "When I'd take him with a group of Jewish leaders to the Rayburn [House Office] Building," he recalled, "he could win over the congressman in a matter of minutes. He would get right to the point. He was the kind of guy who in his own quiet way would end up dominating the conversation." Talisman said that Abram would be the one person who could elicit a conversation about the next steps that needed to be taken. "In a room full of people, many of whom had something to say, he was the one the member or staffer would turn to at the end and ask for his card. That's when you knew it was a done deal."[41]

Not all who worked with Abram during that period were awed by his talents or reluctant to criticize his missteps. Alan Dershowitz recalls his clash with Abram over the latter's defense of the American Bar Association (ABA) in its efforts to develop a relationship with its Soviet counterpart. "I was very critical of the American Bar Association for having very friendly dealings with the Soviet Union at a time when the Soviet Union was discriminating against Jews. Morris attacked me for attacking the American Bar Association because he was an American Bar Association type." Dershowitz says that Abram was angered when the Harvard professor walked out of an

ABA meeting over the issue of Soviet Jewry, adding, "I took a very different approach."[42]

In May 1985 the ABA entered into a cooperative agreement with the Association of Soviet Lawyers (ASL). The debate over the pact intensified the following June when the agreement was strengthened to include exchanges, joint seminars, and statements that both organizations respected the rule of law.[43] Dershowitz was alerted to the ABA's growing outreach to the Association of Soviet lawyers by his refusenik client Natan Sharansky, who had been released from the Soviet Union earlier that year. To Sharansky, the ASL was no more than "a front for the Soviet system of repression" and such an effort to legitimize this official body would create problems for the few independent lawyers with the courage to operate in that environment.[44]

Shortly after the ABA's policy making body rejected a resolution to terminate the agreement in August 1986, Abram, writing as chairman of NCSJ and the Conference of Presidents, defended its action in an op-ed he wrote for the *New York Times*. While acknowledging the ASL's lack of independence and its spreading of "vicious libels" against human rights advocates, including Jews, Abram thought it was important to develop ties to the only Soviet lawyers group "to whom American lawyers could protest the denial of adequate legal procedures for dissidents, refuseniks, and human rights advocates in the Soviet Union and press the Soviet Union on that denial."[45]

Abram believed the relationship offered the potential to educate prominent Americans about Soviet realities and to be effective monitors of Soviet compliance with the Helsinki Accords. But early the following year, in an exchange with Dershowitz over the issue organized by *Moment* magazine, he acknowledged the failure of the exchanges with Soviets—not just with the ASL, but more broadly in the numerous ones that had been agreed to at the summit in Geneva. He blamed these failures on the unwillingness of American participants to challenge their interlocutors.[46]

In his support for the ABA agreement with the Soviet lawyers, Abram was by no means alone. While the American Jewish community was split, the government of Israel was supportive of engaging with the ASL. The head of the Israel Bar Association met with his ASL counterpart on four separate occasions, deeming them "the only chance we have to influence the Soviets."[47]

Abram's ties to Israel had begun to develop during his presidency of the American Jewish Committee in the mid- to late-1960s, highlighted by the rally he addressed in Lafayette Park during the Six-Day War. Those ties only strengthened over time. In 1978 Abram debated the Lebanese-born academic Fouad Ajami on the PBS program "The Advocates" on the question of self-determination for the Palestinians in the context of a Middle East peace settlement. To Abram, the term self-determination, one with a "superficial moralistic appeal," in this case meant nothing less than "a Soviet armed, PLO radical state in the heart of the Middle East." In addition to being unjust, Abram opposed the granting of self-determination to the Palestinians on the grounds that it would be dangerous not only to Israel but also to America and to the peace of the world itself "for which we all pray."[48]

To former Undersecretary of State George Ball, an expert witness supporting self-determination who advocated a UN force to be deployed during an interim period while full self-determination was being implemented, Abram reminded the audience of the disastrous failures of such forces in the region in the past. And to Ball's assertion that terrorism is simply a response to military occupation, Abram pointed out that PLO-sponsored terrorism had taken place within Israel's pre-1967 borders. As Robert W. Tucker of Johns Hopkins remarked under questioning from Abram, terrorism would not stop under a Palestinian state, since states can be their own directors of terrorist acts.[49]

In 1982 the PLO was set to collect on a $30,000 bequest from an eccentric American journalist named Fred Sparks who had died the previous year. Representing the American Jewish Congress, the Anti-Defamation League, and the World Jewish Congress, Abram sought to block the bequest, claiming that compensating a terrorist organization was a violation of public policy. The New York Civil Liberties Organization filed an *amicus* brief in which it argued that a denial would chill the rights of political organizations, to which Abram replied, "It is farcical to describe this band of gangsters as a 'political organization.'" A settlement was reached two years later when the parties signed off on an agreement to donate the money to the International Red Cross to improve the living conditions of the Palestinian people. The three organizations expressed their gratitude that the funds would be used for humanitarian purposes rather than to support terrorist activities.[50]

Wearing his Conference of Presidents and Soviet Jewry hats during the 1980s, Abram's direct contacts with Israel's leadership increased, and both Malcolm Hoenlein and the NCSJ's Jerry Goodman were impressed with his ability to deal with Israel's leaders on an equal footing. According to Hoenlein, "We met with prime ministers and Morris was the only guy I knew who could communicate criticism and everyone would listen and take it seriously, not be resentful. And he loved Israel."[51] To Goodman, Abram's strength was in his extraordinary self-confidence. "He never felt inferior to a Shimon Peres or a Yitzhak Rabin. He dealt with them as equals."[52]

Abram's ability to find the right balance between unequivocal public support for Israel and tough talk to its leadership when called for was tested following the sentencing of American Jonathan Pollard for spying on behalf of the Jewish state in March 1987. Fearing a U.S. backlash against Israel in the aftermath of the incident, American Jewish organizations were harsh in their condemnation of Pollard, with many, including Abram, even supporting his unprecedented life sentence for passing military secrets to an ally.

Jewish leadership was particularly alarmed when the Israeli government promoted two individuals who had been implicated in the incident. A Conference of Presidents delegation led by Abram, Hoenlein, and AIPAC president Robert Asher traveled to Israel in March 1987 to meet with the country's leaders in a trip that had been planned prior to the Pollard episode. In a press conference held in Jerusalem, Abram remarked that Israel had made a serious error in promoting one of Pollard's handlers to a top military position and the other to head a state-run company. Abram called these appointments "a grievous matter" and "a very deep wound that needs to be addressed."[53]

Still, Abram voiced strong confidence in Israel's ability to investigate the matter effectively. He predicted that in the end the episode would amount to no more than a "bump on the road" in the history of strong relations between the United States. and Israel.[54] To Abram, the highlight of the mission was witnessing the flyby of the Lavi, the highly sophisticated Israel-produced, U.S.-funded fighter jet. The delegation was then flown to an airbase in the northern part of the country and witnessed the arrival of six advanced American F-16s, the first batch of seventy-five such planes the United States sent to Israel as part of the strategic cooperation between the two countries.

For Abram, this was "an unforgettable example of friendship between America and Israel and between the air forces of the two countries. When our American airmen flew over the base in these jets, landed one by one and turned over the planes to their Israeli counterparts," he reported, "these were moments that will long remain with me, and I believe with all those who witnessed this spectacular and living example of U.S.-Israel cooperation."[55]

Chairmen of the Conference of Presidents traditionally serve a two-year term. In Abram's case, the term was extended for an additional half year as the date for selecting his successor was moved forward. Although this was done for technical reasons, "everyone," according to Malcolm Hoenlein, "wanted to have him as long as possible."[56]

To one of his former law partners at Paul, Weiss, Abram was "one of my true heroes." Why? Was it his courtroom abilities, his dedication to clients, his oratorical skills? Max Gitter said, "There's a phrase in Yiddish; it's actually in English as well. It's really a term of art; the term is 'a good Jew.' And a good Jew doesn't mean an observant Jew. It's a person who is an advocate for Jews. And a good person. And a good person for Jews and for everybody else. If I had to write a book about Morris Abram I would describe him simply as a good Jew."[57]

By the time his term at the Conference of Presidents had expired, a new administration had taken over in Washington, and it wasn't long before President George H. W. Bush was calling on Abram to resume his public service. It had been over two decades since he had been appointed by President Johnson to represent the United States at the United Nation's Human Rights Commission. The new assignment, as the Permanent U.S. Representative to the European Office of the UN, would require him to move to Geneva, Switzerland. It was there that Morris Abram entered the final chapter of his life.

THIRTEEN

Back to the United Nations

What are you doing that's good for the world?

On January 24, 1989, four days after George H. W. Bush was inaugurated as the forty-first president of the United States, he held a dinner at the White House in honor of Javier Perez de Cuellar, the secretary-general of the United Nations, and his wife Marcella. From the incoming administration the dinner list included Secretary of State James Baker, Chief of Staff John Sununu, and National Security Adviser Brent Scowcroft. Among others on the list were World Bank president Barber Conable, *Washington Post* Editorial Page editor Meg Greenfield, and Senators Robert Dole and George Mitchell. Morris Abram and his daughter Ruth were also in attendance.[1]

One week later, the president appointed Abram to serve as the U.S. ambassador to the European Headquarters of the United Nations in Geneva, Switzerland. Abram, who had recently stepped down as chairman of both the National Conference on Soviet Jewry and the Conference of Presidents of Major American Jewish Organizations, said that his two main priorities as ambassador would be human rights and health.[2] Abram's familiarity with the inner workings of the United Nations and its subsidiary bodies dated back to his UN service during the Kennedy and Johnson administrations. But his views about the organization had become soured by the reality of its more recent record. Following the General Assembly's 1975 resolution equating Zionism with racism, Abram headed up the Ad Hoc

Group on the United Nations, which consisted of academic experts who studied the institution's actions. The group's first report issued the following year expressed its disenchantment "with the publicized behavior which had undermined the institutional capacity of the UN system to deal in an impartial and effective manner with questions of world concern."[3]

In his lecture at Columbia University on the thirtieth anniversary of the adoption of the UN Declaration of Human Rights, Abram harshly criticized the "Alice in Wonderland World" that the United Nations had become. Abram remarked, "Today, the General Assembly, often specialized agencies and sometimes even the secretariat, act as if the overpowering evils affecting mankind were a free press, Apartheid, Arab refugees, and Zionism." He criticized decolonized states that defended repressive policies by blaming their former colonial masters and deplored the creation of a propaganda unit within the UN to advance the agenda of the Palestine Liberation Organization (PLO). "Nothing has been more destructive of the UN's good name and reputation for integrity than the conferring of unprecedented status and resources upon a group whose terrorist acts are feared by innocents throughout the world and even in Arab states."

According to Abram, at the same time they were conferring legitimacy on the PLO, the UN and its human rights bodies were turning their backs on victims of persecution, most recently the boat people fleeing Vietnam. He compared this betrayal to how these bodies "have historically turned their backs on whole nations held in bondage of which they are periodically reminded when the spark of freedom flares, as in Hungary in 1956 and Czechoslovakia in 1968."[4]

Four years later the Ad Hoc Group issued its second report entitled "The United States and the United Nations . . . A Policy for Today." While stressing that "our interdependent world needs the UN, and the principles enunciated in its charter," and that it continues to be in the American interest to use the UN as a significant foreign policy forum, the group urged that the United States be prepared to act alone or with others outside the UN in light of deterioration in the capacity of the world organization to deal impartially and effectively with questions of world concern. "The UN system, with some good works in the cause of peace, economic and social betterment and human rights, also reflects—and occasionally aggravates—the dangerous international environment in which the U.S. finds itself." UN activity, the report asserted, has been increasingly marked by "political behavior and a tyranny of the majority that keeps it from functioning effectively in accord with the purposes enunciated in the UN Charter."

Concerning the work of the UN's human rights bodies, the report said that they still have a long way to go in correcting the "selective morality" that concentrates on violations in a few countries only and ignores others. "Neither authoritarian nor totalitarian regimes," it declared, "should be permitted to subscribe formally to international human rights standards while violating them in practice." The experts urged that the United States consider not attending or withholding financial support from specialized agencies or functional conferences whose purposes it has found—after careful examination, explanation, and warning—to be seriously compromised by the injection of extraneous political issues. The report carried the endorsement of Henry Cabot Lodge, chief delegate under President Eisenhower, and former Secretaries of State Rusk, Vance, and Muskie.[5]

Confirmed by the Senate during the spring of 1989, Abram, now with ambassadorial rank, took up his position as head of the U.S. Mission in Geneva in early May. The mission oversaw U.S. participation in a large array of UN operations, encompassing six specialized agencies, including the World Health Organization and the International Labor Organization, and an equal number of subsidiary bodies, including the UN High Commissioner for Refugees and the UN Conference on Trade and Development.

Abram's predecessors as head of the U.S. mission in Geneva were Gerald Carmen, a businessman whose previous role in the Reagan administration had been as head of the General Services Administration, and Joseph Petrone, a retired Army colonel. According to California attorney David Schwarz, who was Abram's assistant at the mission during the first half of his tenure, by appointing someone with his background and interests, the Bush administration was sending a strong message that human rights would be a top priority for the mission.

Following an administration that placed such a strong emphasis on the issue, this was significant. Schwarz said, "When you have a President like George H. W. Bush come in the question is, are we going to move in a more realpolitik world where the advances made in terms of the human rights agenda are going to take on less significance? I would say that alone, the fact that a guy who cared deeply about these issues was appointed was an important signal."[6] The signal to the diplomatic community was that under Abram's leadership, the United States was placing an emphasis even greater than the previous administration on the work of the UN Commission on Human Rights.

Much of the energy of the U.S. delegation to the commission during Abram's period as ambassador was devoted to promoting resolutions geared toward targeted countries, particularly Cuba, Iran, and China. But it also included fighting off the sustained efforts of the commission's member states to condemn the Jewish state of Israel. During Abram's tenure, Arab countries joined in an effort to elevate the status of the Palestine Liberation Organization (PLO). This was true not only at the commission but also at the other specialized UN agencies and bodies based in Geneva, where the organization and its allies saw opportunities to use the back door to elevate the PLO's position.

Abram's efforts to push back against these maneuvers received strong backing from the U.S. State Department. The official he reported to at the department was John Bolton, then the Assistant Secretary overseeing U.S. participation in international organizations. Bolton and Abram were very much on the same page with respect to Israel and the PLO. In 1991, following a concerted effort on the part of the Bush administration, the UN General Assembly repealed its sixteen-year-old resolution declaring Zionism a form of racism. In congressional testimony eight years later, Abram gave the credit to his former State Department boss. "Without John Bolton in the position he was in," he told a House committee, "there would have been no repeal of the 'Zionism is Racism' resolution."[7]

Abram was highly respected by his staff at the Geneva mission. According to his political counselor Anne Patterson, who later became an ambassador herself to four countries, including Pakistan and Egypt, "He was universally admired. I just don't know any other way to put it. Everyone had a great respect for his intellect and his work ethic and there wasn't anyone who didn't find it an honor to be working for him."[8]

Schwarz saw the efforts Abram and his colleagues at the mission were compelled to exert to prevent the UN from taking harmful actions as ultimately a source of frustration for him. "I think anyone who's dealing with the UN in that setting," he said,

> is going to feel that you're in a defensive crouch and have a palpable sense of an institution that's failed. It's hard for an optimist, an agent of change which Morris was, to devote a lot of energy to a rear-guard action which was a lot of what we did. How do we bar the PLO? How do we stop the 28th resolution against Israel? That's not the kind of thing that would drive a man like that who wanted to accomplish something good as opposed to keeping something really bad from happening.

Abram's view, according to Anne Patterson, was that "the UN had an opportunity to do a transformational job and they were just blowing it."[9] In response to a letter he received from an American academic doing research on U.S. human rights policy, Abram expressed pride that his country publishes an annual survey of human rights policies of countries around the world, even though it often caused considerable harm to U.S. bilateral relationships. This was something he had challenged other countries and regional groupings to do as well, since "we neither claim to have a monopoly or copyright in the field."

While no country is perfect, he wrote, "and certainly not ours," Abram believed it commendable that the United States was willing "to call the shots as we see them on friend and foe alike." This he contrasted with the UN Human Rights Commission, where weeks were spent on Israel and South Africa, while other parts of Africa, "in which human rights are massively violated," as well as Asia and the Arab world, were exempted from criticism.[10]

Following the 1992 presidential election, Abram sent a memorandum to the State Department Transition Team outlining the mission's responsibilities and recent activities. The latter included its success in defeating an "inappropriate" Arab call for a special session of the Human Rights Commission to discuss the situation in the West Bank and Gaza. But not all achievements were of a defensive nature, and he was able to report some notable successes, including the U.S.-led effort to convene the first ever special session of the commission to take up the increasingly grave situation in the former Yugoslavia. The session appointed recently retired Polish prime minister Tadeusz Mazowiecki as special rapporteur, who traveled twice to the war-torn area and issued four reports on human rights violations that were passed on to the Security Council.[11]

Abram's memorandum to the transition team called for U.S. efforts to reform the Human Rights Commission. As Abram pointed out, members such as Iran, Iraq, and Libya sit in judgment of other states as if "those in the dock are sitting on the jury." In addition, the agenda and program of the body were in need of reform, since they were dominated by attention to Apartheid and the Occupied Territories to the exclusion of examining human rights violators such as China.

Within a year of Abram's move to Geneva he met Bruna Molina, an Italian-born human rights lawyer, twenty-two years his junior, who was serving on the staff of Ian Martenson, the UN's under secretary-general responsible for Human Rights, Disarmament, and the Office in Geneva. Abram had needed a female companion for gender balance at a dinner he was organizing in honor of Edgar Bronfman and had tasked a member of his staff to make the choice. The Israeli publication *Maariv* described Molina, a divorcée with two teenage children, as "tall, slim, elegant, and self-assured." The two married during the summer of 1990 in Abram's summer cottage in Dennis Village, Massachusetts, on Cape Cod.[12]

Abram lived the remainder of his life with Molina in Geneva. Their summers were spent on the northern shore of Cape Cod in the eighteenth-century house he once shared with his second wife, Carlyn. He remained associated with Paul, Weiss in an "of counsel" capacity and stayed in touch with former colleagues throughout the decade. His international orientation was best captured by the recollection of his former law partner Max Gitter: "When Morris came back to the firm during the nineties to visit his former colleagues," he recalled, "he never inquired about specific cases we were working on. Rather, he would ask, 'What are you doing that's good for the world?' That was a wonderful thing, and it captured Morris."[13]

Upon the conclusion of his four-year tenure as U.S. ambassador, Abram reflected on the UN's role in the promotion and protection of human rights. He regarded the UN Charter adopted in 1945 as a landmark in international treaties in affirming the dignity and worth of the human person, going far beyond the Covenant of the League of Nations and the post–World War I treaties referring to the rights of minorities in the newly created states.[14] Although the most recent period marked "some advancement," he observed, it also involved "much stagnation and even a reversion of some human rights practices." Abram identified several defects in the human rights apparatus, resulting from "political compromises, poor personnel practices, improper oversight, and the reluctance to restructure organs and procedures to meet conditions that have dramatically changed over the past half century."[15]

To Abram, the UN human rights system faced four essential challenges. The first was the attempt of some states to undermine the notion of the universality of human rights by making their application subject to cultural or historical differences between societies. Despots, he said, will argue that "Western" norms are unfairly used to judge non-Western people. Such arguments reflect "the contempt of dictators for a single standard of justice," and when those in the West seeking "politically correct" approval of such particularisms as African socialism or Islamic democracy, "they are simply demonstrating their reluctance to confront authoritarian regimes."[16]

The second challenge to the human rights system, Abram noted, was the elevation of social and economic rights, the latter including the oft-mentioned claim of a right to development, to the status of civil and political rights such as those enumerated in the U.S. Bill of Rights and the French Declaration of the Rights of Man. Abram contrasted worthy goals, such as reducing inequalities among nations, which require compromise, to rights that are absolute. Raising goals like development to the status of rights, Abram argued, is detrimental to both.[17] Since the inception of the UN's human rights system, it had been weakened by states seeking narrow political objectives. Such politicization, Abram contended, constituted a third major challenge to that system, insofar as it undermined its legitimacy, universality, and effectiveness.

Much of this politicization took the form of a continuous focus by the UN Human Rights Commission on only two countries: South Africa and Israel. While these two agenda items were taking up fully one-third of the commission's time, the human rights abuses of neighboring countries were virtually ignored. And as the racist apartheid system in South Africa was being dismantled, the democratic state of Israel remained the sole country on whom the commission's attention was obsessively concentrated. In 1991, Israel was the object of thirty-two negative UN resolutions. To the extent that the other democracies do not come to Israel's defense, Abram argued, the UN as a whole becomes corrupted by its own weakness, "in a way that a judge will eventually become corrupted if he permits corruption in his own courtroom."[18]

The fourth challenge Abram identified for the UN's human rights system is the building of democracy. He believed this to be the most critical challenge, since the acceptance of universally accepted human rights standards depends on "a world in which more and more states are founded on the moral authority and consent of the governed." Quoting the eighteenth-century British statesman Edmund Burke that democratic development depends upon a tradition of moderation, Abram believed that this reality portended a long wait for the goals of the UN Charter to be realized. "Still," he noted, "there is no other instrument, no other hope, in which to invest our energies than the UN system."[19]

Following the termination of his official duties as U.S. Representative in early 1993, Abram resumed his advocacy, but this time not in any formal sense on behalf of his country but rather in the service of longstanding convictions. According to David Harris, when Abram became the founding chairman of UN Watch, his vision was guided by the fact that, "'Here I have been in Geneva four years as U.S. Ambassador and how is it possible that even I, a well-informed, well-educated, well-read American and Jew had almost no idea what was going on here pretty much behind everyone's back? Only as ambassador did I discover the degree to which anti-Israelism, anti-Zionism, and sometimes anti-Semitism, are part of the main menu. And because there is such little media coverage in Geneva, it becomes a dirty dark little secret among secretariat officials serving in Geneva.'"[20]

Eric Block, a corporate lawyer in Toronto who spent a year working with Abram at UN Watch following his ambassadorship, concurs with Harris's assessment. "Morris believed that anti-Zionism, in the forms it was being talked about at the UN, was indistinguishable from anti-Semitism. And he felt it deeply." Block added,

> Think about it from his perspective. Morris could have gone back to Paul, Weiss or done something else with the remaining years of his life. But here was a guy who really was committed to Israel. And it came from his experience in Geneva. He wasn't Israel's ambassador; he was the U.S. ambassador. But because the function of the U.S. ambassador in Geneva was to deal with all these human rights issues, what caught his eye and his heart the most was how it really was an organization that was dedicated to pounding Israel.[21]

UN Watch had its origin in a conference sponsored by the World Jewish Congress (WJC) on antisemitism in Europe following the fall of Communism. It was held in Brussels in July 1992, toward the end of Abram's term in Geneva. Jonathan Cohen, who was working for the human rights organization Freedom House in Europe, was hired by WJC president Edgar Bronfman to organize the conference.

The gathering attracted representatives from Jewish communities around the world and was addressed by heads of state and senior Vatican officials. With Abram's assistance, Cohen recruited a panel to discuss the role of the United Nations in shaping the human rights agenda and fomenting antisemitism, which turned out to be the conference highlight. Chaired by the Harvard literature professor and essayist Ruth Wisse, the panel included former U.S. UN representative Jean Kirkpatrick, Canadian human rights lawyer Irwin Cotler, and Abram. According to Cohen, the panel brought home to conference participants the extent to which the UN's human rights apparatus had become obsessed with Israel, producing in the process vicious antisemitic statements and resolutions while managing to ignore genuine human rights crises in countries that often sat in judgment of the Jewish state. The panel offered some corrective measures that needed to be taken in response.[22]

By the fall of 1992 Cohen was working full-time for Seagram's, the company headed by Bronfman, where he was handling special projects related to his boss' philanthropic activities. Building upon the ideas that emerged from the Brussels panel on the UN, Cohen submitted a proposal to Bronfman to provide funding for a nongovernmental organization located in Geneva to monitor the UN's human rights apparatus, primarily the Commission on Human Rights. Bronfman agreed to fund the first year of UN Watch, provided it became a formal part of the World Jewish Congress and that the effort was led from Geneva by Morris Abram. Bronfman had cemented his friendship with Abram during their trip to the Soviet Union on Bronfman's plane in the spring of 1987. According to Cohen, "Edgar was not an intellectual, but he was intellectually curious, and he had great respect for writers and thinkers, particularly if they were also men and women of action and influence. And if you flew on Edgar's private plane, you became his friend. That was an important, formative trip for Edgar, a touchstone, really, in his career as a Jewish leader."[23]

Abram readily accepted the offer to serve as the organization's chairman. The WJC agreed to provide an office and staff, including an executive director, a secretary, fellows, and interns. In addition, it provided a housing subsidy to enable Abram and Bruna to live comfortably in Geneva after he left his post as ambassador. To Abram, it was important that the NGO play an activist role. As Anne Patterson notes, "I think what he thought, not to put words in his mouth, was that a lot of this NGO stuff at the UN was just namby-pamby, and he wanted an NGO that would take a position, be more aggressive."[24]

The organization was able to recruit a prestigious international board that included European and American thinkers and activists such as Per Ahlmark from Sweden, Father Stanislaw Musial from Poland, AFL-CIO chief Lane Kirkland, and former UN Ambassador

Jean Kirkpatrick. Also sitting on the board were major Jewish phil-anthropic and community leaders, including Edmund Safra, Nes-sim Gaon, David Wollach, and Branco Weiss.

Foreign Policy editor Jonathan Tepperman recalled that when he began his fellowship, he questioned the whole mission of UN Watch. "I had felt going into the job," he said, "that Jews who complained about Israel's mistreatment at the United Nations were generally crying wolf and were trying to use the anti-Semitism card to explain what in my mind at the time was justified criticism of Israel." The rea-son he felt this way was because he had no idea of "how bad things actually were at the UN. It was an incredibly eye-opening experi-ence to discover the scandalous treatment that Israel was receiving at the UN at the time."[25]

The hostility toward Israel spilled over into the perception of UN Watch on the part of Geneva's large NGO community, much of which regarded its staff as "Zionist lackeys," and according to Tep-perman, were shunned in that community. He recalled a meeting dealing with human rights issues when, following an intervention he contributed, he was called a "Judeo-Nazi" by the representative of a Quaker organization.[26]

One of the first victories of UN Watch was getting the Human Rights Commission to place the issue of antisemitism on its agenda. This was the same battle Abram had fought as the U.S. expert on the Sub-Commission for the Prevention of Discrimination and Protec-tion of Minorities thirty-two years earlier, when he was thwarted by the Soviets and their UN allies.

On March 9, 1994, for the first time in its history, a UN entity offi-cially condemned the world's oldest and most historically destructive form of bigotry. The commission voted to instruct its chief investi-gator of acts of racism to include anti-Jewish incidents and discrim-inatory behavior in his annual reports to the body, which in turn would ask governments to respond to these charges.

This unprecedented inclusion of actions against Jews in a UN reso-lution represented a personal victory for Abram. The U.S. delegation had agreed to help bring the resolution to a vote, but only if intro-duced by another country. Through Abram's behind-the-scenes lobbying, Turkey agreed to include the language on antisemitism in a routine resolution it was introducing condemning racism.[27]

Michael Colson, who served as executive director of UN Watch from 1997 to 2001 recalled a conversation with an Israeli diplomat who had served as his country's ambassador to the Geneva office of the UN during Abram's tenure in the corresponding role. Once your term ends, the diplomat told Colson, the former ambassador becomes irrelevant.[28] But Abram proved to be an exception. Working mostly out of his apartment with a tiny number of aides, as Tepperman noted, "Morris managed to act and project the aura as if he was still running the U.S. embassy with all of this staff or was still a senior partner at Paul, Weiss with an army of associates and assistants."[29]

Many saw Abram's post-ambassadorial activism as a violation of precedent and protocol, which dictate that a retired ambassador leaves the place where he was posted or at least does not steal the spotlight from his successor. In Abram's case, not only did he remain in Geneva, he made use of his previous status to benefit the organization he chaired. Shortly after he began his tenure at UN Watch, Abram hired a former technical writer for a digital equipment company, Hannah Gaywood, as his executive secretary. According to Gaywood, Abram had unusually broad access to UN officials, the diplomatic community, and the Geneva authorities. When a friend with a high-level position with the Federation of the Red Cross and Red Crescent reported to her that no NGO was allowed admission to an important conference, she recalled, "I only smiled. Morris, of course, was there."[30]

In a letter to supporters in May 1995, Abram noted that he had better access to high-level UN officials as the chairman of UN Watch than he did as U.S. ambassador. He speculated that the courteous treatment he and his staff received could be explained by the fact that these officials were unaware of his organization's agenda or what it intended to write afterward. He also noted that one assistant secretary-general who was aware of what the group was up to had advised his staff "to behave with caution and to remember they were being watched by us."[31]

Not all the meetings he scheduled were friendly. During one

with the director-general of the UN Conference on Trade and Development—Colson can't remember the specific issue—but "the guy started to really yell at me. He admonished me. I can't recall what the reason was. And we came out and I said, 'Morris, did I overstep?' And he said, 'Michael, that shows we're having an impact.' He was thrilled. Of course, he said, 'he can't yell at me, so he's going to yell at you. Keep it up!'"[32]

According to Gaywood, "Morris was very respected but also feared in Geneva, especially in UN circles. I had known it when I worked with him and it has been confirmed by UN officials here. He would not remain silent in a single conference, commission, committee, or UN Day that mattered for the cause." His outspokenness was often resented by the objects of his criticism. Colson recalled a tense meeting between Abram and UN High Commissioner for Human Rights Mary Robinson, a frequent critic of Israel, in which she complained that he had spared no opportunity to undermine her work.[33]

Abram's success in maintaining his influence in Geneva after stepping down as U.S. ambassador was at least in part attributable to the frequent dinners he and Bruna hosted at their apartment at 56 Quai-Gustave Ador. On these occasions, Abram would bring together a group of a dozen or so that included ambassadors representing diverse countries, heads of UN agencies, and European business leaders, and which might also include one or two visiting journalists or officials. For example, the director of the European Broadcast Authority and the head of the Telecommunications Union might be invited to meet with a visiting broadcast official.

Colson remembers looking out the window of the Abrams's apartment and seeing the large lineup of diplomatic cars with the drivers standing alongside and thinking how unheard of it was for someone in no official capacity to have that kind of pull. He imagined that new ambassadors were told by their predecessors that these dinners were worth attending. And why not? The high-level group would be relatively small, consisting of ambassadors and other notables they would want to be in touch with; there would be interesting visitors; and they would also meet agency heads in a comfortable environment. Guests would include ambassadors from countries that did not recognize Israel. For example, Colson recalled dinners that included the ambassador of Malaysia, with whom he and Abram held several meetings.[34] UN Watch was, by and large, regarded as a pro-Israel NGO, though its mandate included human rights more broadly. According to Colson, "We never fully resolved the question, are we a pro-Israel NGO that does other stuff as well, or are we an NGO that is focusing on Israel as a case study of broader issues? That was the tension in the organization."[35]

During Block's year as a fellow at UN Watch, the organization carried out a study of women in the UN, both how they were underemployed and how they were mistreated in various parts of the organization, "some of which is only coming to more light now." Block said that this and other studies gave the organization legitimacy, "and frankly they showed we weren't just a one-trick pony."[36]

The organization's impact was not easy to measure. "Certainly, we got attention," Block said, "and I know the U.S. newspapers were now more attuned to the fact that the UN Human Rights Commission was a bit of a gong show. And ironic, in that the President of Syria or Libya or whoever would be chairing these things on the anti-Israel days, while their own human rights record was abhorrent. But those days continue apace today."[37]

An Egyptian expert sitting on the committee overseeing the convention on racial discrimination once expressed in open session his respect for the French communist Roger Garaudy, whose book *The Founding Myths of Modern Israel* denies the Holocaust. When Abram and Colson paid him a visit, the expert said that they were objecting to his comments "because you're Jews." When they took their complaint to the Egyptian Ambassador, a heated confrontation ensued, ending in a plea by the ambassador, "Morris, I'm speaking to you as a friend, stop this!" At that point, Colson says, they knew they had touched a nerve, which Colson considered a success for the organization. A public campaign by UN Watch exposing the expert's comments about Garaudy ensued, which "made people in those committees more careful of what they said."[38]

According to Cohen, who served as a consultant to UN Watch during its formative years, Abram and Colson "developed a sensibility, an approach for how to stand up in human rights councils and counter the kinds of crazy things that were being said, in addition to putting human rights rapporteurs in the hot seat and holding them to account for biased reporting on matters in Gaza and the West Bank. And this is where the model that [executive director] Hillel Neuer has taken to such heights in my opinion really was forged."[39]

Edgar Bronfman was supplying nearly half of the UN Watch annual budget during its initial years as well as providing it with space in the offices of the World Jewish Congress. But the affiliation rested primarily on Bronfman's personal relationship with Abram, and by the latter part of the 1990s the organization decided that it was time to terminate the partnership. Abram's search for a new partner brought him back to the American Jewish Committee, the organization in which he had begun his earliest tie to the Jewish world.

Negotiations for the transfer of UN Watch began in the late 1990s while Abram was still alive. California attorney Bruce Ramer, who was then ACJ president, was involved in the negotiation that led to the incorporation of UN Watch into the organization. He recalled, "As we got more involved in talking to Morris and to UN Watch, it became clear that it was our kind of people, our kind of group, our kind of organization, our kind of goal."[40]

But there were individuals within the American Jewish Committee who were less enthusiastic about the organization taking on UN Watch and others who were flatly opposed. According to Felice Gaer, head of AJC's Blaustein Institute for the Advancement of Human Rights, a number of issues were raised among her colleagues. One had to do with the approach of the two organizations, whether engagement is a better way to bring about change than the "in your face" style of UN Watch. Another was the question of location. Some argued that Brussels would be a more strategic location, given what they considered the centrality of the European Union to the position of the Human Rights Commission on key issues, including the Palestinian question.

Others were concerned about Abram's reliability, whether what they regarded as his self-centeredness might lead him to promise one thing and do another. Gaer said that some of her colleagues were upset that a lifelong Democrat had switched and served as an ambassador in a Republican administration.[41] According to Jonathan Cohen, much of the opposition within the Blaustein Institute was based on a perception of UN Watch as a potential competitor both ideologically and institutionally.[42]

Nevertheless, the days of AJC taking an ambivalent attitude toward the Jewish state were over. When the first Bush administration indicated its support for repealing the Zionism is Racism resolution at the UN in the early 1990s, the committee was ready to make this goal a high priority.[43] By 1999, the negotiation to take over UN Watch had almost concluded, and Abram called upon David Harris shortly before his death in March 2000 to take over its chairmanship. That spring, Harris had a sabbatical scheduled and had signed up to teach at the Bologna, Italy campus of the Johns Hopkins' School of International Studies. "But I had pangs of guilt," he recalled. "In order to keep UN Watch alive, I took the chairmanship for a year, trying to keep Morris' legacy alive."[44]

In the summer of 1999, Morris Abram had a fall at his cottage in Dennis. Four years earlier he had returned from Geneva to Mt. Sinai Hospital, where he had been treated for leukemia two decades earlier, for heart surgery that involved four bypasses and a valve replacement. When Bruna had to leave to resume her work in Geneva, Hannah Gaywood traveled to Cape Cod to care for the increasingly frail Abram. When he went to Cape Cod for the last time, Bruna said, his major concern was how to keep UN Watch afloat financially. "And the American Jewish Committee came forward and offered financial support. And that was very important for him."[45]

Today, under the leadership of former AJC President Alfred Moses and Canadian lawyer Hillel Neuer, the watchdog group is entirely independent, participating at the UN as an accredited NGO in Special Consultative Status to the UN Economic and Social Council, and as an associate NGO to the UN Department of Public Information. True to Morris Abram's vision, it speaks out against the UN's unfair treatment of Israel and calls out dictatorial regimes that abuse their people's human rights in violation of the UN Charter and the Universal Declaration of Human Rights.

When he returned to Geneva in the fall of 1999, Abram resumed his lunch hour swims at the hotel La Reserve to rebuild his weakened muscles. At that point he was down to a single lap. But his frail condition did not stop him from travelling to the city where he achieved his early success as a civil rights lawyer to address the Anti-Defamation League that October. In that speech, Abram compared the UN's treatment of Israel with the treatment of blacks he recalled from living in the Jim Crow South: "Today, after a lifetime in UN affairs, I can say that the United Nations is a vital house, but it too is a house divided. It is divided not only by differences of opinion which is healthy, but by discrimination against Israel, much as the discrimination against blacks of which I have spoken tonight. Israel, the Jewish State, is treated as a pariah within the UN—a fact that we in the Jewish community know. And this treatment, wholly unacceptable, divides the world body and impairs its credibility."[46]

On December 12, 1999, the American Jewish Committee honored Morris Abram with its National Distinguished Leadership Award at the Plaza Hotel in New York. AJC invited UN Secretary-General Kofi Annan to deliver the keynote address. Shortly after the invitation was received, senior members of Annan's staff recommended that he turn down the invitation. Gillian Martin Sorensen, who served as assistant secretary-general for External Affairs, sent a memorandum to Annan noting that "Despite Morris Abram's long United Nations experience, and despite his frequent references to his close friendship with you, United Nations Watch has often been a diatribe [sic], unbalanced and unfair. In particular, it has vilified Mary Robinson. I am concerned that your presence at this dinner will not only bolster Mr. Abram personally but will enhance the stature of United Nations Watch." Sorensen, the wife of Abram's former law partner Theodore Sorensen, recommended that the secretary-general use the event "to address issues of importance to the United Nations and Jewish community with a temperate salute to Ambassador Abram," advice with which her colleague Mary Robinson noted her concurrence in writing.[47]

Rejecting this advice, Annan offered the keynote address at AJC's dinner that December. He described Abram as "a forceful advocate of freedom, who addresses the fate of Jews throughout the world, so they can live their lives without discrimination." U.S. ambassador to the UN Richard Holbrooke hailed Abram's deep commitment to the United Nations, that had pushed the organization "to put a higher priority on human rights."[48]

Morris and Bruna had planned to return to the United States to live following her retirement from her position in December. In February 2000 the two travelled to Israel, where she said, "He wanted to see everything."[49] The Abrams planned a dinner in Geneva for the evening of March 15, 2000, where the invited guest of honor was the outgoing president of the International Red Cross, prominent Swiss lawyer and diplomat Cornelio Sommaruga. But that morning, Abram was taken to the hospital with an intestinal infection. His staff avoided canceling the dinner, since they believed Abram had a good chance of making it home from the hospital in time to host it. They were wrong. Abram died the following afternoon at the age of eighty-one.

FOURTEEN

Legacy

I believe you live on in the acts you do, in the attitudes you transmit.

O n Sunday, March 19, 2000, family, friends, and dignitaries gathered at the Cape Cod synagogue in Hyannis to pay tribute to Morris Abram, who died earlier that week in Geneva. Abram, who was born six months before the end of World War I, died three months after the close of a tumultuous century for America and the world.

The executive director of UN Watch, Michael Colson, spoke of Abram's youthfulness, his vigor, his devotion to ideas, his incomparable warmth and charisma. "He had a love of life," said Colson, "that was unparalleled." Abram's daughter Ann noted her father's enormous desire to connect with people and his insatiable intellectual curiosity. The latter was echoed by his son Joshua. "Until the day of his death," he remarked, "he woke up every morning wondering, 'What can I learn today?'"[1]

One of Abram's earliest law partners, Robert Hicks, told the assembled guests that none of the many obituaries that had been written in the U.S. and European press could possibly capture the "intangibles" that marked his departed friend, among them his wit, his remarkable sense of humor, and his charm, "which enabled everyone in his presence to feel significant." Abram's adopted stepson wept, as did Eric Block and Jonathan Tepperman, both of whom worked for him in Geneva for a single year while embarking on successful careers on which he left an indelible mark.[2] At Abram's request, the family asked that donations in his name be made to three organizations: the United Negro College Fund, UN Watch, and Brandeis University.

Just over a week later, a memorial service was held at Geneva's Hotel President Wilson attended by ambassadors and other notables from around the world. The U.S. ambassador to the UN in Geneva, George Moose, said of Abram that no one had represented his country abroad "with greater dignity and grace." Reviewing Abram's career, Ambassador Moose noted, "Having been a fierce defender of those who had been denied their rights in the United States, he was no less fierce in his conviction that those same rights should be extended to every individual, everywhere." Like his friend Martin Luther King Jr., Moose observed, "the passion Morris brought to his convictions as well as his life left no one indifferent."[3]

This is how David Harris described Morris Abram's legacy: "To this day, and God knows, we have many complex and difficult situations, I say to myself, where is Morris? What would he have said; how can we fill that space? His legacy is indelible in defending the highest Jewish and American values, but also in a way in inevitably creating a vacuum after his death that can't be filled by anyone else on the stage."[4]

At the contentious hearing before the Senate Judiciary Committee in July 1983 as it considered his nomination to the U.S. Commission on Civil Rights, Abram asked himself why he was accepting this assignment amid so much controversy just after receiving his Medicare card, a time when most Americans are looking to slow their lives down. Quoting one of his heroes, Justice Holmes, he answered his own question this way: "It is required of a man," he said, "that he should take part in the actions and passions of his time, at the peril of being judged not to have lived." Abram's friend and AJC colleague Alfred Moses said about him, "Whatever the cause, Morris was passionate in everything he did. What he felt was what he thought. But that's okay: the world could use a few more Morris Abrams."[5]

Abram's passion, not to mention his idealism, often came with a measure of naivete that, at various times in his life, resulted in his having to react to events rather than anticipate them. This quality went all the way back to his boyhood in Fitzgerald. Abram described how he was amazed to learn that an eighth grade teacher whose intelligence he respected harbored prejudice toward Jews, a quality the young Abram had previously associated exclusively with the backwoods. Years later, when he began his legal career in Atlanta, he was crushed to learn that a Rhodes Scholar was unacceptable to the most prestigious law firms because of the same prejudice.

And it was not until the latter part of the 1960s that he began to realize that the progressive views he had held in locales in which they were particularly unwelcome were themselves under siege, this time not from Southern segregationists but from those who were undermining traditional liberalism from the left. During the Six-Day War of June 1967, attacks on Israel from the liberal side of the political spectrum came as a surprise. "I could not believe it," he wrote, "the 'advanced' religious leaders of the Protestant establishment began turning their backs on Israel and Jewish Americans, whose history and fates were intertwined with the survivors of Hitler's gas ovens."[6]

In his inaugural address at Brandeis the following year, he told his audience how amazed he was to hear a professor at a prestigious university voicing agreement with those who thought that certain points of view were so wrong they should not be tolerated within the institution. Three months later, when he found himself challenged by a group of black students who were occupying the building that housed the university's communications system, he tried to convince them that he was on their side.

Jacob Cohen recalled how "he kept telling everyone who would listen, believing the students would be tremendously impressed with this, I can call up Coretta King right now and she would advise you if you want me to do that. I knew Martin Luther King. Over and over, not knowing that by this point, 1969, Martin Luther King had been assassinated and was mourned, but he also had become a laughingstock of the black radicals who were coming into the forefront."[7] That transition in the civil rights movement, Cohen continued, "aggressively colorblind, aggressively integrationist, aggressively nonviolent, that civil rights movement had, by the beginning of 1965 and '66, intensifying in 1967 and 1968, had become, not black and white, we shall overcome, but 'Lookout, Black Power's going to get your mama!'"[8]

"He never quite understood it. He was puzzled by it and hurt," said Norman Podhoretz, whose relationship with Abram went back to his days as the young editor of *Commentary* when Abram became president of the American Jewish Committee, then the publication's sponsoring organization.

> He wasn't the only one who was unable to take the real measure of what was happening on the left as it affected the liberal community in the Democratic Party. I was very close to Pat Moynihan in those years and I remember, I can't tell you how many times he said to me, explain it to me again, why do they hate me? And I believed Morris felt the same way. He didn't understand the radical movement of the sixties. He couldn't understand why they were changing; he couldn't understand why they would be hostile to someone like him.[9]

Mugged by reality, Abram nevertheless refused to relinquish his belief that people of good will could make the world a better place. "He became especially incensed," said Ambassador Moose at the memorial service in Geneva, "by efforts, at times successful, to turn the voice of the United Nations against the very principles on which it was founded. But he never abandoned his faith in the capacity in the community of nations to make a positive difference in the lives of ordinary people."[10]

Abram also believed that despite all the talk of "two Americas" in the 1960s, the United States could truly become a colorblind society where people would be judged, as his friend Martin Luther King dreamed, by the content of their character rather than the color of their skin. Did those from poor backgrounds need financial and other forms of support? Of course they did, but this had to be done without imposing the same kind of invidious racial classifications that had such disastrous results and that Abram had courageously fought in the Jim Crow South.

In accepting the American Liberties award from the American Jewish Committee at a dinner at the Waldorf Astoria in 1975, Abram offered what he regarded as the right way to think about affirmative action:

> Let there be no impediment to development or placement on the grounds of race; let there be careful reexamination of all traditions in respect of entrance and qualification to opportunity; let there be affirmative efforts to move the disadvantaged forward, with "disadvantaged" defined without regard to race, color, creed, or national origin. For eighty-nine years, from 1865 to 1954, people such as those on this dais fought color and religious prejudice and urged the 14th Amendment to the Constitution as support for this equalitarian principle. I think that anyone who, on the grounds of expedience, opportunism, or frustration, seeks today to justify the classification of Americans on the grounds of race is making a serious strategic mistake which, if successful, may someday haunt us all.[11]

Anticipating the end of his life in a letter to his daughter Ruth in March 1999, Abram expressed concern that his political beliefs and actions since 1982, the year in which his autobiography was published, not be misrepresented. He quoted to her the passage from the book on what liberalism meant to him, namely, "while men differ in their natural endowments, they must be treated as equal citizens in the eyes of the law; that they should possess equality of opportunity and be afforded some minimum of social benefits." He noted that these principles, which united liberals for generations, "now divide me from some who seek equality of result and who sanction the preferences imposed by government to attain it."[12]

In fact, Abram was never really a man of the left. As he told Eli Evans, because the issues surrounding civil rights were the defining ones in the South, any integrationist such as himself was considered a liberal. But his views were never that easy to categorize. And though his break with the Carter administration over both its foreign and domestic policies marked a significant political turning point for him, his doubts about many of the assumptions of progressivism had begun years earlier. In 1972 Abram told the graduates of Emory University that during his college years he had been attracted to the view of man as essentially good, with deviations from that goodness attributable to his circumstances. He rejected the Hobbesian concept of man motivated by the search for power and the fear of death as late as the mid-1940s.[13] After twenty-five years of practicing law, he told the graduates, he had concluded that men are neither as good as they pretend to be nor as bad as their enemies paint them. This view had strengthened his belief in democratic government with its built-in balance of interests. "I do not now tend to idolize the governments of any type," he said, "for all are affected to a more or less degree by the frailties and infirmities of human nature."[14]

Thirteen years later, Abram said that he considered himself a practitioner of classical liberalism "that is no longer practiced by a large number of people who call themselves liberal." Far from looking suspiciously at government, they look "fawningly" at it. "I think it's remarkable," he added, "how some people who call themselves liberals will not outrightly condemn the use of a university mob to prevent other people from going to class. They claim they are acting in a moral tradition. This is not liberalism."[15]

In 1986, after he ascended to the chairmanship of the Conference of Presidents, Abram told an interviewer that he considered himself "a transcendental liberal," one who believes in the ultimate freedom of the individual. Devoted to the Bill of Rights, he never believed in treating any person as a member of a group, but as an individual. "Unfortunately," he said, "that has ceased to be the doctrine of the organized liberals. I can't help that, and I am not going to change simply because the doctrine has changed."[16]

Although he never self-identified as a conservative, Abram was drawn to conservative intellectuals in the final two decades of his life. He carried on a friendly correspondence with the economist Thomas Sowell, and he recommended to others the writings of Paul Johnson and Joseph Epstein. He wrote to his son Morris Jr. that Epstein, whom he said had been forced from his position as editor of *The American Scholar* for reasons of political correctness, had become one of his favorite essayists.[17] In Geneva he would look forward to receiving the latest issue of the neoconservative magazine *Commentary* and proceed to read it from cover to cover the morning of its arrival, making notes in the margins of each article.[18]

And he did gravitate to positions advocated by conservatives on issues as diverse as the relationships between the government and the individual, and between church and state. With respect to the former, the Atlanta lawyer who sang the praises of the New Deal before an audience of conservatives at Emory in the early 1960s became the New York lawyer who later told George Goodwin, the public relations counsel, that his views were conservative on economic issues such as the New York fiscal crisis.[19] In an address to the AARP in the mid-1970s, he said, "America was not built on the premise that public employment should be continued when the service is no longer needed or can be more efficiently provided in some other way. Public service is not meant to serve the ends of public servants."[20] And on the threshold of the 1980 presidential election, he wrote to Reagan adviser and future national security adviser Richard Allen, "I believe that men and women in a civilized society can and should do more things for themselves if they are left alone and with untaxed resources to do them. Of course, government has a proper place in any social order, but our government has grown too large, too inefficient, too bureaucratic and too restrictive."[21]

Regarding the separation of church and state, the Jewish student who grew up resentful of having to listen to the New Testament read out loud in his rural Georgia school rooms found a way to justify the use of government funds to support the enrollment of poor children in parochial schools. Although he never retreated from his view that what he experienced in Fitzgerald's schools was unconstitutional, Abram agreed with the Supreme Court's pragmatic accommodation of religion, one mandated by the free exercise clause of the First Amendment and "the need to ensure that separation of church and state does not discriminate against religion."[22]

In an address entitled "In Pursuit of Justice" at Emory Law School, Abram asked why Switzerland, the country he had lived in for the past seven years, one with diverse cultures, languages, and religions, had avoided the centuries of bloodshed experienced by its European neighbors. The country had hung together, he said, because it does not tackle issues like abortion and doctor-assisted suicide without public discussion and the building of a consensus. Quoting his intellectual mentor Justice Holmes, he noted that "Great Constitutional provisions must be administered with caution. Some play must be allowed for the joints of the machine, and it must be remembered that legislatures are ultimate guardians of the liberties and welfare of the people in quite as great a degree as the courts."[23]

After Abram left Atlanta in 1962, it was his growing Jewish identity that helped give definition to much of his worldview. In 1983 he told the Southern Jewish Historical Society that under the influence of his mother, he grew up believing that Judaism was a religion, period. And since there was no synagogue that they could attend, he never received a proper Jewish education.[24]

Fortunately for Abram, in Fitzgerald his neighbor Isadore Gelders exposed him to texts that highlighted Jewish contributions to Western civilization. It was Gelders, the editor of the alternative newspaper in town, who helped set him on a course of learning over time that Judaism was much more than a religion. In discussing the evolution of his own views on Jewish peoplehood in 1983, he asked his audience of Southern Jewish historians to concentrate on four "resounding" themes: first, that in every Jew there is a collective unconscious that echoes the passage from the official story of Passover stating that there are those in every generation "who rise up to destroy us"; second, that there is a linkage among Jews such that each Jew is responsible for one another; third, that in each Jew there is a deep connection with the land of Israel; and finally, that Jews are natural fighters determined to follow the Biblical mandate of choosing life over death.[25] This was his own choice in middle age while overcoming what was for most a life-ending illness.

In the spring of 1985, Abram's daughter Ruth presented him with "what may be the challenge of your life." She was writing to provide the text of prayers that he would be chanting in Hebrew at his granddaughter Anna's Bat Mitzvah service for which she had prepared a tape. "Dear Anna," he wrote after the service, "You and your family have, I feel, restored a tradition in the family which I did not as a young man appreciate but which I now hold dear and precious." He concluded by telling her that she had given him "the greatest birthday gift I can have on my 67th this week."[26]

During one of Morris Abram's trips to Israel as chairman of the Conference of Presidents of Major American Jewish Organizations, he attended a Sabbath service at Jerusalem's Great Synagogue and was given the honor of carrying the Torah, the sacred scrolls containing the Five Books of Moses. He told his traveling companions that it was one of the greatest honors of his life.[27]

In one of his transatlantic flights with his wife Bruna during his years traveling back and forth from Geneva, a passenger recognized Abram while he was reading a book about Jesus Christ. Incredulous, he asked why Morris Abram of Jewish fame was reading such a book. "Simple," Abram replied, "I'm very interested in the story of Jesus from a historical perspective."[28]

In his graduation address at Emory, Abram quoted Socrates's aphorism that he knew nothing "except the fact of my own ignorance." Learning, he told the graduates, is a lifelong process, which often requires one to discard many previously held views. As his wife Bruna said, her husband had an interest in life itself.

According to Anne Patterson, his political counselor in Geneva, "His intellect was what I admired most. And another thing about him, he listened. We could tell him that we thought something wasn't a great idea, and he would listen to it. He was a person who would listen to other opinions even after all the experiences he had."[29]

Jonathan Cohen, who also knew Abram well from his days in Geneva, was impressed by Abram's relentless engagement with others in pursuit of ideas right up to the end of his life. "Morris thought he could still win people over," he recalled. "He was charming, he was a raconteur, he admired people for their intellect, and if you could engage with him in conversation that's all he needed to know. He would never run somebody from the dinner table for taking a point of view he didn't like."[30]

In his Memorial Lecture at King's College, University of London, in 1944, C. S. Lewis warned of the dangers of "The Inner Ring":

> I believe that in all men's lives at certain periods, and in many men's lives at all periods between infancy and extreme old age, one of the most dominant elements is the desire to be inside the local Ring and the

terror of being left outside. . . . The quest of the Inner Ring will break your hearts unless you break it. But if you break it, a surprising result will follow. If in your working hours you make the work your end, you will presently find yourself all unawares inside the only circle in your profession that really matters. . . . And if in your spare time you consort simply with the people you like, you will again find that you have come unawares to a real inside: that you are indeed snug and safe at the center of something which, seen from without, would look exactly like an Inner Ring.[31]

Morris Abram was from his earliest years a man of deep ambition whose aggressive pursuit of the inner ring led him from a small rural town in south central Georgia to comfortable interaction with presidents, prime ministers, and even the pope. But he never forgot why he was following his ambitions.

To Eric Block, who worked for Abram at UN Watch,

he was a down to earth guy, a hard-working guy. That's the other thing: he was not just some chairman-emeritus of this thing. He worked his ass off. He was always plotting: how do I raise more money? How do I get this issue in front of the UN? When he was hosting dinner parties, it wasn't for the glory of Morris Abram. How do I put UN Watch on the map? How do I entrench it further? If he had worked that hard in the private sector, he could have earned millions and millions of more dollars before he died. But he didn't. He was working for the Jewish community.[32]

Block's sentiments were echoed by his UN colleague Jonathan Tepperman. "It was clear," he said,

that [Abram] had had this incredible drive and this incredible work ethic. And had an amazing ability to push himself. But he didn't talk about it in terms of personal ambition. He talked about it in terms of fighting the fight. That's the story we would tell each other all the time, that the job we were in was fighting for principle. It was never defined in specific language, but it was certainly defending Israel at the United Nations, exposing the real and serious flaws of the United Nations, defending Israel from its enemies more broadly, championing the Jewish people.[33]

And his energy level was extraordinary. His archives overflow with boxes and boxes of correspondence. He stayed in touch with everyone from his past and reached out to others he was cultivating for the future: fellow members of the numerous organizations on whose boards he sat and for which he raised money, including Cardozo Law School, the United Negro College Fund, Morehouse University, the Jewish Theological Seminary, and many others; editors and television executives he wanted to write and speak for; old friends he helped by sending their children's resumes to people he knew in academia; and associates past and present from whom he was eager to get their reactions to articles he had just written, speeches he had just delivered, and books he had just read.

Reflecting on Abram's life, Vernon Jordan, who had many sharp disagreements with him in his later years, remarked, "If I were assessing his life, I'd say Morris was a great man who made a great difference. He was a civil rights lawyer, a civil rights leader, and my view is that this is how he ought to be remembered."[34] That sentiment was echoed by John Lewis: "Morris was just one of these individuals that you had to know if you wanted to get something accomplished. Check with Morris Abram. He was a pillar. He was always just so caring. And it was delightful to be in his presence."[35]

Asked what had attracted her to him, Bruna Molina replied, "He was, how should I put this, a straightforward person, with human qualities, very warm as a person, and interesting. He brought all his family to my home, so I would meet them to make sure this was a serious relationship. And he took me to the States to visit Fitzgerald, the place where he was born."[36]

Recalling his battle with leukemia, when he had to face his mortality, Abram told a reporter that "you live on in the acts you do, in the attitudes you transmit."[37] He would be pleased to learn that those who knew him best are grateful for the rich legacy he left behind.

NOTES

Introduction

1. Potter, "Funeral but Few Mourners."
2. AJC Oral History Project, vol. 5, 886.
3. Potter, "Funeral but Few Mourners."
4. Carter, *Turning Point*, 40.
5. Interview with Ted Maloof, July 25, 2017.
6. Interview with Jeh Johnson, February 16, 2018.
7. Conversation with Robert Hicks, August 29, 2018.
8. Interview with Ruth Abram, May 16, 2017.
9. Trippett, "The Walls Came Tumbling Down," 101.
10. AJC Oral History Project, vol. 3, 594.
11. AJC Oral History Project, vol. 3, 421.
12. Interview of Morris Abram by Lorraine Nelson Spritzer, January 4, 1978, Georgia Government Documentation Project, Special Collections and Archives, Georgia State University Library, Atlanta.
13. AJC Oral History Project, vol. 2, 247.
14. AJC Oral History Project, vol. 2, 245–46.
15. Interview with Eric Yoffie, October 16, 2017.
16. Interview with Robert Hicks, December 1, 2017.
17. Abram Papers, box 41.
18. "White Liberals, Black Problems," letter to the *New York Review of Books*, March 6, 1997.
19. Hearings Before the Committee on the Judiciary, United States Senate, July 13, 1983, 17.

1. Childhood

1. AJC Oral History Project, vol. 2, 215–19.
2. Abram, *The Day Is Short*, 10.
3. This and the following three paragraphs are drawn from the following sources: Sparks, "Eden in the Grass"; Smith, "Georgia Yankees"; Sparks, "The Town Yanks and Rebs Built"; and Sheffield, "The Yankee-Reb City."
4. Sheffield, "The Yankee-Reb City," 21.

5. Encyclopedia of Southern Jewish Communities-Fitzgerald, Georgia.

6. AJC Oral History Project, vol. 1, 41–42.

7. Jane Abram to Morris Abram Jr., 1964, Abram Papers, box 91.

8. Adler, *Roots in a Moving Stream*, 43; Ketz, "110 Years of Temple Beth El," pamphlet, Abram Papers, box 79.

9. Adler, *Roots in a Moving Stream*, 44, 46.

10. Adler, *Roots in a Moving Stream*, 46, 48.

11. Adler, *Roots in a Moving Stream*, 49.

12. Adler, *Roots in a Moving Stream*, 50.

13. AJC Oral History Project, vol. 1, 16; Abram, *The Day Is Short*, 13–14.

14. AJC Oral History Project, vol. 1, 14; Abram, *The Day Is Short*, 13–15.

15. Interview with Lamar Perlis, May 31, 2018.

16. Interview with Janice Rothschild Blumberg, February 23, 2018.

17. Interview with Ruth Abram, May 16, 2017.

18. Abram, *The Day Is Short*, 15.

19. AJC Oral History Project, vol. 1, 26.

20. AJC Oral History Project, vol. 2, 221–22.

21. AJC Oral History Project, vol. 1, 46.

22. Interview with Cecily Abram, February 16, 2018.

23. AJC Oral History Project, vol. 1, 40.

24. Abram, "A Jewish Boy Growing Up in Rural Georgia."

25. Letter to the Editor, *American Jewish History*, November 1983.

26. AJC Oral History Project, vol. 1, 50.

27. AJC Oral History Project, vol. 1, 68.

28. AJC Oral History Project, vol. 1, 60.

29. Conversation with Eric Singer, January 18, 2018.

30. AJC Oral History Project, vol. 1, 106.

31. AJC Oral History Project, vol. 2, 221.

32. *Fitzgerald Leader*, 1954, Abram Papers, box 2.

33. Conversation with Penson Kaminsky, May 31, 2018.

34. Abram, *The Day Is Short*, 28.

35. Abram, *The Day Is Short*, 27, 29, 34–35.

36. Interview with Lamar Perlis, May 31, 2018.

37. AJC Oral History Project, vol. 1, 125.

38. Abram, *The Day Is Short*, 37.

39. Abram, "The Southernness of Jimmy Carter."

40. Morris Abram Oral History Interview 1, March 20, 1984, by Michael L. Gillette, internet copy, LBJ Library, Interview 1, 1–2.

41. Interview with Andrew Young, March 21, 2018.

42. Smith, "Morris Abram, Foe of Unfairness."

43. AJC Oral History Project, vol. 1, 12; vol. 2, 226.

44. AJC Oral History Project, 223; Abram, *The Day Is Short*, 48.

45. Evans, *The Provincials*, 96–97.

46. Abram, "A Jewish Boy Growing Up in Rural Georgia."

47. AJC Oral History Project, vol. 1, 91.

48. Abram, *The Day Is Short*, 17–18.

49. Conversation with Joshua Abram, June 21, 2018; AJC Oral History Project, vol. 1, 92.

50. AJC Oral History Project, vol. 1, 95–97.

2. Education

1. "History of UGA," University of Georgia, http://www.uga.edu/profile/history/.

2. Abram, *The Day Is Short*, 42.

3. AJC Oral History Project, vol. 2, 260.

4. Abram, *The Day Is Short*, 43.

5. AJC Oral History Project, vol. 2, 255; Abram, *The Day Is Short*, 44.

6. AJC Oral History Project, vol. 2, 293; Abram, *The Day Is Short*, 53.

7. AJC Oral History Project, vol. 2, 293–94.

8. Abram, *The Day Is Short*, 53–54. See also Abram, "Ethics and the New Medicine," in which Abram discusses the limitations in medicine when his brother began his practice during the 1930s.

9. Abram, *The Day Is Short*, 46.

10. Abram, *The Day Is Short*, 52–53.

11. AJC Oral History Project, vol. 2, 274.

12. AJC Oral History Project, vol. 2, 274.

13. Conversation with Joshua Abram, June 22, 2018.

14. Abram, *The Day Is Short*, 55; AJC Oral History Project, vol. 2, 272.

15. Morris Abram to Bobby Troutman, October 11, 1939, Abram Papers, box 22.

16. Abram, *The Day Is Short*, 58.

17. Abram to Troutman, October 21, 1939.

18. Abram to Troutman, October 21, 1939.

19. Abram to Troutman, November 14, 1939.

20. Abram to Troutman, October 21, 1939; Abram, *The Day Is Short*, 60.

21. Abram to Troutman, February 16, 1940.

22. Interview with Janice Rothschild Blumberg, February 23, 2018.

23. AJC Oral History Project, vol. 2, 279; Abram to Troutman, October 21, 1940.

24. AJC Oral History Project, vol. 2, 279–81.

25. AJC Oral History Project, vol. 2, 263.

26. Interview with Miles Alexander, July 19, 2018.

27. AJC Oral History Project, vol. 2, 266.

28. Abram to Troutman, date unknown, 1940.

29. Abram to Troutman, 1940; Abram, *The Day Is Short*, 60–61; AJC Oral History Project, vol. 2, 774.

30. Abram, *The Day Is Short*, 51.

31. William Anderson, *The Wild Man from Sugar Creek*, 169.

32. AJC Oral History Project, vol. 4, 771.

33. AJC Oral History Project, vol. 4, 786.

34. Montgomery, "Bias Dread Sent Abram from Banking to Law."

35. Abram to Troutman, October 21, 1940.

36. AJC Oral History Project, vol. 4, 771; Abram, *The Day Is Short*, 62.

37. Abram to Troutman, January 16, 1941.

38. Abram to Troutman, March 28, 1941.

39. Abram, *The Day Is Short*, 66.

40. *Orlando Reporter-Star*, January 4, 1944.

41. AJC Oral History Project, vol. 2, 343–44.

42. Abram, *The Day Is Short*, 67.

43. Abram, *The Day Is Short*, 65–66.

44. Abram, *The Day Is Short*, 69–70.

45. AJC Oral History Project, vol. 2, 296.

46. Interview with Ruth Abram, May 16, 2017

47. Abram, *The Day Is Short*, 71.

48. AJC Oral History Project, vol. 2, 296.

49. AJC Oral History Project, vol. 2, 298–99.

50. Abram, *The Day Is Short*, 74.

51. Abram, *The Day Is Short*, 75.

52. AJC Oral History Project, vol. 2, 294–308.

53. Abram, *The Day Is Short*, 59.

54. Interview with Eric Block, May 21, 2018.

55. AJC Oral History Project, vol. 2, 294. Jane Abram later underwent a conversion to Judaism.

3. Atlanta Lawyer

1. Hugo Black lecture, University of Alabama Law School, March 30, 1977, Abram Papers, box 2.

2. AJC Oral History Project, vol. 4, 787.

3. Interview with Robert Hicks, December 1, 2018.

4. AJC Oral History Project, vol. 4, 788.

5. Interview with Andrew Young, March 21, 2018.

6. Abram, "What I Have Learned in Thirty Years."

7. *Amicus* Brief in the case of Franklin v. Harper, Number 16759, Supreme Court of Georgia, Abram Papers, box 89.

8. Elbert Tuttle to Morris Abram, August 22, 1949, Abram Papers, box 89.

9. Ellis Arnall to Morris Abram, August 24, 1949, Abram Papers, box 89.

10. Rep. Grace Towns Hamilton to Senator Edward Kennedy, June 23, 1983, Abram Papers, box 91.

11. Hamilton to Kennedy, June 23, 1983.

12. Spritzer and Bergmark, *Grace Towns Hamilton*, 90.

13. Spritzer and Bergmark, *Grace Towns Hamilton*, 95.

14. Interview with Ted Maloof, July 25, 2017.

15. Interview with Miles Alexander, July 19, 2018.

16. Interview with Ted Maloof, July 25, 2017.

17. AJC Oral History Project, vol. 2, 258.

18. Interview with Ted Maloof, July 25, 2017.

19. Interview with Ted Maloof, July 25, 2017.

20. Interview with Elliott Levitas, August 7, 2017.

21. Interview with Grace Pauley, July 18, 1974, interview G-0046. Southern Oral History Program Collection (#4007) http://docsouth.unc.edu/sohp/g-0046/g-0046.html.

22. AJC Oral History Project, vol. 3, 402–3.

23. AJC Oral History Project, vol. 3, 418.

24. Spritzer and Bergmark, *Grace Towns Hamilton*, 97.

25. Abram, *The Day Is Short*, 86.

26. *Atlanta Journal*, May 15, 1952.

27. Spencer, "Abram Invades Rockdale."

28. Spencer, "Abram Invades Rockdale."

29. Abram Papers, box 2.

30. Abram Papers, box 2.

31. Abram, "Your Stake in the County Unit Amendment."

32. Abram, *The Day Is Short*, 89.

33. Abram, *The Day Is Short*, 90.

34. AJC Oral History Project, vol. 3, 420.

35. Interview with Miles Alexander, July 17, 2017.

36. Talmadge, *You and Segregation*, 22–23.

37. McGill, "New York's Southerner."

38. Oral Argument of Morris Abram, *Gray v. Sanders*.

39. AJC Oral History Project, vol. 4, 419.

40. Martin, *William Berry Hartsfield: Mayor of Atlanta*, 137.

41. Interview with Joseph Lefkoff, September 27, 2017.

42. Interview with Joseph Lefkoff, September 27, 2017

43. Abram, *The Day Is Short*, 86–87.

44. Smith, "Moral but not Moralistic"; interview with Robert Hicks, December 1, 2017.

45. Interview with Joseph Lefkoff, September 27, 2017

46. Email from Joseph Lefkoff, December 9, 2017.

47. Letter from Morris Abram to Fred Orr, September 20, 1988, Abram Papers, box 82.

48. Interview with Ted Maloof, July 25, 2017.

49. Conversation with Joseph Lefkoff, August 21, 2018.

50. AJC Oral History Project, vol. 2, 318–19.

51. Interview with Robert Hicks, December 1, 2017.

52. Interview with Ted Maloof, July 25, 2017.

53. Interview with Ruth Abram, May 16, 2017.

54. Transcript, Morris Abram Oral History Interview 1, March 20, 1984, LBJ Library, 7.

55. *Papers of Martin Luther King, Jr.*, vol. 5, 522.

56. Branch, *Parting the Waters*, 207, 353.

57. Oliphant and Wilkie, *The Road to Camelot*, 338.

58. Abram, *The Day Is Short*, 126.

59. Abram, *The Day Is Short*, 128.

60. Branch, *Parting the Waters*, 362; Coretta Scott King, *My Life*, 93.

61. Henderson, *Ernest Vandiver*, 124.

62. Branch, *Parting the Waters*, 376; Abram, *The Day Is Short*, 132.

63. Levingston, *Kennedy, and King*, 114; The president's first choice was Paul Freund of Harvard Law School. Cox, Abram, and Carl McGowan were on the short list after Freund turned down the offer. Abram Chayes, recorded interview by Eugene Gordon, June 22, 1964, 6–7, John F. Kennedy Library Oral History Program.

64. AJC Oral History Project, vol. 2, 359.

65. "The Founding Moment," U.S. Peace Corps, https://www.peacecorps.gov/about/history/founding-moment/.

66. "Peace Corps Role Hailed," *Tulsa Sunday World*.

67. "Peace Corps Role Hailed," *Tulsa Sunday World*.

68. Morris, "Buckley and Abram Clash in Spirited Emory Debate."

69. "Buckley and Abram Collide in Liberal-Conservative Duel," *Atlanta Constitution*, October 19, 1962.

4. Victory

1. Bulloch III and Gaddie, *Georgia Politics in a State of Change*, 135.

2. Spritzer, *The Belle of Ashby Street*, 89.

3. Spritzer, *The Belle of Ashby Street*, 89.

4. *Colegrove v. Green*, 328 U.S. 549 (1946).

5. Spritzer, *The Belle of Ashby Street*, 146.

6. Spritzer, *The Belle of Ashby Street*, 146.

7. Interview of Morris Abram by Lorraine Nelson Spritzer, January 4, 1978, Georgia Government Documentation Project, Special Collections and Archives, Georgia State University Library, Atlanta.

8. Spritzer, *The Belle of Ashby Street*, 147.

9. Interview of Morris Abram by Lorraine Nelson Spritzer, January 4, 1978, Georgia Government Documentation Project, Special Collections and Archives, Georgia State University Library, Atlanta.

10. Abram, *The Day Is Short*, 83.

11. *South v. Peters*, 339 U.S. 276 (1950).

12. *South v. Peters*, 339 U.S. 276 (1950).

13. *South v. Peters*, 339 U.S. 276 (1950); Smith, *On Democracy's Doorstep*, 104.

14. Abram, "The County Unit System Is Unconstitutional," 36–37.

15. Abram, "The County Unit System Is Unconstitutional," 35.

16. Abram, "The County Unit System Is Unconstitutional," 36.

17. Abram, *The Day Is Short*, 101.

18. *Cox v. Peters*, 208 Ga. 498 (1951).

19. *Cox v. Peters*, 208 Ga. 498 (1951).

20. 342 U.S. 936 (1952).

21. *New Georgia Encyclopedia*, https://www.georgiaencyclopedia.org/articles/government-politics/william-b-hartsfield-1890-1971.

22. AJC Oral History Project, vol. 5, 862.

23. Interview of Morris Abram by Lorraine Nelson Spritzer, January 4, 1978, Georgia Government Documentation Project, Special Collections and Archives, Georgia State University Library, Atlanta.

24. AJC Oral History Project, vol. 5, 864.

25. Davis, "No Federal Issue, 5–4 Decision Says."

26. *Atlanta Constitution*, "I'm Tired of Fighting, Mayor Says."

27. Interview of Morris Abram by Lorraine Nelson Spritzer, January 4, 1978, Georgia Government Documentation Project, Special Collections and Archives, Georgia State University Library, Atlanta.

28. Abram, *The Day Is Short*, 103–4.

29. Abram, *The Day Is Short*, 104.

30. Lefkoff, "The Georgia County Unit Case."

31. Interview of Morris Abram by Lorraine Nelson Spritzer, January 4, 1978, Georgia Government Documentation Project, Special Collections and Archives, Georgia State University Library, Atlanta.

32. Carter, *Turning Point*, 33.

33. *Toombs v. Fortson*, 205 F. Supp. 248 (N.D. Ga. 1962).

34. Carter, *Turning Point*, 38–40.

35. Abram, *The Day Is Short*, 106; AJC Oral History Project, vol. 5, 882–83.

36. Carter, *Turning Point*, 40.

37. *Gray v. Sanders*, Oral Argument, January 17, 1963, Part 2.

38. Archibald Cox to Morris Abram, December 21, 1962, Abram Papers, box 14.

39. Cox to Abram, January 4, 1963, Abram Papers, box 14.

40. Smith, *On Democracy's Doorstep*, 107.

41. Ferris, "Attorney General Kennedy vs. Solicitor General Cox: The Formulation of the Federal Government's Position in the Reapportionment Cases."

42. Smith, *On Democracy's Doorstep*, 107.

43. Interview with Joseph Lefkoff, September 27, 2017.

44. Henderson, *Ernest Vandiver, Governor of Georgia*, 167. At Abram's request to Archibald Cox, Mayor Hartsfield was also sworn in that day. Archibald Cox to Morris Abram, January 1963, Abram Papers, box 14.

45. *Gray v. Sanders*, Oral Argument, January 17, 1963, Part 2.

46. *Gray v. Sanders*, Oral Argument, January 17, 1963, Part 2.

47. *Gray v. Sanders*, Oral Argument, January 17, 1963, Part 2.

48. *Gray v. Sanders*, Oral Argument, January 17, 1963, Part 2.

49. Tye, *Robert Kennedy, The Making of a Liberal Icon*, 166.

50. *Gray v. Sanders*, Oral Argument, January 17, 1963, Part 2.

51. Interview of Morris Abram by Lorraine Nelson Spritzer, January 4, 1978, Georgia Government Documentation Project, Special Collections and Archives, Georgia State University Library, Atlanta.

52. Abram letter to *Time* magazine, February 22, 1963.

53. *Gray v. Sanders*, Oral Argument, January 17, 1963, Part 2.

54. *Gray v. Sanders*, 372 U.S. 368 (1963).

5. Jewish Imperatives

1. Interview with Ruth Abram, May 16, 2017.

2. Interview with Ted Maloof, July 25, 2017.

3. LBJ Library Oral History Project, Interview 2, May 3, 1984.

4. AJC Oral History Project, vol. 2, 364.

5. Interview with Robert Rifkind, May 15, 2018.

6. AJC Oral History Project, vol. 2, 359.

7. Abram, *The Day Is Short*, 134.

8. Trippett, "The Walls Came Tumbling Down," 43–44.

9. Sanua, *Let Us Prove Strong*, 3–9.

10. Sanua, *Let Us Prove Strong*, 104–05.

11. Interview with David Harris, May 2, 2017

12. AJC Oral History Project, vol. 2, 368.

13. AJC Oral History Project, vol. 2, 368.

14. Sanua, *Let Us Prove Strong*, 111.

15. Loeffler, *Rooted Cosmopolitans*, 250–53.

16. Statement by Morris Abram, U.S. Member of the Sub-Commission for the Prevention of Discrimination and Protection of Minorities, Abram Papers, box 92.

17. Statement by Morris Abram, U.S. Member of the Sub-Commission for the Prevention of Discrimination and Protection of Minorities, Abram Papers, box 92.

18. Chernin, "Making Soviet Jews an Issue," 35.

19. Statement by Morris Abram, U.S. Member of the Sub-Commission for the Prevention of Discrimination and Protection of Minorities, Abram Papers, box 92.

20. Statement by Morris Abram, U.S. Member of the Sub-Commission for the Prevention of Discrimination and Protection of Minorities, Abram Papers, box 92.

21. The Academy quietly withdrew the book from publication.

22. Statement by Morris Abram, U.S. Member of the Sub-Commission for the Prevention of Discrimination and Protection of Minorities, Abram Papers, box 92.

23. State Department Press Release, March 25, 1965, Abram Papers, box 68.

24. Memorandum for the President from Secretary of State Dean Rusk, March 12, 1965, Abram Papers, box 68.

25. Loeffler, *Rooted Cosmopolitans*, 266.

26. Loeffler, *Rooted Cosmopolitans*, 267, 273; Feingold, *Silent No More*, 64n, 328–29.

27. Interview with David Harris, May 2, 2017; Abram, *The Day Is Short*, 151.

28. Sanua, *Let Us Prove Strong*, 123.

29. Sanua, *Let Us Prove Strong*, 126–27.

30. Sanua, *Let Us Prove Strong*, 131; AJC News Release, Monday, June 1, 1964.

31. Abram, *The Day Is Short*, 144; Sanua, *Let Us Prove Strong*, 131.

32. Abram, *The Day Is Short*, 146.

33. AJC Press release, June 3, 1964.

34. Interview with Miles Alexander, July 17, 2017.

35. Letter from Abram to White House Assistant Lee White, September 2, 1965, Abram Papers, box 92.

36. Sanua, *Let Us Prove Strong*, 132.

37. Interview with Steven Bayne, December 26, 2017.

38. Cushing to Abram, Abram Papers, box 92.

39. Sanua, *Let Us Prove Strong*, 132–33.

40. Sanua, *Let Us Prove Strong*, 26.

41. Interview with Steven Bayme, December 26, 2017.

42. Interview with Steven Bayme, December 26, 2017.

43. Abram, *The Day Is Short*, 149–50.

44. Interview with Steven Bayme, December 26, 2017.

45. Abram, *The Day Is Short*, 142.

46. The Field Foundation of Illinois, http://www.fieldfoundation.org/about/history.

47. Abram, *The Day Is Short*, 123–24.

48. American Jewish Committee, a conversation with Case, Kennedy, and Abram conducted by Herb Brubaker at WTTG Studios of Metromedia Television Network on Sunday May 15, 1966. Abram Papers, box 22.

49. Interview with Steven Bayne, December 26, 2017.

50. "Panel Selects Three for First Shield of Jerusalem Prizes," *New York Times*.

51. Abram, "A Jewish Boy Growing Up in Rural Georgia."

52. Interview with Steven Bayne, December 26, 2017.

6. Continuing the Struggle

1. Branch, *Parting the Waters*, 864.

2. Branch, *Parting the Waters*, 865.

3. "Sedition Trial, Americus, GA," Civil Rights Digital Library, last modified April 25, 2019, http://crdl.usg.edu/events/sedition_trial_americus/.

4. *Hague v. Committee for Industrial Organization*, 307 U.S. 496 (1939); interview with Sidney Rosdeitcher, November 7, 2018.

5. Interview with Sidney Rosdeitcher, November 7, 2018.

6. Interview with Sidney Rosdeitcher, November 7, 2018.

7. Lewis, "American Lawyers Gideon's Army," 159.

8. Lewis, "American Lawyers Gideon's Army," 159.

9. Interview of Morris Abram by Lorraine Nelson Spritzer, January 4, 1978, Georgia Government Documentation Project, Special Collections and Archives, Georgia State University Library, Atlanta. Regarding Carter, a sympathetic biographer who served in his presidential administration later wrote that "feelings were so inflamed, and the pressure on all politicians to make ill-conceived pro-segregation comments so strong, that his very silence was itself a measure of courage." Bourne, *Jimmy Carter*, 136.

10. Abram, *The Day Is Short*, 139–40.

11. Allen, *Mayor: Notes on the Sixties*, 104.

12. Allen, *Mayor: Notes on the Sixties*, 104–06.

13. Allen, *Mayor: Notes on the Sixties*, 133, 241.

14. The American Presidency Project.

15. The American Presidency Project.

16. Geary, *Beyond Civil Rights*, 76.

17. Memorandum to the President from the Vice President, September 1, 1965, Abram Papers, box 68.

18. Memorandum to the President from Lee White, September 28, 1965, Abram Papers, box 68. Both LaFollette and Burke Marshall had also been considered.

19. Califano, *The Triumph and Tragedy of Lyndon Johnson,* 47–48.

20. McPherson, *A Political Education,* 344.

21. Weissman, *Daniel Patrick Moynihan,* 90.

22. Weissman, *Daniel Patrick Moynihan,* 92–93.

23. Geary, *Beyond Civil Rights,* 79.

24. Geary, *Beyond Civil Rights,* 80.

25. Moynihan, "The President and the Negro."

26. Geary, *Beyond Civil Rights,* 149.

27. Weissman, *Daniel Patrick Moynihan,* 108.

28. McPherson, *A Political Education,* 245.

29. Oral Interview with Morris Abram, LBJ Library, Interview 1, March 20, 1984.

30. LBJ Oral History Project, Interview 1.

31. LBJ Oral History Project, Interview 2, May 3, 1984.

32. Address by Morris B. Abram, co-chairman, at the Opening of the White House Conference "To Fulfill These Rights," November 4, 1965, Abram Papers, box 90.

33. McPherson, *A Political Education,* 345.

34. LBJ Oral History; Otten, "Administration Hopes for Best in June Civil Rights Parley."

35. Branch, *Parting the Waters,* 471.

36. Interview with John Lewis, December 12, 2017.

37. Abram, *The Day Is Short,* 154, 158.

38. Friedman, *What Went Wrong,* 209–10.

39. Friedman, *What Went Wrong,* 210–11.

40. Friedman, *What Went Wrong,* 214.

41. Friedman, *What Went Wrong,* 226.

42. Friedman, *What Went Wrong,* 220.

43. Friedman, *What Went Wrong,* 230.

44. Martin L. King Jr. to Morris Abram, September 20, 1967, Abram Papers, box 91. According to historian Murray Friedman, when King began to give his speech, he was jeered by a group of black militants, shouting "Kill Whitey." And when an SCLC member tried to speak out against the resolution on Zionism, which was eventually dropped, his life was threatened. Friedman, *What Went Wrong,* 232–34.

45. King letter to Morris Abram.

46. King letter to Morris Abram.

47. Sanua, *Let Us Prove Strong,* 178–79.

48. Sanua, *Let Us Prove Strong,* 179–80.

49. Sanua, *Let Us Prove Strong,* 180.

50. O'Neill, "City Hall"; Katcher, *New York Post,* October 25, 1967.

51. McColl, "In the Morris Chair."

52. Witkin, "Democrats View a '68 Possibility." *New York Times,* Oct 25, 1967.

53. Sanua, *Let Us Prove Strong*, 232.

54. Abram, *The Day Is Short*, 165–67.

55. Friedman, *What Went Wrong*, 258–62.

56. Friedman, *What Went Wrong*, 263.

57. Sanua, *Let Us Prove Strong*, 180.

7. Brandeis

1. Abram, *The Day Is Short*, 167.

2. Jewish Telegraphic Agency, February 22, 1968.

3. Abram Papers, box 92.

4. Interview with Kenneth Sweder, April 3, 2018.

5. Abram Sachar Brandeis University Presidential Papers, box 44.

6. Sachar Presidential Papers.

7. Giguere, "End Violence, Mrs. King Appeals"; Krasner, "Seventeen Months in the President's Chair," 45.

8. Interview with Kenneth Sweder, April 3, 2018.

9. Abram, *The Day Is Short*, 191.

10. AJC Oral History Project, vol. 5, 919.

11. Interview with David Squire, October 13, 2017.

12. Interview with Jacob Cohen, October 19, 2017.

13. Fripp and Jordan, "Brandeis Students Seize Hall."

14. Kitch, "Building Taken by Blacks in Dispute with Brandeis."

15. Abram, "Odyssey of a Southern Liberal."

16. Interview with Jacob Cohen, October 19, 2017.

17. Krasner, "Seventeen Months in the President's Chair," 52.

18. Kitch, "Building Taken by Blacks in Dispute with Brandeis."

19. Interview with Herbert Teitelbaum, May 9, 2017.

20. Interview with Ruth Abram, May 16, 2017.

21. Fellman Collection, Minutes of Faculty Meetings; Special Faculty meeting, January 8, 1969, box 1, Folder 16.

22. Interview with Gordon Fellman, September 28, 2017.

23. Roche, *Sentenced to Life*, 150.

24. Interview with Kenneth Sweder, April 3, 2018; Fenton, "Brandeis Quiet Despite Student Sit-In." One journalist on the scene reportedly quipped that the incident demonstrated that "even the black students at Brandeis have Jewish mothers."

25. *Christian Science Monitor*, "Abram Draws Faculty Praise."

26. Fenton, "Negroes at Brandeis Seek New Talk on 'Racist' Issue."

27. Gordon Fellman Collection, box 1, Ford Hall Occupation, Folder 5.

28. Abram, "Odyssey of a Southern Liberal."

29. "The Justice," January 14, 1969.

30. Fripp, "Brandeis Library Disrupted as Blacks Reject Afro Department Bid."

31. Interview with Jacob Cohen, October 19, 2017.

32. Interview with Eric Yoffie, October 16, 2017.

33. Interview with Eric Yoffie, October 16, 2017.

34. Fellman Collection, box 1, Folder 17.

35. Interview with Jacob Cohen, October 19, 2017.

36. Interview with Morton Keller, September 27, 2017.

37. Interview with Gordon Fellman, September 28, 2017.

38. Abram, "The Eleven Days at Brandeis—as seen from the President's Chair."

39. Interview with Eric Yoffie, October 16, 2017.

40. Interview with Kenneth Sweder, April 3, 2018.

41. Krasner, "Seventeen Months in the President's Chair," 67.

42. Sachar Presidential Papers, box 44.

43. Abram, "Odyssey of a Southern Liberal"; Grossman, "College Protestors Didn't Always Have Football Team Behind Them."

44. Abram, "Odyssey of a Southern Liberal."

45. Interview with David Squire, October 13, 2017.

46. Fellman Collection, FBI Files, box 1.

47. Krasner, "Seventeen Months in the President's Chair," 67–68.

48. Abram, *The Day Is Short*, 189.

49. Interview with David Squire, October 13, 2017.

50. Interview with Ruth Abram, May 16, 2017.

51. Interview with David Squire, October 13, 2017.

52. Abram, "Reflections on the University in the New Revolution."

53. Interview with David Squire, October 13, 2017.

54. Interview with Eric Yoffie, October 16, 2017.

55. Interview with Kenneth Sweder, April 3, 2018.

56. Interview with Jacob Cohen, October 19, 2017.

57. *Atlanta Constitution*, "Morris Abram Quits Post at Brandeis, Studies Senate."

58. Interview with Alfred Moses, April 5, 2017.

59. Interview with Robert Hicks, December 1, 2017.

60. Abram, *The Day Is Short*, 164.

61. Abram, *The Day Is Short*, 189.

8. Values

1. AJC Oral History Project, vol. 2, 349–50.

2. Interview with Ruth Abram, May 16, 2017.

3. Spritzer and Bergman, *Grace Towns Hamilton*, 218.

4. Interview with Hamilton Fish, May 18, 2018.

5. Conversation with Joshua Abram, June 22, 2018.

6. Interview with Hamilton Fish, May 18, 2018.

7. Interview with Hamilton Fish, May 18, 2018.

8. Interview with Hamilton Fish, May 18, 2018.

9. Conversation with Joshua Abram, June 22, 2018.

10. Maguire, *On Shares: Ed Brown's Story*.

11. Interview with Hamilton Fish, May 18, 2017.

12. Interview with Hamilton Fish, May 18, 2017.

13. Interview with Hamilton Fish, May 18, 2017.

14. Interview with Ruth Abram, May 16, 2017.

15. Abram, *The Day Is Short*, 30.

16. Interview with Deborah Forman, June 9, 2017.

17. Interview with Joseph Lefkoff, September 27, 2017.

18. Interview with Jeh Johnson, February 26, 2017.

19. Conversation with Joshua Abram, June 22, 2018.

20. Conversation with Robert Hicks, August 29, 2018.

21. Interview with Michael Colson, April 26, 2018; Mulcahy, "A Brilliant and Caring Heart."

22. AJC Oral History Project, vol. 2, 356.

23. Abram, *The Day Is Short*, 203.

24. Handwritten letter to Morris Abram, October 25, 1983, Abram Papers, box 81.

25. Handwritten letter to Lewis Abram et al, December 24, 1985, Abram Papers, box 81.

26. Interview with Deborah Forman, June 9, 2017.

27. Interview with Michael Colson, April 26, 2018.

28. Forman, "A Good Friend Who Made the World a Better Place."

29. Interview with Max Gitter, August 23, 2017.

30. Interview with Sidney Rosdeitcher, November 7, 2017.

31. Interview with Mark Levin, May 23, 2017.

32. Interview with Mark Levin, May 23, 2017.

33. Interview with Jonathan Tepperman, May 10, 2018.

34. Interview with Jonathan Tepperman, May 10, 2018.

35. Interview with Jonathan Tepperman, May 10, 2018.

36. Interview with Jonathan Tepperman, May 10, 2018.

37. Lazar, "Abram: An Outsider Who Served Four Presidents May Serve Bush."

38. Abram, "What I Have Learned in Thirty Years."

9. New York Lawyer

1. Interview with Jacob Cohen, October 19, 2017.

2. Knowles, "Abram Eligibility Is Held in Dispute"; Ronan, "Abram Abandons Race for Senate."

3. AJC Oral History Project, vol. 3, 444–45.

4. Goldstein, "The Law Firm that Stars in Court."

5. Hoffman, *Lions of the Eighties*, 152–54.

6. Interview with Sidney Rosdeitcher, November 7, 2017.

7. Rifkind actually outlasted Abram at the firm, working right up to the year of his death. Pace, "Simon Rifkind, Celebrated Lawyer, Dies at 94."

8. AJC Oral History Project, vol. 3, 439.

9. AJC Oral History Project, vol. 3, 617.

10. Denniston, "Super Lawyer, Bad Book."

11. Interview with Jeh Johnson, February 26, 2017.

12. Abram, *The Day Is Short*, 95.

13. Interview with Max Gitter, August 23, 2017. The case, on behalf of Western Union, was the first important one Abram argued after joining the Heyman law firm. Abram, *The Day Is Short*, 98–99.

14. Gitter interview; Michael Kramer, "Son of Bob vs. Son of Jerry."

15. Interview with Sidney Rosdeitcher, November 7, 2017.

16. AJC Oral History Project, vol. 2, 235–37.

17. AJC Oral History Project, vol. 2, 242, 244.

18. AJC Oral History Project, vol. 2, 243.

19. Abram, "The Challenge of the Courtroom."

20. Auerbach, "Don't Call Us, We'll Call You."

21. Interview with Robert Destro, February 13, 2018.

22. Interview with Alan Dershowitz, March 22, 2018.

23. Interview with Robert Rifkind, May 15, 2018.

24. "Judge: Bias a 'No-No' in Partner Promotion," 613–14.

25. Interview with Robert Rifkind, May 15, 2018.

26. Interview with Robert Destro, February 13, 2018.

27. Abram, "Living with Leukemia," 160.

28. Interview with Robert Hicks, December 1, 2017.

29. Interview with Robert Hicks, December 1, 2017.

30. Lerner, "The Patient Who Tried to Cure His Own Cancer," 11.

31. Abram, "Living with Leukemia," 162.

32. Abram, "Living with Leukemia," 162–63.

33. Abram, "Living with Leukemia," 165.

34. Abram, "Ethics and the New Medicine," 94.

35. Abram, *The Day Is Short*, 205.

36. Abram, "Living with Leukemia," 166; Abram, *The Day Is Short*, 217.

37. *New York Times*, "Acute Leukemia Most Malignant, Is Usually Fatal, Authorities Say."

38. Abram, "Living with Leukemia," 168.

39. Abram, "Living with Leukemia," 169–70.

40. Gupte, "Noted Lawyer Free of Symptoms Four Years After Getting Leukemia."

41. Lerner, "The Patient Who Tried to Cure His Own Cancer," 13.

42. "Stein Tells Jews Not to Be Paranoid About Probes of Jewish-Owned Nursing Homes," Jewish Telegraphic Agency; Abram, *The Day Is Short*, 227, 237.

43. AJC Oral History Project, vol. 3, 457–8; Abram, *The Day Is Short*, 227.

44. Auletta, *Hard Feelings*, location 3330.

45. Auletta, *Hard Feelings*, location 3358; Abram, *The Day Is Short*, 232–33.

46. Auletta, *Hard Feelings*, location 3358–68.

47. Abram, *The Day Is Short*, 234.

48. Abram, *The Day Is Short*, 235.

49. Auletta, *Hard Feelings*, location 3407–36; Abram, *The Day Is Short*, 236.

50. Hess, "Moreland Report Cites Rockefeller"; *New York Times*, "Moreland Panel's Record."

51. Abram Papers, box 2.

52. Peters and Woolley, "The American Presidency Project."

53. Jimmy Carter Presidential Library, Office of Staff Secretary.

54. Abram, "Ethics and the New Medicine," 68.

55. Abram, "Ethics and the New Medicine," 68; Peters and Woolley, "The American Presidency Project."

56. The President's Commission for the Study of Ethical Problems in Medicine and in Biomedical and Behavioral Research.

57. The President's Commissions, 2001–2009; Former Bioethics Commissions, https://bioethicsarchive.georgetown.edu/pcbe/reports/pastcommissions/index.html.

58. Abram, "Ethics and the New Medicine," 68, 100.

10. Transition

1. Interview with Vernon Jordan, May 5, 2017.

2. Vernon Jordan to Morris Abram, June 22, 1970, Abram Papers, box 10.

3. Interview with Vernon Jordan, May 5, 2017.

4. Gasman, *Envisioning Black Colleges*, 134.

5. Gasman, *Envisioning Black Colleges*, 135–36.

6. Interview with David Harris, May 2, 2017.

7. Abram, "What I Have Learned in Thirty Years."

8. Abram, "What I Have Learned in Thirty Years."

9. Abram, "What I Have Learned in Thirty Years."

10. Interview with Norman Podhoretz, June 21, 2017.

11. Abram, *The Day Is Short*, 248.

12. Bourne, *Jimmy Carter*, 197.

13. Letter from Abram to Governor Carter, January 14, 1971, Abram Papers, box 8.

14. Jimmy Carter to Morris Abram, December 21, 1974, Abram Papers, box 8.

15. AJC Oral History Project, vol. 3, 625–26.

16. AJC Oral History Project, vol. 3, 626.

17. "Jimmy Carter's Big Breakthrough." *Time*, May 10, 1976.

18. Abram, "Carter and Baptists."

19. Abram, "Carter and Baptists."

20. Abram, "The Southernness of Jimmy Carter."

21. Abram, Memorandum to Jimmy Carter during 1976 campaign Subject: "How to Space Yourself from Ford," Abram Papers, box 8.

22. Abram to Carter.

23. Interview with Vernon Jordan, May 5, 2017.

24. Letter from Morris Abram to President Carter, "Why Portions of the American Jewish Community are Concerned with the Present Posture of U.S./Israel/Arab Relations," July 5, 1977, cited in Strieff, "Jimmy Carter and the Domestic Politics of Arab-Israeli Diplomacy 1977–80," 80.

25. Abram, *The Day Is Short*, 252–53.

26. Abram, *The Day Is Short*, 254.

27. Gershman, "The World According to Andrew Young."

28. Gershman, "The World According to Andrew Young."

29. Abram, Typewritten speech at Columbia University, December 7, 1978, Abram Papers, box 2.

30. *Time Magazine*, "The Fall of Andy Young."

31. Abram, Typewritten op-ed submitted to *the New York Times*, Abram Papers, box 91. The piece eventually ran in the *Atlanta Constitution* on October 30, 1979 under the title "On Fighting Anti-Semitism."

32. Abram, "On Fighting Anti-Semitism."

33. Abram, *The Day Is Short*, 257–58.

34. Abram Papers, box 8.

35. Leon, "Stars Shine in Alzheimer Gala."

36. Abram to Elliott Abrams, October 20, 1980; Abram to Richard Allen, October 21, 1980, box 54.

37. Dodson, "Beating the Odds," 13.

38. Abram, *The Day Is Short*, 262–63; Leon, "Stars Shine in Alzheimer Gala."

39. Carter, *The Shame of Southern Politics*, xvi.

40. Abram, *The Day Is Short*, 268.

11. Challenging New Definitions of Civil Rights

1. Abram, "The Odyssey of a Southern Liberal."

2. *Regents of the University of California v. Bakke*, 438 U.S. 265, 1978.

3. Abram, "Odyssey of a Southern Liberal."

4. Abram, "Odyssey of a Southern Liberal."

5. "Liberalism and the Jews."

6. "Liberalism and the Jews."

7. "Liberalism and the Jews."

8. Sawyer, "Senate Panel Starts Hearings on Constitutionality of Affirmative Action."

9. Abram, "Skewing Affirmative Action's Purpose."

10. Abram, "Misguided Black Political Strategy."

11. Abram, "Misguided Black Political Strategy."

12. Abram Papers, box 95.

13. Abram to Norman Redlich, April 16, 1981, Abram Papers, box 74.

14. *Luevano v. Campbell*, 93 F.R.D. 68 (D.D.C. 1981).

15. U.S. Commission on Civil Rights, http://www.usccr.gov/about/index.php.

16. Williams, "Beyond the Lunch Counter Victories."

17. Williams, "Beyond the Lunch Counter Victories."

18. Interview with Linda Chavez, December 12, 2017.

19. Clines, "Reagan Chooses Three for Civil Rights Panel."

20. Interview with Marshall Breger, May 8, 2018.

21. Hearings Before the Committee on the Judiciary, United States Senate, July 13, 1983, 10.

22. Hearings Before the Committee on the Judiciary, United States Senate, July 13, 1983, 17; Georgia Senator Sam Nunn also submitted a letter in support of Abram's nomination, which can be found on page 15.

23. Kahlenberg, *Tough Liberal*, 240–41, 245.

24. Kahlenberg, *Tough Liberal*, 243.

25. Hearings Before the Committee on the Judiciary, United States Senate, July 13, 1983, 33.

26. Interview with Linda Chavez, December 12, 2017.

27. Williams, "Middle Ground on Civil Rights."

28. Interview with Robert Destro, February 13, 2018.

29. Hearings Before the Committee on the Judiciary, United States Senate, July 13, 1983, 132.

30. Letter from Grace Towns Hamilton to Senator Edward Kennedy, June 23, 1983, Abram Papers, box 91.

31. Gailey, "Leaders of Rights Coalition Call for Rejection of Three Reagan Nominees."

32. Hearings Before the Committee on the Judiciary, United States Senate, July 13, 1983, 130.

33. Jewish Telegraphic Agency, August 30, 1983.

34. Douglas, "Black and Jewish Leaders Call for New Harmony."

35. Gailey, "Leaders of Rights Coalition Call for Rejection of Three Reagan Nominees."

36. Nathan Perlmutter to Ralph Neas, May 27, 1983, Abram Papers, box 42.

37. Abram, "What Is a Civil Right?," 52.

38. Gailey, "Leaders of Rights Coalition Call for Rejection of Three Reagan Nominees."

39. Bond, "Who Helped King get out of Jail?"

40. Hearings Before the Committee on the Judiciary, United States Senate, July 13, 1983, 42.

41. Hearings Before the Committee on the Judiciary, United States Senate, July 13, 1983, 109–10.

42. Lardner, "Compromise Apparently Reconstitutes Civil Rights Commission."

43. Kurtz, "Rights Panel's Critics Try to put it out of Business."

44. Interview with Linda Chavez, December 12, 2017.

45. Interview with Linda Chavez, December 12, 2017.

46. Interview with Linda Chavez, December 12, 2017.

47. Interview with Robert Destro, February 13, 2018.

48. Abram, "Against Comparable Worth."

49. Abram, "Against Comparable Worth."

50. Schroeder and Snowe, "Comparable Worth is the American Way."

51. Pear, "Civil Rights Agency Splits in Debate on Narrowing Definition of Equality."

52. Abram, "Against Goals and Timetables in Hiring and Recruitment."

53. Abram, "Against Goals and Timetables in Hiring and Recruitment."

54. *New York Times*, "The Dispute over Affirmative Action."

55. Pear, "Civil Rights Agency Splits in Debate on Narrowing Definition of Equality."

56. Abram, "What Constitutes a Civil Right?," 52.

57. Abram, "What Constitutes a Civil Right?," 54.

58. Abram, "What Constitutes a Civil Right?," 54.

59. Abram, "What Constitutes a Civil Right?," 60.

60. Mariano, "New York and NAACP Agree on Racial Quotas for Housing."

61. Goodman, "Dispute over Housing Quotas at Starrett City: Complex Mix of Principle and Politics."

62. Mariano, "New York and NAACP Agree on Racial Quotas for Housing."

63. Morris Abram to Hon. William Bradford Reynolds, June 19, 1984, Abram Papers, box 77.

64. Reynolds to Abram, July 10, 1984, box 77.

65. Paul, Weiss Office Memorandum, June 16, 1988, Abram Papers, box 77.

66. Morley, "Double Reverse Discrimination," 16; *Village Voice*, January 3, 1984.

67. Abram, "Affirmative Action: Fair Shakers and Social Engineers," 1312, 1326.

68. Abram, "Affirmative Action: Fair Shakers and Social Engineers," 1314.

69. Abram, "Affirmative Action: Fair Shakers and Social Engineers," 1315.

70. Abram, "Affirmative Action: Fair Shakers and Social Engineers," 1318–19.

71. Abram, "Affirmative Action: Fair Shakers and Social Engineers," 1321–23.

72. Abram, "Affirmative Action: Fair Shakers and Social Engineers," 1326.

73. Morris Abram to President Ronald Reagan, Abram Papers, box 41.

74. Abram Papers, box 104.

12. Leadership

1. Hoffman, "How We Freed Soviet Jewry."

2. Beckerman, *When They Come for Us We'll Be Gone*, 515–16, 527.

3. Abram, *The Day Is Short*, 76, 141.

4. Forman, "Jewish Leader Says Summit Must Address Human Rights."

5. Forman, "Jewish Leader Says Summit Must Address Human Rights."

6. Interview with Richard Schifter, June 5, 2017.

7. Lazin, *The Struggle for Soviet Jewry in American Politics*, 28–29.

8. Golden, *O Powerful Western Star*, 170–71.

9. Chernin, *A Second Exodus*, 2–3.

10. Interview with Shulamit Bahat, June 6, 2017.

11. Beckerman, *When They Come for Us We'll be Gone*, 279.

12. Interview with Malcolm Hoenlein, May 10, 2017.

13. Interview with Jerry Goodman, May 15, 2017.

14. Interview with Jerry Goodman, May 15, 2017.

15. Interview with Mark Talisman, July 13, 2017.

16. Altshuler, *From Exodus to Freedom*, 75–77.

17. Interview with Mark Levin, May 23, 2017.

18. Interview with Mark Levin, May 23, 2017.

19. Interview with George Shultz, May 26, 2017.

20. *Daily Journal*, October 28, 1988.

21. Fred Lazin, "We Are Not One: American Jews, Israel, and the Struggle for Soviet Jewry."

22. Interview with Herbert Teitelbaum, May 9, 2017.

23. Interview with Jerry Goodman, May 15, 2017.

24. "The American Bar and the Soviet Bear—an Exchange."

25. "The American Bar and the Soviet Bear—an Exchange." The Executive Director of the National Jewish Community Relations Council claimed it was his organization that had prodded NCSJ into action prior to Reykjavik. Lazin, *Struggle*, 247.

26. Beckerman, *When They Come for Us We'll Be Gone*, 513–16.

27. Shipler, "Two Say Soviet Plans to let Jews Leave in Larger Numbers."

28. Lazin, *Struggle*, 222.

29. Lazin, *Struggle*, 214. It was the Bronfman-Abram mission that led to Josef Mendelevich's outburst at the Solidarity Day rally in New York that May. Feingold, *Silent No More*, 271.

30. Interview with David Harris, May 2, 2017.

31. Morris Abram to President Ronald Reagan, April 9, 1984, box 61.

32. Abram, "Don't be Misled by the Bitburg Trip."

33. Interview with Abraham Foxman, May 16, 2017.

34. Interview with Abraham Foxman, May 16, 2017.

35. Interview with Billy Keyserling, May 25, 2017.

36. Interview with Malcolm Hoenlein, May 10, 2017.

37. Interview with Malcolm Hoenlein, May 10, 2017.

38. Interview with Malcolm Hoenlein, May 10, 2017.

39. Conversation with Mark Talisman, July 13, 2017.

40. Interview with Malcolm Hoenlein, May 10, 2017.

41. Conversation with Mark Talisman, July 13, 2017.

42. Interview with Alan Dershowitz, March 22, 2018.

43. Shipp, "ABA Maintains an Agreement with Soviet Lawyers' Group."

44. Dershowitz, *Chutzpah*, 264–65.

45. Abram, "For Ties with Soviet Lawyers."

46. "The American Bar and the Soviet Bear—an Exchange."

47. Altshuler, *From Exodus to Freedom*, 84–85.

48. *The Advocates*, "Should the United States Support 'Self-Determination'?"

49. *The Advocates*, "Should the United States Support 'Self-Determination'?" Abram's other expert witness was Ben Nitay (now Benjamin Netanyahu) of the Boston Consulting Group.

50. Margolick, "Those Against Bequest to Attack PLO Aims"; Shenon, "Settlement Reached on Bequest to PLO."

51. Interview with Malcolm Hoenlein, May 10, 2017.

52. Interview with Jerry Goodman, May 15, 2017.

53. Greenberg, "U.S. Jewish Leaders Walk Tightrope on Pollard Case."

54. Frankel, "U.S. Jews Press Israel on Pollard."

55. "1987 Mission to Jerusalem." Typewritten report of the Conference of Presidents in the wake of the Pollard case, March 17–22, 1987, Abram Papers, box 66.

56. Email from Malcolm Hoenlein, June 22, 2017.

57. Interview with Max Gitter, August 23, 2017.

13. Back to the United Nations

1. Romano, "The President and His Parties."

2. Nomination of Morris Berthold Abram To Be United States Representative to the European Office of the United Nations, February 2, 1989, Public Papers of the Presidents, The American Presidency Project; "Abram Officially Named US Envoy to UN in Geneva," Jewish Telegraphic Agency, February 5, 1989.

3. Abram Papers, box 73.

4. Typewritten speech at Columbia University, December 7, 1978, Abram Papers, box 2.

5. Release from the Ad Hoc Group on the United Nations, March 16, 1982, Abram Papers, box 73; Nossiter, "Private US Group Says UN Sometimes Heightens World Tensions."

6. Interview with David Schwarz, April 10, 2018.

7. "The Treatment of Israel by the United Nations," Hearing Before the House Committee on International Relations," July 14, 1999, 34.

8. Interview with Anne Patterson, April 23, 2018.

9. Interview with David Schwarz, April 10, 2018; interview with Anne Patterson, April 23, 2018.

10. Morris Abram to Dr. Christiana Nichols, January 31, 1991, Abram Papers, box 91.

11. "The United Nations Office in Geneva and the Role of the U.S. Mission," Memorandum from Morris Abram, U.S. Permanent Representative to the United Nations and Other International Organizations to the State Department Transition Team, December 16, 1992, Abram Papers, box 91.

12. *Maariv Style Supplement*, "Romantic Encounter in Geneva."

13. Interview with Max Gitter, August 23, 2017.

14. Abram, "The United Nations, the United States, and International Human Rights," 114.

15. Abram, "The United Nations, the United States, and International Human Rights," 115.

16. Abram, "The United Nations, the United States, and International Human Rights," 117–18.

17. Abram, "The United Nations, the United States, and International Human Rights," 118–19.

18. Abram, "The United Nations, the United States, and International Human Rights," 122.

19. Abram, "The United Nations, the United States, and International Human Rights," 122–23.

20. Interview with David Harris, May 2, 2017.

21. Interview with Eric Block, May 21, 2018.

22. Interview with Jonathan Cohen, April 20, 2018.

23. Interview with Jonathan Cohen, April 20, 2018.

24. Interview with Anne Patterson, April 23, 2018.

25. Interview with Jonathan Tepperman, May 10, 2018.

26. Interview with Jonathan Tepperman, May 10, 2018.

27. Lewis, "A First at UN, a Panel Condemns Anti-Semitism"; *New York Post*, "A Condemnation Long Overdue," March 10, 1994; Flash Report from the United Nations Watch, "The United Nations Has Finally Condemned Anti-Semitism," Abram Papers, box 22.

28. Interview with Michael Colson, April 26, 2018.

29. Interview with Jonathan Tepperman, May 10, 2018.

30. Interview with Hannah Gaywood, May 17, 2018.

31. "Dear Friend" letter from the Chairman, UN Watch, May 1, 1995, Abram Papers, box 22.

32. Interview with Michael Colson, April 26, 2018.

33. Interview with Hannah Gaywood, May 17, 2018; interview with Michael Colson, April 26, 2018.

34. Interview with Michael Colson, April 26, 2018.

35. Interview with Michael Colson, April 26, 2018.

36. Interview with Eric Block, May 21, 2018.

37. Interview with Eric Block, May 21, 2018.

38. Interview with Michael Colson, April 26, 2018.

39. Interview with Jonathan Cohen, April 20, 2018.

40. Interview with Bruce Ramer, January 10, 2018.

41. Interview with Felice Gaer, September 17, 2018.

42. Interview with Jonathan Cohen, April 20, 2018.

43. Sanua, *Let Us Prove Strong*, 337.

44. Interview with David Harris, May 2, 2017.

45. Interview with Bruna Molina, July 3, 2018.

46. Abram, "A House Divided Can't Stand; A House United Will Stand."

47. Memorandum to the Secretary General from Gillian Martin Sorensen.

48. UN Watch Press Release, "Kofi Annan Honors UN Watch Founder Morris Abram."

49. Interview with Bruna Molina, July 3, 2018.

14. Legacy

1. Mulcahy, "A Brilliant Intellect and Caring Heart."

2. Interview with Jonathan Tepperman, May 10, 2018.

3. Moose, George. "Remarks."

4. Interview with David Harris, May 2, 2017.

5. Hearings before the Committee on Judiciary, July 13, 1983; interview with Alfred Moses, April 5, 2017.

6. Abram, *The Day Is Short*, 149–50.

7. Interview with Jacob Cohen, October 19, 2017.

8. Interview with Jacob Cohen, October 19, 2017.

9. Interview with Norman Podhoretz, June 21, 2017.

10. Moose, George. "Remarks."

11. Abram, Typewritten Text of Remarks, May 1, 1975, Abram Papers, box 2.

12. Morris Abram to Ruth Abram, March 30, 1999, Abram Papers, box 104.

13. Abram, "What I Have Learned in Thirty Years."

14. Abram, "What I have Learned in Thirty Years."

15. Magida, "Morris Abram, a Confusion of Labels."

16. Goldberg, "Questions of Life."

17. Morris Abram to Morris Abram Jr., February 2, 2000, Abram Papers, box 104.

18. Interview with Michael Colson, April 26, 2017.

19. AJC Oral History Project, vol. 3, 619.

20. Abram Papers, box 2.

21. Morris Abram to Richard Allen, October 21, 1980, Abram Papers, box 54.

22. Abram, "Is Strict Separation Too Strict?," 32–34.

23. Abram, "In Pursuit of Justice."

24. Abram, "A Jewish Boy Growing Up in Rural Georgia."

25. Abram, "A Jewish Boy Growing Up in Rural Georgia."

26. Abram Papers, box 91.

27. Conversation with Max Green, October 9, 2017.

28. Interview with Bruna Molina, July 3, 2018.

29. Interview with Anne Patterson, April 23, 2018.

30. Interview with Jonathan Cohen, April 20, 2018.

31. I am grateful to Robert Hicks for calling my attention to Lewis's address and its connection to Abram's quest.

32. Interview with Eric Block, May 21, 2018.

33. Interview with Jonathan Tepperman, May 10, 2018.

34. Interview with Vernon Jordan, May 5, 2017.

35. Interview with John Lewis, December 13, 2017

36. Interview with Bruna Molina July 3, 2018.

37. Gupte, "Noted Lawyer Free of Symptoms Four Years After Getting Leukemia."

BIBLIOGRAPHY

Manuscripts and Archives

"1987 Mission to Jerusalem." Typewritten report of the Conference of Presidents in the wake of the Pollard case, March 17–22, 1987.

American Presidency Project, by Gerhard Peters and John T. Woolley

    Lyndon B. Johnson, Commencement Address at Howard University: "To Fulfill These Rights," June 4, 1965. http://www.presidency.ucsb.edu/ws/?pid=27021.

Georgia Government Documentation Project, Special Collections and Archives, Georgia State University Library, Atlanta.

    Interview by Lorraine Nelson Spritzer, January 4, 1978, P1978–02, Series G: "The Belle of Ashby Street."

Kennedy Institute of Ethics, Georgetown University, Washington DC

    The President's Commission for the Study of Ethical Problems in Medicine and in biomedical and Behavioral Research. A Guide to the Records in the Bioethics Research Library. https://bioethics.georgetown.edu/archives/Presidents-Commission-for-Study-of-Ethical-Problems-in-Medicine-and-in-Biomedical-and-Behavioral-Research- original-Archive-Finding-Aid.pdf.

Jimmy Carter Presidential Library

    Records of the Office of the Staff Secretary, Container 124, July 16, 1979. http://www.jimmycarterlibrary.gov/library/findingaids/Staff_Secretary.pdf.

LBJ Library

    Transcript, Morris B. Abram Oral History Interview 1, March 20, 1984, by Michael L. Gillette, Internet Copy.

    Transcript, Morris B. Abram Oral History Interview 2, May 3, 1984, by Michael L. Gillette, Internet Copy, http://www.lbjlibrary.net/assets/documents/archives/oral_histories/abram_m/ABRAM02.pdf.

Southern Oral History Program Collection (#4007) Talmadge Amendment

    Interview with Frances Pauley, July 18, 1974, no. G-0046. http://www.lbjlibrary.net/assets/documents/archives/oral_histories/abram_m/ABRAM01.pdf.

Bibliography

Stuart A. Rose Manuscript, Archives, and Rare Book Library, Emory University

"A Jewish Boy Growing Up in Rural Georgia." Presented at the Eighth Annual Meeting of the Southern Jewish Historical Society, December 4, 1983.

Morris B. Abram Papers, mss 514:

American Jewish Committee: A Conversation with Case, Kennedy, and Abram conducted by Herb Brubaker at wttg Studios of Metromedia Television Network, Sunday, May 15, 1966.

Morris B. Abram Oral Memoir: William E. Wiener, 1974–76, Volumes 1–5.

"The Southernness of Jimmy Carter," July 1976.

"What I Have Learned in Thirty Years as Expressed in Thirty Minutes." Commencement Address, Emory University, June 12, 1972.

John F. Kennedy Library Oral History Program

Recorded interview of Abram Chayes by Eugene Gordon, June 22, 1964, https://archive1.jfklibrary.org/JFKOH/Chayes,%20Abram%20J/JFKOH-ABJC-02/JFKOH-ABJC-02-TR.pdf.

Hoover Institution

Firing Line, "The Odyssey of a Southern Liberal," June 23, 1982, Record # 80040, 650–723–1754, https://digitalcollections.hoover.org/images/Collections/80040/80040_s0513_trans.pdf.

wgbh Media Library & Archives

"Should the United States Support 'Self-Determination' for Palestinians in a Middle East Peace Settlement?" *The Advocates*, June 6, 1978, http://openvault.wgbh.org/catalog/V_98F4072381BB439F8ECE8DC747297DBE.

"Your Stake in the County Unit Amendment," Pamphlet circulated in favor of Amendment No. 1 in the Georgia General Election of November 4, 1952.

Published Works

Abram, Morris B. "Affirmative Action: Fair Shakers and Social Engineers." *Harvard Law Review* 99, no. 6 (April 1986): 1312–26.

———. "Against Goals and Timetables in Hiring and Recruitment." *BNA's Employee Relations Weekly* 2, no. 39 (October 8, 1984).

———. "The Challenge of the Courtroom: Reflections on the Adversary System." *The Law School Record*, University of Chicago, Autumn 1963.

———. "The County Unit System Is Unconstitutional." *Georgia Bar Journal* 14, no. 1 (August 1951): 28–39.

———. *The Day Is Short*. New York: Harcourt, Brace, Jovanovich, 1982.

———. "Don't Be Misled by the Bitburg Trip." *New York Times*, May 10, 1985.

———. "The Eleven Days at Brandeis, as Seen from the President's Chair." *New York Times Magazine*, February 16, 1969, 28–29, 113–16.

———. "Ethics and the New Medicine." *New York Times Magazine*, June 5, 1983, 68–69, 94, 100.

———. "For Ties with Soviet Lawyers." *New York Times*, August 26, 1986.

———. "In Pursuit of Justice," Emory Law School, May 13, 1966. http://secure.unwatch.org/site/apps/nlnet/content2.aspx?c=bdkkisnqEmG&b=1330827&ct=1748059&notoc=1

————. "Is Strict Separation Too Strict?" *The Public Interest* 82 (Winter 1986): 81–90.

————. "Living with Leukemia." *Encyclopedia Britannica Health Annual,* 1979, 158–70.

————. "Reflections on the University in the New Revolution." *Daedalus* 99, no. 1 (Winter 1970): 122–40.

————. "The United Nations, the United States, and International Human Rights." In *US Policy and the Future of the United Nations,* edited by Roger A. Coate. Brookings, 1994.

————. "The U.N. and Human Rights." *Foreign Affairs* 47, no. 2 (January 1969): 363–74.

————. "What Constitutes a Civil Right?" *New York Times Magazine,* June 10, 1984, 52–64.

"Abram Draws Faculty Praise." *Christian Science Monitor,* January 15, 1969.

"Abram Officially Named US Envoy to UN in Geneva." *Jewish Telegraphic Agency,* February 5, 1989.

"Acute Leukemia Most Malignant, Is Usually Fatal, Authorities Say." *New York Times,* August 15, 1977.

Adler, Frank. *Roots in a Moving Stream: The Centennial History of Congregation B'nai Jehudah of Kansas City, 1870–1970.* Kansas City MO: The Temple, Congregation B'nai Jehudah, 1972.

Allen, Ivan Jr. with Paul Hemphil. *Mayor: Notes on the Sixties.* New York: Simon and Schuster, 1971.

Altshuler, Stuart. *From Exodus to Freedom: A History of the Soviet Jewry Movement.* Lanham MD: Rowman and Littlefield, 2005.

Amaker, Norman. *Civil Rights and the Reagan Administration.* Washington DC: Urban Institute Press, 1988.

"The American Bar and the Soviet Bear—an Exchange." *Moment,* January-February 1987.

Anderson, William. *The Wild Man from Sugar Creek: The Political Career of Eugene Talmadge.* Baton Rouge: Louisiana State University Press, 1975.

Auerbach, Jerold S. "Don't Call Us, We'll Call You." *New York Times,* April 13, 1976.

Auletta, Ken. *Hard Feelings: Reporting on the Pols, the Press, the People and the City.* New York: Random House, 1980.

Beckerman, Gal. *When They Come for Us, We'll Be Gone: The Epic Struggle to Save Soviet Jewry.* Boston: Houghton, Mifflin, Harcourt, 2010.

Bond, Julian. "Who Helped King Get Out of Jail?" *Columbus Citizen-Journal,* July 18, 1983.

Bourne, Peter. *Jimmy Carter: A Comprehensive Biography from Plains to Post-Presidency.* New York: Scribner, 1997.

Branch, Taylor. *At Canaan's Edge: America in the King Years, 1965–68.* New York: Simon and Schuster, 2006.

————. *Parting the Waters: America in the King Years 1954–63.* New York: Simon and Schuster, 1988.

"Buckley and Abram Collide in Liberal-Conservative Duel." *Atlanta Constitution,* October 19, 1962.

Bulloch, Charles III, and Ronald Gaddie. *Georgia Politics in a State of Change.* New York: Pearson, 2013.

Califano, Joseph. *The Triumph and Tragedy of Lyndon Johnson: The White House Years.* New York: Touchstone, 1991.

Bibliography

Carter, Dan. "Introduction." In *The Shame of Southern Politics, Essays and Speeches*, by Leslie Dunbar. Lexington: University Press of Kentucky, 2002.

Carter, David. *The Music Has Gone Out of the Movement: Civil Rights and the Johnson Administration, 1965–68*. Chapel Hill: University of North Carolina Press, 2012.

Carter, Jimmy. *Turning Point: A Candidate, a State, and a Nation Come of Age*. New York: Times Books, 1994.

Chernin, Albert D. "Making Soviet Jews an Issue: A History." In *A Second Exodus: The American Movement to Free Soviet Jews*, edited by Murray Friedman and Albert D. Chernin, 15–69. Waltham MA: Brandeis University Press, 1999.

Clines, Francis X. "Reagan Chooses Three for Civil Rights Panel." *New York Times*, May 26, 1983.

Daily Journal, Los Angeles, California, October 28, 1988, Abram Papers, box 22.

Davis, Harold. "No Federal Issue, 5–4 Decision says." *Atlanta Journal*, June 16, 1958.

Denniston, Lyle. "Super Lawyer, Bad Book." Abram Papers, box 22, 1982.

Dershowitz, Alan. *Chutzpah*. New York: Simon and Schuster, 1991.

Dodson, James. "Beating the Odds." *Atlanta Weekly*, October 17, 1982, 10–13.

Dorsen, David. "Paul, Weiss, Goldberg—What Kind of Ticket Is That?" *New York*, April 13, 1970, 44–46.

Douglas, Carlyle. "Black and Jewish Leaders Call for New Harmony." *New York Times*, June 26, 1985.

Editorial, *Atlanta Journal*, May 15, 1952.

Emanuel, Anne. *Elbert Parr Tuttle: Chief Jurist of the Civil Rights Revolution*. Athens: University of Georgia Press, 2011.

Encyclopedia of Southern Jewish Communities-Fitzgerald, Georgia. http://www.isjl.org/georgia-fitzgerald-encyclopedia.html.

Evans, Eli. *The Provincials: A Personal History of Jews in the South*. New York: Atheneum, 1980.

Feingold, Henry. *Silent No More: Saving the Jews of Russia, the American Jewish Effort, 1967–1989*. Syracuse: Syracuse University Press, 2007.

Fenton, John. "Brandeis Quiet Despite Student Sit-In." *New York Times*, January 14, 1969.

———. "Negroes at Brandeis Seek New Talk on 'Racist' Issue." *New York Times*, January 12, 1969.

Ferris, Bruce J. "Attorney General Kennedy vs. Solicitor General Cox: The Formulation of the Federal Government's Position in the Reapportionment Cases." *Journal of Supreme Court History* (December 2007): 335–45.

Forman, Debbie. "A Good Friend Who Made the World a Better Place." *Cape Cod Times*, March 23, 2000.

———. "Jewish Leader Says Summit Must Address Human Rights." *Cape Cod Times*, December 8, 1987.

Fowler, Harper, and George Pratt. "What the Supreme Court Did Not Do During the 1951 Term." *Pennsylvania Law Review* 101, no. 4 (January 1953).

Frankel, Glenn. "U.S. Jews Press Israel on Pollard." *Washington Post*, March 18, 1987.

Friedman, Murray. *What Went Wrong? The Creation and Collapse of the Black-Jewish Alliance*. New York: Free Press, 1994.

Fripp, William, and Robert Jordan. "Brandeis Library Disrupted as Blacks Reject Afro Department Bid." *Boston Globe*, January 16, 1969.

———. "Brandeis Students Seize Hall." *Boston Globe*, January 9, 1969.

Gailey, Phil. "Leaders of Rights Coalition Call for Rejection of Three Reagan Nominees." *New York Times*, June 10, 1983.

Gasman, Marybeth. *Envisioning Black Colleges: A History of the United Negro College Fund*. Baltimore MD: Johns Hopkins Press, 2007.

Geary, Daniel. *Beyond Civil Rights: The Moynihan Report and its Legacy*. Philadelphia: University of Pennsylvania Press, 2015.

Gershman, Carl. "The World According to Andrew Young." *Commentary*, August 1978.

Giguere, Paul. "End Violence, Mrs. King Appeals." *Boston Herald-Traveler*, October 5, 1968.

Goldberg, J. J. "Questions of Life: US Jewry's Top Spokesman Finds Personal Lessons in a Crusading Career." *Jewish Week*, October 14, 1986.

Golden, Peter. *O Powerful Western Star: American Jews, Russian Jews and the Final Battle of the Cold War*. Jerusalem: Gefen, 2012.

Goldstein, Tom. "The Law Firm that Stars in Court." *New York Times*, December 19, 1976.

Goodman, Walter. "Dispute Over Housing Quotas at Starrett City: Complex Mix of Principle and Politics." *New York Times*, July 14, 1984.

Gray v. Sanders, Oral Argument, January 17, 1963, Part 2, https://apps.oyez.org/player/#/warren11/oral_argument_audio/14491.

Greenberg, Joel. "U.S. Jewish Leaders Walk Tightrope on Pollard Case." *Christian Science Monitor*, March 18, 1987.

Grossman, "College Protestors Didn't Always Have Football Team Behind Them." *Chicago Tribune*, November 13, 2015.

Gupte, Pranay. "Noted Lawyer Free of Symptoms Four Years After Getting Leukemia." *New York Times*, August 15, 1977.

Hellman, Peter. "A Dilemma Grows in Brooklyn." *New York*, October 17, 1988.

Henderson, Harold. *Ernest Vandiver, Governor of Georgia*. Athens: University of Georgia Press, 2000.

Hess, John. "Moreland Report Cites Rockefeller." *New York Times*, February 26, 1976.

Hoffman, Allison. "How We Freed Soviet Jewry." *Tablet*, December 6, 2017.

Hoffman, Paul. *Lions in the Street*. New York: Saturday Review/Dutton, 1973.

———. *Lions of the Eighties: The Inside Story of the Powerhouse Law Firms*. New York: Doubleday, 1982.

"I'm Tired of Fighting, Mayor Says." *Atlanta Constitution*, June 16, 1958.

"Jimmy Carter's Big Breakthrough." *Time*, May 10, 1976.

"Judge: Bias a 'no-no' in Partner Promotions." *American Bar Association Journal* 63, May 1977.

Justia, U.S. Supreme Court, *Gray v. Sanders*, 372 U.S. 381 (1963), https://supreme.justia.com/cases/federal/us/372/368/.

Kahlenberg, Richard D. *Tough Liberal: Albert Shanker and the Battles over Schools, Unions, Race, and Democracy*. New York: Columbia University Press, 2007.

King, Coretta Scott. *My Life, My Love, My Legacy*. New York: Henry Holt, 2017.

Bibliography

King, Martin Luther, Jr. *Papers, Volume 5: Threshold of a New Decade, January 1959–December 1960*. Berkeley: University of California Press, 2005.

Kitch, James. "Building Taken by Blacks in Dispute with Brandeis." *Harvard Crimson*, January 9, 1969.

Knowles, Clayton. "Abram Eligibility is Held in Dispute." *New York Times*, February 25, 1970.

"Kofi Annan Honors UN Watch Founder Morris Abram." UN Watch Press Release, December 15, 1999. http://secure.unwatch.org/site/c.bdkkisnqEmG/b.2148793/k.e748/Kofi_Annan_Honors_un_Watch_Founder_Morris_Abram.htm.

Kramer, Michael. "Son of Bob vs. Son of Jerry." *New York*, November 7, 1977, 41–47.

Krasner, Jonathan. "Seventeen Months in the President's Chair: Morris Abram, Brandeis University, and the Anatomy of a Failed Presidency." *American Jewish History* 99, no. 1 (January 2015): 27–77.

Kurtz, Howard. "Rights Panel's Critics Try to Put It Out of Business." *Washington Post*, July 11, 1986.

Lardner, George. "Compromise Apparently Reconstitutes Civil Rights Commission." *Washington Post*, June 11, 1983.

Lazar, Kay. "Abram: An Outsider who Served Four Presidents May Serve Bush." *New York Observer*, January 23, 1989.

Lazin, Fred A. "The Role of Ethnic Politics in U.S. Immigration and Refugee Policy: The Case of Soviet Jewry." The Center for Comparative Immigration Studies, University of California, San Diego Working Paper 175, February 2009.

———. *The Struggle for Soviet Jewry in American Politics*. Lanham MD: Lexington, 2005.

Lee, David. Review of "Jane Maguire, On Shares: Ed Brown's Story." *Georgia Historical Quarterly* 61, no. 2 (Summer 1977): 180–90.

Lefkoff, Merle. "The Georgia County Unit Case: One Man, One Vote." MA Thesis, Emory University, 1965.

Leon, Masha. "Stars Shine in Alzheimer Gala." *Forward*, December 5, 2006.

Lerner, Barron. "The Patient Who Tried to Cure His Own Cancer: Revisiting the Story of Morris Abram's Leukemia." *The Pharos*, Autumn 2007.

Levingston, Stephen. *Kennedy and King*. New York: Hachette, 2017.

Lewis, Anthony. "American Lawyers Gideon's Army." *Cornell Law Review* 50, no. 2 (Winter 1965): 155–60.

Lewis, Paul. "A First at UN, a Panel Condemns Anti-Semitism." *New York Times*, March 10, 1994.

"Liberalism and the Jews: A Symposium." *Commentary*, January 1980.

Loeffler, James. *Rooted Cosmopolitans: Jews and Human Rights in the 20th Century*. New Haven: Yale University Press, 2018.

Magida, Arthur. "Morris Abram, a Confusion of Labels," *Baltimore Jewish Times*, June 28, 1985.

Maguire, Jane. *On Shares: Ed Brown's Story*. New York: W. W. Norton, 1975.

Margolick, David. "Those Against Bequest to Attack PLO Aims." *New York Times*, May 23, 1982.

Mariano, Ann. "New York and NAACP Agree on Racial Quotas for Housing." *Washington Post*, May 2, 1984.

Martin, Harold. *William Berry Hartsfield: Mayor of Atlanta*. Athens: University of Georgia Press, 1978.

McColl, Patricia. "In the Morris Chair." *Women's Wear Daily*, Monday, October 9, 1967.

McGill, Ralph. "New York's Southerner." *Atlanta Constitution*, September 13, 1967.

McPherson, Harry. *A Political Education*. New York: Atlantic-Little Brown, 1972.

Memorandum to the Secretary General from Gillian Martin Sorensen, September 22, 1999, https://search.archives.un.org/uploads/r/united-nations-archives/9/0/f/90f9fd4c00 62cd2384a7bfbc9ce76e894e53ec4545c38a21833177603b6db41c/s-1100–0033 –02–00021.pdf.

Montgomery, Jim. "Bias Dread sent Abram from Banking to Law." *Atlanta Constitution*, September 27, 1967.

Moose, George. "Remarks." Hotel President Wilson, March 27, 2000.

"Moreland Panel's Record." *New York Times*, May 20, 1976.

Morley, Jefferson. "Double Reverse Discrimination." *New Republic*, July 9, 1984, 14–18.

"Morris Abram Quits Post at Brandeis, Studies Senate." *Atlanta Constitution*, February 24, 1970.

Morris, Ann. "Buckley and Abram Clash in Spirited Emory Debate." *Atlanta Journal*, October 19, 1962.

Moynihan, Daniel P. "The President and the Negro." *Commentary*, February 1967.

Mulcahy, M. W. "A Brilliant and Caring Heart." *Cape Cod Times*, March 20, 2000.

Nossiter, Bernard. "Private US Group Says UN Sometimes Heightens World Tensions." *New York Times*, March 16, 1982.

Oliphant, Thomas, and Curtis Wilkie. *The Road to Camelot: Inside JFK's Five-Year Campaign*. New York: Simon and Schuster, 2017.

O'Neill, Edward. "City Hall." *New York Daily News*, October 2, 1967.

On Nomination of Morris B. Abram, John A. Bunzel, Robert A. Destro, and Linda Chavez to Serve on the U.S. Commission on Civil Rights: Hearings Before the Committee on the Judiciary, United States Senate, 98th Congress, First Session, July 13 and 26, 1983. U.S. Government Printing Office.

Pace, Eric. "Simon Rifkind, Celebrated Lawyer, Dies at 94." *New York Times*, November 15, 1995.

"Panel Selects Three for First Shield of Jerusalem Prizes." *New York Times*, November 14, 1983.

"Peace Corps Role Hailed." *Tulsa Sunday World*, March 5, 1961.

Pear, Robert. "Civil Rights Agency Splits in Debate on Narrowing Definition of Equality." *New York Times*, October 14, 1985.

Potter, Pat. "Funeral but Few Mourners." *Atlanta Journal*, April 29, 1962.

Roche, John P. *Sentenced to Life: Reflections on Politics, Education and Law*. New York: MacMillan, 1974.

Romano, Lois. "The President and his Parties." *Washington Post*, May 11, 1989.

"Romantic Encounter in Geneva." *Maariv Style Supplement*, November 21, 1990.

Ronan, Thomas. "Abram Abandons Race for Senate." *New York Times*, April 10, 1970.

Rosenthal, Stephen T. *Irreconcilable Differences: The Waning of the American Jewish Love Affair with Israel*. Waltham MA: Brandeis University Press, 2001.

Bibliography

Sanua, Marianne R. *Let Us Prove Strong: The American Jewish Committee, 1945–2006.* Waltham MA: Brandeis University Press, 2007.

Sawyer, Kathy. "Senate Panel Starts Hearings on Constitutionality of Affirmative Action." *Washington Post,* May 5, 1981.

Schroeder, Patricia, and Olympia Snowe. "Comparable Worth Is the American Way." *New York Times Letters,* November 17, 1985.

Sheffield, Donna. "The Yankee-Reb City." *Georgia Voyager,* Spring 1998.

Shenon, Phillip. "Settlement Reached on Bequest to PLO." *New York Times,* February 7, 1984.

Shipler, David K. "Two Say Soviet Plans to Let Jews Leave in Larger Numbers." *New York Times,* March 31, 1987.

Shipp, E. R. "ABA Maintains an Agreement with Soviet Lawyers' Group." *New York Times,* August 12, 1986.

Smith, Charlotte. "Georgia Yankees." *Savannah Morning News,* November 29, 1950.

Smith, J. Douglas. *On Democracy's Doorstep: The Inside Story of How the Supreme Court Brought "One Person, One Vote" to the United States.* New York: Hill and Wang, 2014.

Smith, Lee. "Moral but not Moralistic: In Long Career, Osgood O. Williams Took on President, Governor, Mayor." *Fulton County Daily Report,* January 20, 1988.

Smith, Phil. "Morris Abram, Foe of Unfairness." *Atlanta Journal-Constitution,* April 29, 1962.

Sparks, Andrew. "Eden in the Grass." *Atlanta Journal-Constitution Magazine,* July 16, 1950.

———. "The Town Yanks and Rebs Built." *Atlanta Journal-Constitution Magazine,* June 4, 1961.

Spencer, Bert. "Abram Invades Rockdale, Blasts Davis GOP Record." *Atlanta Constitution,* Sunday August 1, 1954.

Spritzer, Lorraine Nelson. *The Belle of Ashby Street: Helen Douglas Mankin and Georgia Politics.* Athens: University of Georgia Press, 1982.

Spritzer, Lorraine Nelson, and Jean Bergmark. *Grace Towns Hamilton and the Politics of Southern Change.* Athens: University of Georgia Press, 1997.

"Stein Tells Jews Not to Be Paranoid About Probes of Jewish-Owned Nursing Homes." *Jewish Telegraphic Agency,* October 17, 1975.

Strieff, Daniel Patrick. "Jimmy Carter and the Domestic Politics of Arab-Israeli Diplomacy 1977–80." Thesis submitted to the London School of Economics, October 2013.

Supreme Court of Georgia. *David Franklin, Plaintiff in Error v. J. Walker Harper, C. Nolan Bowden, and G. E. Murphy.* Defendants in Error, Brief of Herman Heyman, Elbert Tuttle, Morris Abram, Heyman, Howell and Heyman and Sutherland, Tuttle, and Brennan amicus curiae, Number 16759.

Talmadge, Herman. *You and Segregation.* Birmingham AL: Vulcan, 1955.

Taylor, Telford. *The Anatomy of the Nuremberg Trials.* New York: Alfred A. Knopf, 1952.

The American Bar and the Soviet Bear—an Exchange." *Moment,* January-February 1987.

"The Dispute over Affirmative Action: Whose Civil Rights?" *New York Times,* Week in Review, March 10, 1985.

"The Fall of Andy Young." *Time Magazine,* August 27, 1979.

The Treatment of Israel by the United Nations. Hearing Before the Committee on International Relations, U.S. House of Representatives, 106th Congress, First Session, July 14, 1999, U.S. Government Printing Office.

Trippett, Frank. "The Walls Came Tumbling Down." *Atlanta Magazine*, February 1966.

Tye, Larry. *Robert Kennedy: The Making of a Liberal Icon*. New York: Random House, 2017.

Wedding Announcement, *Orlando Reporter-Star*, January 4, 1944, email from Joshua Abram to author, August 24, 2018.

Weissman, Steven, ed. *Daniel Patrick Moynihan: A Portrait in Letters of an American Visionary*. New York: Public Affairs, 2010.

Whitfield, Stephen, and Jonathan B. Krasner, "Jewish Liberalism and Racial Grievance in the Sixties: The Case of Brandeis University." *Modern Judaism* 35, no. 1 (February 2015): 18–41.

Williams, Juan. "Beyond the Lunch Counter Victories." *Washington Post*, June 1, 1983.

———. "Middle Ground on Civil Rights." *Washington Post*, July 20, 1983.

Witkin, Richard. "Democrats View a '68 Possibility." *New York Times*, October 25, 1967.

INDEX

Index

Index

Cox, Archibald, 59, 72, 73, 74, 76–77
Cox v. Peters, 67–68
Cravath, Swain and Moore, 152–53
Cushing, Cardinal Richard, 90

Daedalus, 130
Dakota Apartment Building, 137
D'Amato, Alfonse, 184
Davis, James, 49, 50, 51–52, 64, 65, 67, 72
DeFunis v. Odegaard, 196
Democratic National Convention of 1964, 108
Democratic Party, 167, 224
Denniston, Lyle, 149
Dershowitz, Alan, 8, 152–53, 211–12
Destro, Robert, 151–53, 183, 186, 190
Dole, Robert, 217
Dorminey, Elijah, 23, 170
Douglas, Frederick, 196
Douglas, Hamilton, III, 65
Douglas, William, 66, 68, 69, 73, 77, 148, 196
Dunbar, Leslie, 107, 175

Ebeneezer Baptist Church, 59
Eisenhower, Dwight, 39, 69
Electoral College, 75, 77
Elson, Harry, 56
Eppstein, Elias, 14, 15, 16, 24
Epstein, Joseph, 240
Equal Employment Opportunity Commission, 221
Evans, Eli, 5, 6, 19, 20, 24, 34, 47, 52, 56, 140, 149, 151, 239
"Extremism in America Today" (TV interview), 92

Fair Housing Act of 1968, 194
Farmer, James, 102, 104
Fellman, Gordon, 122, 127
Fenton, John, 123
Ferris, Bruce, 73
Field, Marshall, III, 91
Field, Ruth, 92
Field Foundation, 80, 81, 91, 107, 175, 176
Finch, Atticus, 44
Fish, Hamilton, 136–38, 140
Fitzgerald, Georgia, 4, 49, 200, 236, 242, 245;
    Carnegie Free Library of, 21; and the *Fitzger-*

ald Herald, 20; Hebrew Commercial Alliance,
    20; history of, 11–13; Jews of, 13, 19–21; and
    the *Leader, Enterprise, and Press*, 20–21; liber-
    alism of, 23
Fitzgerald, Phylander, 12
Fleming, Harold, 65
Florida State College for Women, 37
Ford, Gerald, 171, 172
Ford Foundation, 112
Foreign Policy, 144, 227
Farmer, James, 102, 104
Forman, Deborah, 141–42
Forman, James, 109
The Founding Myths of Modern Israel
    (Garaudy), 230
Fourteenth Amendment, 239; equal protection
    clause, 29, 196–97. *See also* county unit system
Foxman, Abraham, 209
Frank, Leo, 24, 51
Frankfurter, Felix, 64–65, 73, 75
Franklin v. Harper, 45
Freedom House, 225
Freund, Paul, 252n63
Friedman, Murray, 113
Fuchs, Lawrence, 123
Fullilove v. Klutznick, 178, 182

Gaer, Felice, 231–32
Gaon, Nessim, 227
Garaudy, Roger, 230
Garrison, Lloyd, 81, 92, 116
Gaywood, Hannah, 228, 229, 232
Gelders, Isadore, 20–21, 242
Geneva Summit, 259
George, Walter, 50
Georgia Bar (journal), 67
Gitter, Joe, 28
Gitter, Max, 150, 171, 215, 222
Gitter, Naomi, 28
Glazer, Nathan, 197
Gloster, Hugh, 128
Goldberg, Arthur, 81, 91, 116, 147–48, 186, 202, 226
Goldenberg, Isadore, 13
Goodell, Charles, 132, 147
Goodhardt, Arthur Lehman, 38, 39
Goodman, Jerry, 203–4, 206, 214
Goodwin, George, 241

282

Index

Index